A Guide to
Convolutional Neural Networks
for Computer Vision

Synthesis Lectures on Computer Vision

Editors
Gérard Medioni, *University of Southern California*
Sven Dickinson, *University of Toronto*

Synthesis Lectures on Computer Vision is edited by Gérard Medioni of the University of Southern California and Sven Dickinson of the University of Toronto. The series publishes 50–150 page publications on topics pertaining to computer vision and pattern recognition. The scope will largely follow the purview of premier computer science conferences, such as ICCV, CVPR, and ECCV. Potential topics include, but not are limited to:

- Applications and Case Studies for Computer Vision

- Color, Illumination, and Texture

- Computational Photography and Video

- Early and Biologically-inspired Vision

- Face and Gesture Analysis

- Illumination and Reflectance Modeling

- Image-Based Modeling

- Image and Video Retrieval

- Medical Image Analysis

- Motion and Tracking

- Object Detection, Recognition, and Categorization

- Segmentation and Grouping

- Sensors

- Shape-from-X

- Stereo and Structure from Motion

- Shape Representation and Matching

- Statistical Methods and Learning

- Performance Evaluation

- Video Analysis and Event Recognition

A Guide to Convolutional Neural Networks for Computer Vision
Salman Khan, Hossein Rahmani, Syed Afaq Ali Shah, and Mohammed Bennamoun
2018

Covariances in Computer Vision and Machine Learning
Hà Quang Minh and Vittorio Murino
2017

Elastic Shape Analysis of Three-Dimensional Objects
Ian H. Jermyn, Sebastian Kurtek, Hamid Laga, and Anuj Srivastava
2017

The Maximum Consensus Problem: Recent Algorithmic Advances
Tat-Jun Chin and David Suter
2017

Extreme Value Theory-Based Methods for Visual Recognition
Walter J. Scheirer
2017

Data Association for Multi-Object Visual Tracking
Margrit Betke and Zheng Wu
2016

Ellipse Fitting for Computer Vision: Implementation and Applications
Kenichi Kanatani, Yasuyuki Sugaya, and Yasushi Kanazawa
2016

Computational Methods for Integrating Vision and Language
Kobus Barnard
2016

Background Subtraction: Theory and Practice
Ahmed Elgammal
2014

Vision-Based Interaction
Matthew Turk and Gang Hua
2013

A Guide to Convolutional Neural Networks for Computer Vision

Salman Khan, Hossein Rahmani, Syed Afaq Ali Shah, and Mohammed Bennamoun

ISBN: 978-3-031-00693-7   paperback
ISBN: 978-3-031-01821-3   ebook
ISBN: 978-3-031-00078-2   hardcover

DOI 10.1007/978-3-031-01821-3

A Publication in the Springer series
SYNTHESIS LECTURES ON COMPUTER VISION

Lecture #15
Series Editors: Gérard Medioni, *University of Southern California*
               Sven Dickinson, *University of Toronto*
Series ISSN
Print 2153-1056   Electronic 2153-1064

A Guide to Convolutional Neural Networks for Computer Vision

Salman Khan
Data61-CSIRO and Australian National University

Hossein Rahmani
The University of Western Australia, Crawley, WA

Syed Afaq Ali Shah
The University of Western Australia, Crawley, WA

Mohammed Bennamoun
The University of Western Australia, Crawley, WA

SYNTHESIS LECTURES ON COMPUTER VISION #15

ABSTRACT

Computer vision has become increasingly important and effective in recent years due to its wide-ranging applications in areas as diverse as smart surveillance and monitoring, health and medicine, sports and recreation, robotics, drones, and self-driving cars. Visual recognition tasks, such as image classification, localization, and detection, are the core building blocks of many of these applications, and recent developments in Convolutional Neural Networks (CNNs) have led to outstanding performance in these state-of-the-art visual recognition tasks and systems. As a result, CNNs now form the crux of deep learning algorithms in computer vision.

This self-contained guide will benefit those who seek to both understand the theory behind CNNs and to gain hands-on experience on the application of CNNs in computer vision. It provides a comprehensive introduction to CNNs starting with the essential concepts behind neural networks: training, regularization, and optimization of CNNs. The book also discusses a wide range of loss functions, network layers, and popular CNN architectures, reviews the different techniques for the evaluation of CNNs, and presents some popular CNN tools and libraries that are commonly used in computer vision. Further, this text describes and discusses case studies that are related to the application of CNN in computer vision, including image classification, object detection, semantic segmentation, scene understanding, and image generation.

This book is ideal for undergraduate and graduate students, as no prior background knowledge in the field is required to follow the material, as well as new researchers, developers, engineers, and practitioners who are interested in gaining a quick understanding of CNN models.

KEYWORDS

deep learning, computer vision, convolution neural networks, perception, back-propagation, feed-forward networks, image classification, action recognition, object detection, object tracking, video processing, semantic segmentation, scene understanding, 3D processing

SK: *To my parents and my wife Nusrat*

HR: *To my father Shirzad, my mother Rahimeh, and my wife Shahla*

AS: *To my parents, my wife Maleeha, and our children Abiya, Maryam, and Muhammad. Thanks for always being there for me.*

MB: *To my parents: Mostefa and Rabia Bennamoun and to my nuclear family: Leila, Miriam, Basheer, and Rayaane Bennamoun*

Contents

Preface

The primary goal of this book is to provide a comprehensive treatment to the subject of convolutional neural networks (CNNs) from the perspective of computer vision. In this regard, this book covers basic, intermediate and well as advanced topics relating to both the theoretical and practical aspects.

This book is organized into nine chapters. The first chapter introduces the computer vision and machine learning disciplines and presents their highly relevant application domains. This sets up the platform for the main subject of this book, "Deep Learning", which is first defined towards the later part of first chapter. The second chapter serves as a background material, which presents popular hand-crafted features and classifiers which have remained popular in computer vision during the last two decades. These include feature descriptors such as Scale-Invariant Feature Transform (SIFT), Histogram of Oriented Gradients (HOG), Speeded-Up Robust Features (SURF), and classifiers such as Support Vector Machines (SVM), and Random Decision Forests (RDF).

Chapter 3 describes neural networks and covers preliminary concepts related to their architecture, basic building blocks, and learning algorithms. Chapter 4 builds on this and serves as a thorough introduction to CNN architecture. It covers its layers, including the basic ones (e.g., sub-sampling, convolution) as well as more advanced ones (e.g., pyramid pooling, spatial transform). Chapter 5 comprehensively presents techniques to learn and regularize CNN parameters. It also provides tools to visualize and understand the learned parameters.

Chapter 6 and onward are more focused on the practical aspects of CNNs. Specifically, Chapter 6 presents state-of-the-art CNN architectures that have demonstrated excellent performances on a number of vision tasks. It also provides a comparative analysis and discusses their relative pros and cons. Chapter 7 goes in further depth regarding applications of CNNs to core vision problems. For each task, it discusses a set of representative works using CNNs and reports their key ingredients for success. Chapter 8 covers popular software libraries for deep learning such as Theano, Tensorflow, Caffe, and Torch. Finally, in Chapter 9, open problems and challenges for deep learning are presented along with a succinct summary of the book.

The purpose of the book is not to provide a literature survey for the applications of CNNs in computer vision. Rather, it succinctly covers key concepts and provides a bird's eye view of recent state-of-the-art models designed for practical problems in computer vision.

Salman Khan, Hossein Rahmani, Syed Afaq Ali Shah, and Mohammed Bennamoun
January 2018

Acknowledgments

We would like to thank Gerard Medioni and Sven Dickinson, the editors of this Synthesis Lectures on Computer Vision series, for giving us an opportunity to contribute to this series. We greatly appreciate the help and support of Diane Cerra, Executive Editor at Morgan & Claypool, who managed the complete book preparation process. We are indebted to our colleagues, students, collaborators, and co-authors we worked with during our careers, who contributed to the development of our interest in this subject. We are also deeply thankful to the wider research community, whose work has led to major advancements in computer vision and machines learning, a part of which is covered in this book. More importantly, we want to express our gratitude toward the people who allowed us to use their figures or tables in some portions of this book. This book has greatly benefited from the constructive comments and appreciation by the reviewers, which helped us improve the presented content. Finally, this effort would not have been possible without the help and support from our families.

We would like to acknowledge support from Australian Research Council (ARC), whose funding and support was crucial to some of the contents of this book.

Salman Khan, Hossein Rahmani, Syed Afaq Ali Shah, and Mohammed Bennamoun
January 2018

CHAPTER 1

Introduction

Computer Vision and Machine Learning have played together decisive roles in the development of a variety of image-based applications within the last decade (e.g., various services provided by Google, Facebook, Microsoft, Snapchat). During this time, the vision-based technology has transformed from just a sensing modality to intelligent computing systems which can understand the real world. Thus, acquiring computer vision and machine learning (e.g., deep learning) knowledge is an important skill that is required in many modern innovative businesses and is likely to become even more important in the near future.

1.1   WHAT IS COMPUTER VISION?

Humans use their eyes and their brains to *see* and *understand* the 3D world around them. For example, given an image as shown in Fig. 1.1a, humans can easily see a "cat" in the image and thus, categorize the image (classification task); localize the cat in the image (classification plus localization task as shown in Fig. 1.1b); localize and label all objects that are present in the image (object detection task as shown in Fig. 1.1c); and segment the individual objects that are present in the image (instance segmentation task as shown in Fig. 1.1d). Computer vision is the science that aims to give a similar, if not better, capability to computers. More precisely, computer vision seeks to develop methods which are able to replicate one of the most amazing capabilities of the human visual system, i.e., inferring characteristics of the 3D real world purely using the light reflected to the eyes from various objects.

However, recovering and understanding the 3D structure of the world from two-dimensional images captured by cameras is a challenging task. Researchers in computer vision have been developing mathematical techniques to recover the three-dimensional shape and appearance of objects/scene from images. For example, given a large enough set of images of an object captured from a variety of views (Fig. 1.2), computer vision algorithms can reconstruct an accurate dense 3D surface model of the object using dense correspondences across multiple views. However, despite all of these advances, understanding images at the same level as humans still remains challenging.

1.1.1   APPLICATIONS

Due to the significant progress in the field of computer vision and visual sensor technology, computer vision techniques are being used today in a wide variety of real-world applications, such as intelligent human-computer interaction, robotics, and multimedia. It is also expected

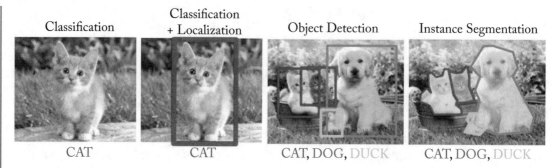

Classification   Classification + Localization   Object Detection   Instance Segmentation

CAT   CAT   CAT, DOG, DUCK   CAT, DOG, DUCK

Figure 1.1: What do we want computers to do with the image data? To look at the image and perform classification, classification plus localization (i.e., to find a bounding box around the main object (CAT) in the image and label it), to localize all objects that are present in the image (CAT, DOG, DUCK) and to label them, or perform semantic instance segmentation, i.e., the segmentation of the individual objects within a scene, even if they are of the same type.

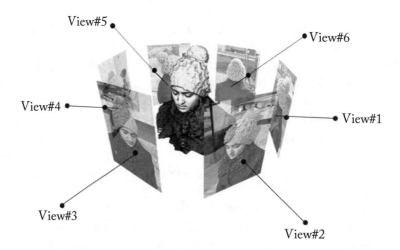

Figure 1.2: Given a set of images of an object (e.g., upper human body) captured from six different viewpoints, a dense 3D model of the object can be reconstructed using computer vision algorithms.

that the next generation of computers could even understand human actions and languages at the same level as humans, carry out some missions on behalf of humans, and respond to human commands in a smart way.

Human-computer Interaction

Nowadays, video cameras are widely used for human-computer interaction and in the entertainment industry. For instance, hand gestures are used in sign language to communicate, transfer messages in noisy environments, and interact with computer games. Video cameras provide a natural and intuitive way of human communication with a device. Therefore, one of the most important aspects for these cameras is the recognition of gestures and short actions from videos.

Robotics

Integrating computer vision technologies with high-performance sensors and cleverly designed hardware has given rise to a new generation of robots which can work alongside humans and perform many different tasks in unpredictable environments. For example, an advanced humanoid robot can jump, talk, run, or walk up stairs in a very similar way a human does. It can also recognize and interact with people. In general, an advanced humanoid robot can perform various activities that are mere reflexes for humans and do not require a high intellectual effort.

Multimedia

Computer vision technology plays a key role in multimedia applications. These have led to a massive research effort in the development of computer vision algorithms for processing, analyzing, and interpreting multimedia data. For example, given a video, one can ask "What does this video mean?", which involves a quite challenging task of image/video understanding and summarization. As another example, given a clip of video, computers could search the Internet and get millions of similar videos. More interestingly, when one gets tired of watching a long movie, computers would automatically summarize the movie for them.

1.1.2 IMAGE PROCESSING VS. COMPUTER VISION

Image processing can be considered as a preprocessing step for computer vision. More precisely, the goal of image processing is to extract fundamental image primitives, including edges and corners, filtering, morphology operations, etc. These image primitives are usually represented as images. For example, in order to perform semantic image segmentation (Fig. 1.1), which is a computer vision task, one might need to apply some filtering on the image (an image processing task) during that process.

Unlike image processing, which is mainly focused on processing raw images without giving any knowledge feedback on them, computer vision produces semantic descriptions of images. Based on the abstraction level of the output information, computer vision tasks can be divided into three different categories, namely low-level, mid-level, and high-level vision.

Low-level Vision

Based on the extracted image primitives, low-level vision tasks could be preformed on images/videos. Image matching is an example of low-level vision tasks. It is defined as the automatic identification of corresponding image points on a given pair of the same scene from different view points, or a moving scene captured by a fixed camera. Identifying image correspondences is an important problem in computer vision for geometry and motion recovery.

Another fundamental low-level vision task is optical flow computation and motion analysis. Optical flow is the pattern of the apparent motion of objects, surfaces, and edges in a visual scene caused by the movement of an object or camera. Optical flow is a 2D vector field where each vector corresponds to a displacement vector showing the movement of points from one frame to the next. Most existing methods which estimate camera motion or object motion use optical flow information.

Mid-level Vision

Mid-level vision provides a higher level of abstraction than low-level vision. For instance, inferring the geometry of objects is one of the major aspects of mid-level vision. Geometric vision includes multi-view geometry, stereo, and structure from motion (SfM), which infer the 3D scene information from 2D images such that 3D reconstruction could be made possible. Another task of mid-level vision is visual motion capturing and tracking, which estimate 2D and 3D motions, including deformable and articulated motions. In order to answer the question "How does the object move?," image segmentation is required to find areas in the images which belong to the object.

High-level Vision

Based on an adequate segmented representation of the 2D and/or 3D structure of the image, extracted using lower level vision (e.g., low-level image processing, low-level and mid-level vision), high-level vision completes the task of delivering a coherent interpretation of the image. High-level vision determines what objects are present in the scene and interprets their interrelations. For example, object recognition and scene understanding are two high-level vision tasks which infer the semantics of objects and scenes, respectively. How to achieve robust recognition, e.g., recognizing object from different viewpoint is still a challenging problem.

Another example of higher level vision is image understanding and video understanding. Based on information provided by object recognition, image and video understanding try to answer questions such as "Is there a tiger in the image?" or "Is this video a drama or an action?," or "Is there any suspicious activity in a surveillance video?" Developing such high-level vision tasks helps to fulfill different higher level tasks in intelligent human-computer interaction, intelligent robots, smart environment, and content-based multimedia.

1.2   WHAT IS MACHINE LEARNING?

Computer vision algorithms have seen a rapid progress in recent years. In particular, combining computer vision with machine learning contributes to the development of flexible and robust computer vision algorithms and, thus, improving the performance of practical vision systems.

For instance, Facebook has combined computer vision, machine learning, and their large corpus of photos, to achieve a robust and highly accurate facial recognition system. That is how Facebook can suggest who to tag in your photo. In the following, we first define machine learning and then describe the importance of machine learning for computer vision tasks.

Machine learning is a type of artificial intelligence (AI) which allows computers to learn from data without being explicitly programmed. In other words, the goal of machine learning is to design methods that automatically perform learning using observations of the real world (called the "training data"), without explicit definition of rules or logic by the humans ("trainer"/"supervisor"). In that sense, machine learning can be considered as *programming by data samples*. In summary, machine learning is about learning to do better in the future based on what was experienced in the past.

A diverse set of machine learning algorithms has been proposed to cover the wide variety of data and problem types. These learning methods can be mainly divided into three main approaches, namely *supervised*, *semi-supervised*, and *unsupervised*. However, the majority of practical machine learning methods are currently supervised learning methods, because of their superior performance compared to other counter-parts. In supervised learning methods, the training data takes the form of a collection of (data:x, label:y) pairs and the goal is to produce a prediction y^* in response to a query sample x. The input x can be a features vector, or more complex data such as images, documents, or graphs. Similarly, different types of output y have been studied. The output y can be a binary label which is used in a simple binary classification problem (e.g., "yes" or "no"). However, there has also been numerous research works on problems such as multi-class classification where y is labeled by one of k labels, multi-label classification where y takes on simultaneously the K labels, and general structured prediction problems where y is a high-dimensional output, which is constructed from a sequence of predictions (e.g., semantic segmentation).

Supervised learning methods approximate a mapping function $f(x)$ which can predict the output variables y for a given input sample x. Different forms of mapping function $f(.)$ exist (some are briefly covered in Chapter 2), including decision trees, Random Decision Forests (RDF), logistic regression (LR), Support Vector Machines (SVM), Neural Networks (NN), kernel machines, and Bayesian classifiers. A wide range of learning algorithms has also been proposed to estimate these different types of mappings.

On the other hand, **unsupervised learning** is where one would only have input data X and no corresponding output variables. It is called unsupervised learning because (unlike supervised learning) there are no ground-truth outputs and there is no teacher. The goal of unsupervised learning is to model the underlying structure/distribution of data in order to discover an interesting structure in the data. The most common unsupervised learning method is the clustering approach such as hierarchical clustering, k-means clustering, Gaussian Mixture Models (GMMs), Self-Organizing Maps (SOMs), and Hidden Markov Models (HMMs).

Semi-supervised learning methods sit in-between supervised and unsupervised learning. These learning methods are used when a large amount of input data is available and only some of the data is labeled. A good example is a photo archive where only some of the images are labeled (e.g., dog, cat, person), and the majority are unlabeled.

1.2.1   WHY DEEP LEARNING?

While these machine learning algorithms have been around for a long time, the ability to automatically apply complex mathematical computations to large-scale data is a recent development. This is because the increased power of today's computers, in terms of speed and memory, has helped machine learning techniques evolve to learn from a large corpus of training data. For example, with more computing power and a large enough memory, one can create neural networks of many layers, which are called deep neural networks. There are three key advantages which are offered by deep learning.

- **Simplicity:** Instead of problem specific tweaks and tailored feature detectors, deep networks offer basic architectural blocks, network layers, which are repeated several times to generate large networks.

- **Scalability:** Deep learning models are easily scalable to huge datasets. Other competing methods, e.g., kernel machines, encounter serious computational problems if the datasets are huge.

- **Domain transfer:** A model learned on one task is applicable to other related tasks and the learned features are general enough to work on a variety of tasks which may have scarce data available.

Due to the tremendous success in learning these deep neural networks, deep learning techniques are currently state-of-the-art for the detection, segmentation, classification and recognition (i.e., identification and verification) of objects in images. Researchers are now working to apply these successes in pattern recognition to more complex tasks such as medical diagnoses and automatic language translation. Convolutional Neural Networks (ConvNets or CNNs) are a category of deep neural networks which have proven to be very effective in areas such as image recognition and classification (see Chapter 7 for more details). Due to the impressive results of CNNs in these areas, this book is mainly focused on CNNs for computer vision tasks. Figure 1.3 illustrates the relation between computer vision, machine learning, human vision, deep learning, and CNNs.

1.3   BOOK OVERVIEW

CHAPTER 2

The book begins in Chapter 2 with a review of the traditional feature representation and classification methods. Computer vision tasks, such as image classification and object detection, have

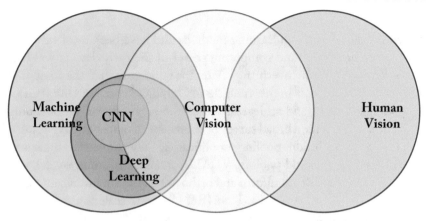

Figure 1.3: The relation between human vision, computer vision, machine learning, deep learning, and CNNs.

traditionally been approached using hand-engineered features which are divided into two different main categories: global features and local features. Due to the popularity of the low-level representation, this chapter first reviews three widely used low-level hand-engineered descriptors, namely Histogram of Oriented Gradients (HOG) [Triggs and Dalal, 2005], Scale-Invariant Feature Transform (SIFT) [Lowe, 2004], and Speed-Up Robust Features (SURF) [Bay et al., 2008]. A typical computer vision system feeds these hand-engineered features to machine learning algorithms to classify images/videos. Two widely used machine learning algorithms, namely SVM [Cortes, 1995] and RDF [Breiman, 2001, Quinlan, 1986], are also introduced in details.

CHAPTER 3

The performance of a computer vision system is highly dependent on the features used. Therefore, current progress in computer vision has been based on the design of feature learners which minimizes the gap between high-level representations (interpreted by humans) and low-level features (detected by HOG [Triggs and Dalal, 2005] and SIFT [Lowe, 2004] algorithms). Deep neural networks are one of the well-known and popular feature learners which allow the removal of complicated and problematic hand-engineered features. Unlike the standard feature extraction algorithms (e.g., SIFT and HOG), deep neural networks use several hidden layers to hierarchically learn the high level representation of an image. For instance, the first layer might detect edges and curves in the image, the second layer might detect object body-parts (e.g., hands or paws or ears), the third layer might detect the whole object, etc. In this chapter, we provide an introduction to deep neural networks, their computational mechanism and their historical background. Two generic categories of deep neural networks, namely feed-forward and feed-back networks, with their corresponding learning algorithms are explained in detail.

CHAPTER 4

CNNs are a prime example of deep learning methods and have been most extensively studied. Due to the lack of training data and computing power in the early days, it was hard to train a large high-capacity CNN without overfitting. After the rapid growth in the amount of annotated data and the recent improvements in the strengths of Graphics Processor Units (GPUs), research on CNNs has emerged rapidly and achieved state-of-the-art results on various computer vision tasks. In this chapter, we provide a broad survey of the recent advances in CNNs, including state-of-the-art layers (e.g., convolution, pooling, nonlinearity, fully connected, transposed convolution, ROI pooling, spatial pyramid pooling, VLAD, spatial transformer layers), weight initialization approaches (e.g., Gaussian, uniform and orthogonal random initialization, unsupervised pre-training, Xavier, and Rectifier Linear Unit (ReLU) aware scaled initialization, supervised pre-training), regularization approaches (e.g., data augmentation, dropout, drop-connect, batch normalization, ensemble averaging, the ℓ^1 and ℓ^2 regularization, elastic net, max-norm constraint, early stopping), and several loss functions (e.g., soft-max, SVM hinge, squared hinge, Euclidean, contrastive, and expectation loss).

CHAPTER 5

The CNN training process involves the optimization of its parameters such that the loss function is minimized. This chapter reviews well-known and popular gradient-based training algorithms (e.g., batch gradient descent, stochastic gradient descent, mini-batch gradient descent) followed by state-of-the-art optimizers (e.g., Momentum, Nesterov momentum, AdaGrad, AdaDelta, RMSprop, Adam) which address the limitations of the gradient descent learning algorithms. In order to make this book a self-contained guide, this chapter also discusses the different approaches that are used to compute differentials of the most popular CNN layers which are employed to train CNNs using the error back-propagation algorithm.

CHAPTER 6

This chapter introduces the most popular CNN architectures which are formed using the basic building blocks studied in Chapter 4 and Chapter 7. Both early CNN architectures which are easier to understand (e.g., LeNet, NiN, AlexNet, VGGnet) and the recent CNN ones (e.g., GoogleNet, ResNet, ResNeXt, FractalNet, DenseNet), which are relatively complex, are presented in details.

CHAPTER 7

This chapter reviews various applications of CNNs in computer vision, including image classification, object detection, semantic segmentation, scene labeling, and image generation. For each application, the popular CNN-based models are explained in detail.

CHAPTER 8

Deep learning methods have resulted in significant performance improvements in computer vision applications and, thus, several software frameworks have been developed to facilitate these implementations. This chapter presents a comparative study of nine widely used deep learning frameworks, namely Caffe, TensorFlow, MatConvNet, Torch7, Theano, Keras, Lasagne, Marvin, and Chainer, on different aspects. This chapter helps the readers to understand the main features of these frameworks (e.g., the provided interface and platforms for each framework) and, thus, the readers can choose the one which suits their needs best.

CHAPTER 2

Features and Classifiers

Feature extraction and classification are two key stages of a typical computer vision system. In this chapter, we provide an introduction to these two steps: their importance and their design challenges for computer vision tasks.

Feature extraction methods can be divided into two different categories, namely hand-engineering-based methods and feature learning-based methods. Before going into the details of the feature learning algorithms in the subsequent chapters (i.e., Chapter 3, Chapter 4, Chapter 5, and Chapter 6), we introduce in this chapter some of the most popular traditional hand-engineered features (e.g., HOG [Triggs and Dalal, 2005], SIFT [Lowe, 2004], SURF [Bay et al., 2008]), and their limitations in details.

Classifiers can be divided into two groups, namely shallow and deep models. This chapter also introduces some well-known traditional classifiers (e.g., SVM [Cortes, 1995], RDF [Breiman, 2001, Quinlan, 1986]), which have a single learned layer and are therefore shallow models. The subsequent chapters (i.e., Chapter 3, Chapter 4, Chapter 5, and Chapter 6) cover the deep models, including CNNs, which have multiple hidden layers and, thus, can learn features at various levels of abstraction.

2.1 IMPORTANCE OF FEATURES AND CLASSIFIERS

The accuracy, robustness, and efficiency of a vision system are largely dependent on the quality of the image features and the classifiers. An ideal feature extractor would produce an image representation that makes the job of the classifier trivial (see Fig. 2.1). Conversely, unsophisticated features extractors require a "perfect" classifier to adequately perform the pattern recognition task. However, ideal features extraction and a perfect classification performance are often impossible. Thus, the goal is to extract informative and reliable features from the input images, in order to enable the development of a largely domain-independent theory of classification.

2.1.1 FEATURES

A feature is any distinctive aspect or characteristic which is used to solve a computational task related to a certain application. For example, given a face image, there is a variety of approaches to extract features, e.g., mean, variance, gradients, edges, geometric features, color features, etc.

The combination of n features can be represented as a n-dimensional vector, called a feature vector. The quality of a feature vector is dependent on its ability to discriminate image samples from different classes. Image samples from the same class should have similar feature

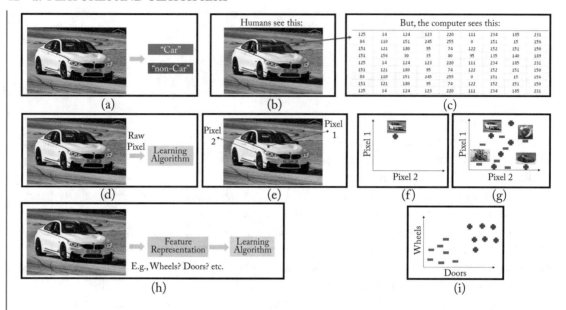

Figure 2.1: (a) The aim is to design an algorithm which classifies input images into two different categories: "Car" or "non-Car." (b) Humans can easily see the car and categorize this image as "Car." However, computers see pixel intensity values as shown in (c) for a small patch in the image. Computer vision methods process all pixel intensity values and classify the image. (d) The straightforward way is to feed the intensity values to the classifiers and the learned classifier will then perform the classification job. For better visualization, let us pick only two pixels, as shown in (e). Because pixel 1 is relatively bright and pixel 2 is relatively dark, that image has a position shown in blue plus sign in the plot shown in (f). By adding few positive and negative samples, the plot in (g) shows that the positive and negative samples are extremely jumbled together. So if this data is fed to a linear classifier, the subdivision of the feature space into two classes is not possible. (h) It turns out that a proper feature representation can overcome this problem. For example, using more informative features such as the number of wheels in the images, the number of doors in the images, the data looks like (i) and the images become much easier to classify.

values and images from different classes should have different feature values. For the example shown in Fig. 2.1, all cars shown in Fig. 2.2 should have similar feature vectors, irrespective of their models, sizes, positions in the images, etc. Thus, a good feature should be informative, invariant to noise and a set of transformations (e.g., rotation and translation), and fast to compute. For instance, features such as the number of wheels in the images, the number of doors in the images could help to classify the images into two different categories, namely "car" and "non-car." However, extracting such features is a challenging problem in computer vision and machine learning.

Figure 2.2: Images of different classes of cars captured from different scenes and viewpoints.

2.1.2   CLASSIFIERS

Classification is at the heart of modern computer vision and pattern recognition. The task of the classifier is to use the feature vector to assign an image or region of interest (RoI) to a category. The degree of difficulty of the classification task depends on the variability in the feature values of images from the same category, relative to the difference between feature values of images from different categories. However, a perfect classification performance is often impossible. This is mainly due to the presence of noise (in the form of shadows, occlusions, perspective distortions, etc.), outliers (e.g., images from the category "buildings" might contain people, animal, building, or car category), ambiguity (e.g., the same rectangular shape could correspond to a table or a building window), the lack of labels, the availability of only small training samples, and the imbalance of positive/negative coverage in the training data samples. Thus, designing a classifier to make the best decision is a challenging task.

2.2   TRADITIONAL FEATURE DESCRIPTORS

Traditional (hand-engineered) feature extraction methods can be divided into two broad categories: global and local. The global feature extraction methods define a set of global features which effectively describe the entire image. Thus, the shape details are ignored. The global features are also not suitable for the recognition of partially occluded objects. On the other hand, the local feature extraction methods extract a local region around keypoints and, thus, can handle occlusion better [Bayramoglu and Alatan, 2010, Rahmani et al., 2014]. On that basis, the focus of this chapter is on local features/descriptors.

Various methods have been developed for detecting keypoints and constructing descriptors around them. For instance, local descriptors, such as HOG [Triggs and Dalal, 2005], SIFT [Lowe, 2004], SURF [Bay et al., 2008], FREAK [Alahi et al., 2012], ORB [Rublee et al., 2011], BRISK [Leutenegger et al., 2011], BRIEF [Calonder et al., 2010], and LIOP [Wang et al., 2011b] have been used in most computer vision applications. The considerable recent progress that has been achieved in the area of recognition is largely due to these features, e.g., optical flow estimation methods use orientation histograms to deal with large motions; image retrieval and structure from motion are based on SIFT descriptors. It is important to note that CNNs, which will be discussed in Chapter 4, are not that much different than the traditional hand-engineered features. The first layer in the CNNs learn to utilize gradients in a way that is similar to hand-engineered features such as HOG, SIFT and SURF. In order to have a better understanding of CNNs, we describe next, three important and widely used feature detectors and/or descriptors, namely HOG [Triggs and Dalal, 2005], SIFT [Lowe, 2004], and SURF [Bay et al., 2008] in some details. As you will see in Chapter 4, CNNs are also able to extract similar hand-engineered features (e.g., gradients) in their lower layers but through an automatic feature learning process.

2.2.1 HISTOGRAM OF ORIENTED GRADIENTS (HOG)

HOG [Triggs and Dalal, 2005] is a feature descriptor that is used to automatically detect objects from images. The HOG descriptor encodes the distribution of directions of gradients in localized portions of an image.

HOG features have been introduced by Triggs and Dalal [2005] who have studied the influence of several variants of HOG descriptors (R-HOG and C-HOG), with different gradient computation and normalization methods. The idea behind the HOG descriptors is that the object appearance and the shape within an image can be described by the histogram of edge directions. The implementation of these descriptors consists of the following four steps.

Gradient Computation
The first step is the computation of the gradient values. A 1D centered point discrete derivative mask is applied on an image in both the horizontal and vertical directions. Specifically, this method requires the filtering of the gray-scale image with the following filter kernels:

$$f_x = [-1 \ 0 \ +1] \quad \text{and} \quad f_y = [-1 \ 0 \ +1]^T. \tag{2.1}$$

Thus, given an image I, the following convolution operations (denoted by $*$) result in the derivatives of the image I in the x and y directions:

$$I_x = I * f_x \quad \text{and} \quad I_y = I * f_y. \tag{2.2}$$

Thus, the orientation θ and the magnitude $|g|$ of the gradient are calculated as follows:

$$\theta = \arctan \frac{I_y}{I_x} \quad \text{and} \quad |g| = \sqrt[2]{I_x^2 + I_y^2}. \tag{2.3}$$

As you will see in Chapter 4, just like the HOG descriptor, CNNs also use convolution operations in their layers. However, the main difference is that instead of using hand-engineered filters, e.g., f_x, f_y in Eq. (2.1), CNNs use trainable filters which make them highly adaptive. That is why they can achieve high accuracy levels in most applications such as image recognition.

Cell Orientation Histogram
The second step is the calculation of the cell histograms. First, the image is divided into small (usually 8×8 pixels) cells. Each cell has a fixed number of gradient orientation bins, which are evenly spread over 0–180° or 0–360°, depending on whether the gradient is *unsigned* or *signed*. Each pixel within the cell casts a weighted vote for a gradient orientation bin based on the gradient magnitude at that pixel. For the vote weight, the pixel contribution can be the gradient magnitude, or the square root of the gradient magnitude or the square of the gradient magnitude.

Block Descriptor
To deal with changes in illumination and contrast, the gradient strengths are locally normalized by grouping the cells together into larger, spatially connected blocks. The HOG descriptor is then the vector of the components of the normalized cell histograms from all of the block regions.

Block Normalization
The final step is the normalization of the block descriptors. Let $\mathbf{v}$ be the non-normalized vector containing all histograms in a given block, $||\mathbf{v}||_k$ be its k-norm for $k = 1, 2$, and ϵ be a small constant. Then the normalization factor can be one of the following:

$$\text{L2-norm:} \quad \mathbf{v} = \frac{\mathbf{v}}{\sqrt{||\mathbf{v}||_2^2 + e^2}}, \tag{2.4}$$

or

$$\text{L1-norm:} \quad \mathbf{v} = \frac{\mathbf{v}}{||\mathbf{v}||_1 + \epsilon}, \tag{2.5}$$

or

$$\text{L1-sqrt:} \quad \mathbf{v} = \sqrt{\frac{\mathbf{v}}{||\mathbf{v}||_1 + \epsilon}}. \tag{2.6}$$

There is another normalization factor, L2-Hys, which is obtained by clipping the L2-norm of $\mathbf{v}$ (i.e., limiting the maximum values of $\mathbf{v}$ to 0.2) and then re-normalizing.

The final image/RoI descriptor is formed by concatenating all normalized block descriptors. The experimental results in Triggs and Dalal [2005] show that all four block normalization methods achieve a very significant improvement over the non-normalized one. Moreover, the L2-norm, L2-Hys, and L1-sqrt normalization approaches provide a similar performance, while the L1-norm provides a slightly less reliable performance.

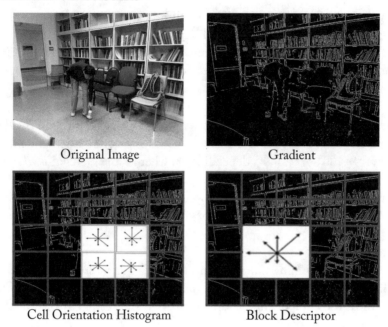

Original Image   Gradient

Cell Orientation Histogram   Block Descriptor

Figure 2.3: HOG descriptor. Note that for better visualization, we only show the cell orientation histogram for four cells and a block descriptor corresponding to those four cells.

2.2.2   SCALE-INVARIANT FEATURE TRANSFORM (SIFT)

SIFT [Lowe, 2004] provides a set of features of an object that are are robust against object scaling and rotations. The SIFT algorithm consists of four main steps, which are discussed in the following subsections.

Scale-space Extrema Detection

The first step aims to identify potential keypoints that are invariant to scale and orientation. While several techniques can be used to detect keypoint locations in the scale-space, SIFT uses the Difference of Gaussians (DoG), which is obtained as the difference of Gaussian blurring of an image with two different scales, σ, one with scale k times the scale of the other, i.e., $k \times \sigma$. This process is performed for different octaves of the image in the Gaussian Pyramid, as shown in Fig. 2.4a.

Then, the DoG images are searched for local extrema over all scales and image locations. For instance, a pixel in an image is compared with its eight neighbors in the current image as well as nine neighbors in the scale above and below, as shown in Fig. 2.4b. If it is the minimum or maximum of all these neighbors, then it is a potential keypoint. It means that a keypoint is best represented in that scale.

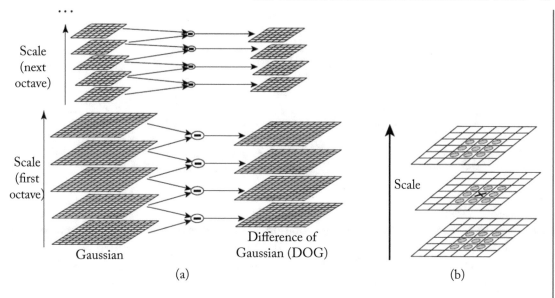

Figure 2.4: Scale-space feature detection using a sub-octave DoG pyramid. (a) Adjacent levels of a sub-octave Gaussian pyramid are subtracted to produce the DoG; and (b) extrema in the resulting 3D volume are detected by comparing a pixel to its 26 neighbors. (Figure from Lowe [2004], used with permission.)

Accurate Keypoint Localization

This step removes unstable points from the list of potential keypoints by finding those that have low contrast or are poorly localized on an edge. In order to reject low contrast keypoints, a Taylor series expansion of the scale space is computed to get more accurate locations of extrema, and if the intensity at each extrema is less than a threshold value, the keypoint is rejected.

Moreover, the DoG function has a strong response along the edges, which results in a large principal curvature across the edge but a small curvature in the perpendicular direction in the DoG function. In order to remove the keypoints located on an edge, the principal curvature at the keypoint is computed from a 2×2 Hessian matrix at the location and scale of the keypoint. If the ratio between the first and the second eigenvalues is greater than a threshold, the keypoint is rejected.

Remark: In mathematics, the Hessian matrix or Hessian is a square matrix of second-order partial derivatives of a scalar-valued function. Specifically, suppose $f(x_1, x_2, \cdots, x_n)$ is a function outputting a scalar, i.e., $f : \mathbb{R}^n \to \mathbb{R}$; if all the second partial derivatives of f exist and are continuous over the domain of the function, then the Hessian H of f is a square $n \times n$ matrix, defined as follows:

$$H = \begin{bmatrix} \frac{\partial^2 f}{\partial x_1^2} & \frac{\partial^2 f}{\partial x_1 \partial x_2} & \cdots & \frac{\partial^2 f}{\partial x_1 \partial x_n} \\ \frac{\partial^2 f}{\partial x_2 \partial x_1} & \frac{\partial^2 f}{\partial x_2^2} & \cdots & \frac{\partial^2 f}{\partial x_2 \partial x_n} \\ \vdots & \vdots & \ddots & \vdots \\ \frac{\partial^2 f}{\partial x_n \partial x_1} & \frac{\partial^2 f}{\partial x_n \partial x_2} & \cdots & \frac{\partial^2 f}{\partial x_n^2} \end{bmatrix}. \tag{2.7}$$

Orientation Assignment

In order to achieve invariance to image rotation, a consistent orientation is assigned to each keypoint based on its local image properties. The keypoint descriptor can then be represented relative to this orientation. The algorithm used to find an orientation consists of the following steps.

1. The scale of the keypoint is used to select the Gaussian blurred image with the closest scale.

2. The gradient magnitude and orientation are computed for each image pixel at this scale.

3. As shown in Fig. 2.5, an orientation histogram, which consists of 36 bins covering the 360° range of orientations, is built from the gradient orientations of pixels within a local region around the keypoint.

4. The highest peak in the local orientation histogram corresponds to the dominant direction of the local gradients. Moreover, any other local peak that is within 80% of the highest peak is also considered as a keypoint with that orientation.

Keypoint Descriptor

The dominant direction (the highest peak in the histogram) of the local gradients is also used to create keypoint descriptors. The gradient orientations are rotated relative to the orientation of the keypoint and then weighted by a Gaussian with a variance of $1.5 \times keypoint scale$. Then, a 16×16 neighborhood around the keypoint is divided into 16 sub-blocks of size 4×4. For each sub-block, an 8 bin orientation histogram is created. This results in a feature vector, called SIFT descriptor, containing 128 elements. Figure 2.6 illustrates the SIFT descriptors for keypoints extracted from an example image.

Complexity of SIFT Descriptor

In summary, SIFT tries to standardize all images (if the image is blown up, SIFT shrinks it; if the image is shrunk, SIFT enlarges it). This corresponds to the idea that if a keypoint can

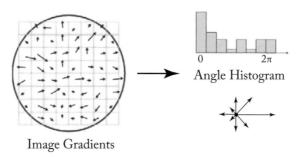

Image Gradients

Figure 2.5: A dominant orientation estimate is computed by creating a histogram of all the gradient orientations weighted by their magnitudes and then finding the significant peaks in this distribution.

Figure 2.6: An example of the SIFT detector and descriptor: (left) an input image, (middle) some of the detected keypoints with their corresponding scales and orientations, and (right) SIFT descriptors–a 16 × 16 neighborhood around each keypoint is divided into 16 sub-blocks of 4 × 4 size.

be detected in an image at scale σ, then we would need a larger dimension $k\sigma$ to capture the same keypoint, if the image was up-scaled. However, the mathematical ideas of SIFT and many other hand-engineered features are quite complex and require many years of research. For example, Lowe [2004] spent almost 10 years on the design and tuning of the SIFT parameters. As we will show in Chapters 4, 5, and 6, CNNs also perform a series of transformations on the image by incorporating several convolutional layers. However, unlike SIFT, CNNs learn these transformation (e.g., scale, rotation, translation) from image data, without the need of complex mathematical ideas.

2.2.3 SPEEDED-UP ROBUST FEATURES (SURF)

SURF [Bay et al., 2008] is a speeded up version of SIFT. In SIFT, the Laplacian of Gaussian is approximated with the DoG to construct a scale-space. SURF speeds up this process by approximating the LoG with a box filter. Thus, a convolution with a box filter can easily be computed with the help of integral images and can be performed in parallel for different scales.

Keypoint Localization

In the first step, a blob detector based on the Hessian matrix is used to localize keypoints. The determinant of the Hessian matrix is used to select both the location and scale of the potential keypoints. More precisely, for an image I with a given point $p = (x, y)$, the Hessian matrix $H(\mathbf{p}, \sigma)$ at point $\mathbf{p}$ and scale σ, is defined as follows:

$$H(\mathbf{p}, \sigma) = \begin{bmatrix} L_{xx}(\mathbf{p}, \sigma) & L_{xy}(\mathbf{p}, \sigma) \\ L_{xy}(\mathbf{p}, \sigma) & L_{yy}(\mathbf{p}, \sigma) \end{bmatrix}, \tag{2.8}$$

where $L_{xx}(\mathbf{p}, \sigma)$ is the convolution of the second-order derivative of the Gaussian, $\frac{\partial^2}{\partial x^2} g(\sigma)$, with the image I at point $\mathbf{p}$. However, instead of using Gaussian filters, SURF uses approximated Gaussian second-order derivatives, which can be evaluated using integral images at a very low computational cost. Thus, unlike SIFT, SURF does not require to iteratively apply the same filter to the output of a previously filtered layer, and scale-space analysis is done by keeping the same image and varying the filter size, i.e., 9×9, 25×15, 21×21, and 27×27.

Then, a non-maximum suppression in a $3 \times 3 \times 3$ neighborhood of each point in the image is applied to localize the keypoints in the image. The maxima of the determinant of the Hessian matrix are then interpolated in the scale and image space, using the method proposed by Brown and Lowe [2002].

Orientation Assignment

In order to achieve rotational invariance, the Haar wavelet responses in both the horizontal x and vertical y directions within a circular neighborhood of radius $6s$ around the keypoint are computed, where s is the scale at which the keypoint is detected. Then, the Haar wavelet responses in both the horizontal dx and vertical dy directions are weighted with a Gaussian centered at a keypoint, and represented as points in a 2D space. The dominant orientation of the keypoint is estimated by computing the sum of all the responses within a sliding orientation window of angle $60°$. The horizontal and vertical responses within the window are then summed. The two summed responses is considered as a local vector. The longest orientation vector over all the windows determines the orientation of the keypoint. In order to achieve a balance between robustness and angular resolution, the size of the sliding window need to be chosen carefully.

Keypoint Descriptor

To describe the region around each keypoint $\mathbf{p}$, a $20s \times 20s$ square region around $\mathbf{p}$ is extracted and then oriented along the orientation of $\mathbf{p}$. The normalized orientation region around $\mathbf{p}$ is split into smaller 4×4 square sub-regions. The Haar wavelet responses in both the horizontal dx and vertical dy directions are extracted at 5×5 regularly spaced sample points for each sub-region. In order to achieve more robustness to deformations, noise and translation, The Haar wavelet responses are weighted with a Gaussian. Then, dx and dy are summed up over each sub-region and the results form the first set of entries in the feature vector. The sum of the absolute values of the responses, $|dx|$ and $|dy|$, are also computed and then added to the feature vector to encode information about the intensity changes. Since each sub-region has a 4D feature vector, concatenating all 4×4 sub-regions results in a 64D descriptor.

2.2.4   LIMITATIONS OF TRADITIONAL HAND-ENGINEERED FEATURES

Until recently, progress in computer vision was based on hand-engineering features. However, feature engineering is difficult, time-consuming, and requires expert knowledge on the problem domain. The other issue with hand-engineered features such as HOG, SIFT, SURF, or other algorithms like them, is that they are too sparse in terms of information that they are able to capture from an image. This is because the first-order image derivatives are not sufficient features for the purpose of most computer vision tasks such as image classification and object detection. Moreover, the choice of features often depends on the application. More precisely, these features do not facilitate learning from previous learnings/representations (transfer learning). In addition, the design of hand-engineered features is limited by the complexity that humans can put in it. All these issues are resolved using automatic feature learning algorithms such as deep neural networks, which will be addressed in the subsequent chapters (i.e., Chapters 3, 4, 5, and 6).

2.3   MACHINE LEARNING CLASSIFIERS

Machine learning is usually divided into three main areas, namely *supervised*, *unsupervised*, and *semi-supervised*. In the case of the supervised learning approach, the goal is to learn a mapping from inputs to outputs, given a **labeled** set of input-output pairs. The second type of machine learning is the unsupervised learning approach, where we are only given inputs, and the goal is to automatically find interesting patterns in the data. This problem is not a well-defined problem, because we are not told what kind of patterns to look for. Moreover, unlike supervised learning, where we can compare our label prediction for a given sample to the observed value, there is no obvious error metric to use. The third type of machine learning is semi-supervised learning, which typically combines a small amount of labeled data with a large amount of unlabeled data to generate an appropriate function or classifier. The cost of the labeling process of a large corpus of data is infeasible, whereas the acquisition of unlabeled data is relatively inexpensive. In such cases, the semi-supervised learning approach can be of great practical value.

Another important class of machine learning algorithms is "reinforcement learning," where the algorithm allows agents to automatically determine the ideal behavior given an observation of the world. Every agent has some impact on the environment, and the environment provides reward feedback to guide the learning algorithm. However, in this book our focus is mainly on the supervised learning approach, which is the most widely used machine learning approach in practice.

A wide range of supervised classification techniques has been proposed in the literature. These methods can be divided into three different categories, namely **linear** (e.g., SVM [Cortes, 1995]; logistic regression; Linear Discriminant Analysis (LDA) [Fisher, 1936]), **nonlinear** (e.g., Multi Layer Perceptron (MLP), kernel SVM), and **ensemble-based** (e.g., RDF [Breiman, 2001, Quinlan, 1986]; AdaBoost [Freund and Schapire, 1997]) classifiers. The goal of ensemble methods is to combine the predictions of several base classifiers to improve generalization over a single classifier. The ensemble methods can be divided into two categories, namely *averaging* (e.g., Bagging methods; Random Decision Forests [Breiman, 2001, Quinlan, 1986]) and *boosting* (e.g., AdaBoost [Freund and Schapire, 1997]; Gradient Tree Boosting [Friedman, 2000]). In the case of the averaging methods, the aim is to build several classifiers independently and then to average their predictions. For the boosting methods, base "weak" classifiers are built sequentially and one tries to reduce the bias of the combined overall classifier. The motivation is to combine several weak models to produce a powerful ensemble.

Our definition of a machine learning classifier that is capable of improving computer vision tasks via experience is somewhat abstract. To make this more concrete, in the following we describe three widely used linear (SVM), nonlinear (kernel SVM) and ensemble (RDF) classifiers in some detail.

2.3.1   SUPPORT VECTOR MACHINE (SVM)

SVM [Cortes, 1995] is a supervised machine learning algorithm used for classification or regression problems. SVM works by finding a linear hyperplane which separates the training dataset into two classes. As there are many such linear hyperplanes, the SVM algorithm tries to find the optimal separating hyperplane (as shown in Fig. 2.7) which is intuitively achieved when the distance (also known as the *margin*) to the nearest training data samples is as large as possible. It is because, in general, the larger the margin the lower the generalization error of the model.

Mathematically, SVM is a maximum margin linear model. Given a training dataset of n samples of the form $\{(\mathbf{x}_1, y_1), \cdots, (\mathbf{x}_n, y_n)\}$, where $\mathbf{x}_i$ is an m-dimensional feature vector and $y_i = \{1, -1\}$ is the class to which the sample $\mathbf{x}_i$ belongs to. The goal of SVM is to find the maximum-margin hyperplane which divides the group of samples for which $y_i = 1$ from the group of samples for which $y_i = -1$. As shown in Fig. 2.7b (the bold blue line), this hyperplane can be written as the set of sample points satisfying the following equation:

$$\mathbf{w}^T \mathbf{x}_i + b = 0, \tag{2.9}$$

where $\mathbf{w}$ is the normal vector to the hyperplane. More precisely, any samples above the hyperplane should have label 1, i.e., $\mathbf{x}_i$ s.t. $\mathbf{w}^T \mathbf{x}_i + b > 0$ will have corresponding $y_i = 1$. Similarly, any samples below the hyperplane should have label -1, i.e., $\mathbf{x}_i$ s.t. $\mathbf{w}^T \mathbf{x}_i + b < 0$ will have corresponding $y_i = -1$.

Notice that there is some space between the hyperplane (or decision boundary, which is the bold blue line in Fig. 2.7b) and the nearest data samples of either class. Thus, the sample data is rescaled such that anything on or above the hyperplane $\mathbf{w}^T \mathbf{x}_i + b = 1$ is of one class with label 1, and anything on or below the hyperplane $\mathbf{w}^T \mathbf{x}_i + b = -1$ is of the other class with label -1. Since these two new hyperplanes are parallel, the distance between them is $\frac{2}{\sqrt{\mathbf{w}^T \mathbf{w}}}$, as shown in Fig. 2.7c.

Recall that SVM tries to maximize the distance between these two new hyperplanes demarcating two classes, which is equivalent to minimizing $\frac{\mathbf{w}^T \mathbf{w}}{2}$. Thus, SVM is learned by solving the following primal optimization problem:

$$\min_{\mathbf{w},b} \frac{\mathbf{w}^T \mathbf{w}}{2} \qquad (2.10)$$

subject to:

$$y_i(\mathbf{w}^T \mathbf{x}_i + b) \geq 1 \quad (\forall \ \text{samples} \ \mathbf{x}_i). \qquad (2.11)$$

Soft-margin Extension

In the case where the training samples are not perfectly linearly separable, SVM can allow some samples of one class to appear on the other side of the hyperplane (boundary) by introducing *slack variables*, an ξ_i for each sample $\mathbf{x}_i$ as follows:

$$\min_{\mathbf{w},b,\xi} \frac{\mathbf{w}^T \mathbf{w}}{2} + C \sum_i \xi_i, \qquad (2.12)$$

subject to:

$$y_i(\mathbf{w}^T \mathbf{x}_i + b) \geq 1 - \xi_i \ \text{and} \ \xi_i \geq 0 \ (\forall \ \text{samples} \ \mathbf{x}_i). \qquad (2.13)$$

Unlike deep neural networks, which will be introduced in Chapter 3, linear SVMs can only solve problems that are linearly separable, i.e., where the data samples belonging to class 1 can be separated from the samples belonging to class 2 by a hyperplane as shown in Fig. 2.7. However, in many cases, the data samples are not linearly separable.

Nonlinear Decision Boundary

SVM can be extended to nonlinear classification by projecting the original input space ($\mathbb{R}^d$) into a high-dimensional space ($\mathbb{R}^D$), where a separating hyperplane can hopefully be found. Thus, the formulation of the quadratic programming problem is as above (Eq. (2.12) and Eq. (2.13)), but with all $\mathbf{x}_i$ replaced with $\phi(\mathbf{x}_i)$, where ϕ provides a higher-dimensional mapping.

$$\min_{\mathbf{w},b,\xi} \frac{\mathbf{w}^T \mathbf{w}}{2} + C \sum_i \xi_i, \qquad (2.14)$$

subject to:

$$y_i(\mathbf{w}^T \phi(\mathbf{x}_i) + b) \geq 1 - \xi_i \ \text{and} \ \xi_i \geq 0 \ (\forall \ \text{samples} \ \mathbf{x}_i). \qquad (2.15)$$

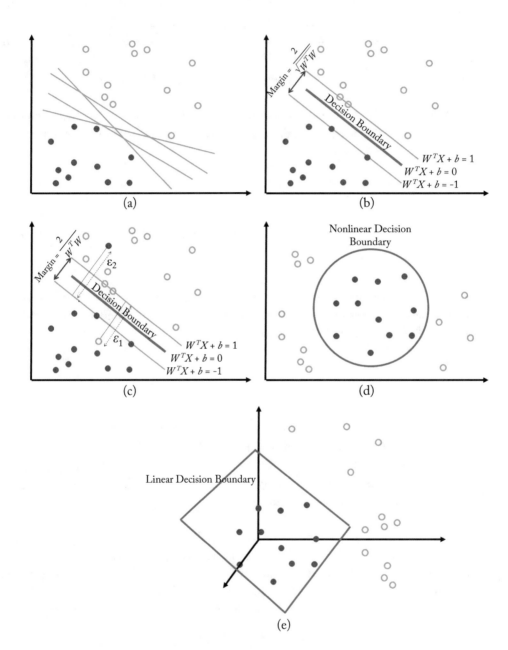

Figure 2.7: (*Continues.*)

Figure 2.7: (*Continued.*) For two classes, separable training datasets, such as the one shown in (a), there are lots of possible linear separators as shown with the blue lines in (a). Intuitively, a separating hyperplane (also called decision boundary) drawn in the middle of the void between the data samples of the two classes (the bold blue line in (b)) seems better than the ones shown in (a). SVM defines the criterion for a decision boundary that is maximally far away from any data point. This distance from the decision surface to the closest data point determines the margin of the classifier as shown in (b). In the hard-margin SVM, (b), a single outlier can determine the decision boundary, which makes the classifier overly sensitive to the noise in the data. However, a soft margin SVM classifier, shown in (c), allows some samples of each class to appear on the other side of the decision boundary by introducing slack variables ξ_i for each sample. (d) Shows an example where classes are not separable by a linear decision boundary. Thus, as shown in (e), the original input space $\mathbb{R}^2$ is projected onto $\mathbb{R}^3$, where a linear decision boundary can be found, i.e., using the kernel trick.

Dual Form of SVM

In the case that $D \gg d$, there are many more parameters to learn for $\mathbf{w}$. In order to avoid that, the *dual form* of SVM is used for optimization problem.

$$\max_{\alpha} \sum_i \alpha_i - \frac{1}{2} \sum_{i,j} \alpha_i \alpha_j \, y_i \, y_j \phi(\mathbf{x}_i)^T \phi(\mathbf{x}_j), \tag{2.16}$$

subject to:

$$\sum_i \alpha_i \, y_i = 0 \ \text{ and } \ 0 \leq \alpha_i \leq C, \tag{2.17}$$

where C is a hyper-parameter which controls the degree of misclassification of the model, in case classes are not linearly separable.

Kernel Trick

Since $\phi(\mathbf{x}_i)$ is in a high-dimensional space (even infinite-dimensional space), calculating $\phi(\mathbf{x}_i)^T \cdot \phi(\mathbf{x}_j)$ may be intractable. However, there are special kernel functions, such as linear, polynomial, Gaussian, and Radial Basis Function (RBF), which operate on the lower dimension vectors $\mathbf{x}_i$ and $\mathbf{x}_j$ to produce a value equivalent to the dot-product of the higher-dimensional vectors. For example, consider the function $\phi : \mathbb{R}^3 \longrightarrow \mathbb{R}^{10}$, where

$$\phi(\mathbf{x}) = (1, \sqrt{2}\mathbf{x}^{(1)}, \sqrt{2}\mathbf{x}^{(2)}, \sqrt{2}\mathbf{x}^{(3)}, [\mathbf{x}^{(1)}]^2, [\mathbf{x}^{(2)}]^2, [\mathbf{x}^{(3)}]^2, \sqrt{2}\mathbf{x}^{(1)}\mathbf{x}^{(2)}, \sqrt{2}\mathbf{x}^{(1)}\mathbf{x}^{(3)}, \sqrt{2}\mathbf{x}^{(2)}\mathbf{x}^{(3)}). \tag{2.18}$$

It is interesting to note that for the given function ϕ in Eq. (2.18),

$$K(\mathbf{x}_i, \mathbf{x}_j) = (1 + \mathbf{x}_i^T \mathbf{x}_j)^2 = \phi(\mathbf{x}_i)^T \cdot \phi(\mathbf{x}_j). \tag{2.19}$$

Thus, instead of calculating $\phi(\mathbf{x}_i)^T \cdot \phi(\mathbf{x}_j)$, the polynomial kernel function $K(\mathbf{x}_i, \mathbf{x}_j) = (1 + \mathbf{x}_i^T \mathbf{x}_j)^2$ is calculated to produce a value equivalent to the dot-product of the higher-dimensional vectors, $\phi(\mathbf{x}_i)^T \cdot \phi(\mathbf{x}_j)$.

Note that the dual optimization problem is exactly the same, except that the dot product $\phi(\mathbf{x}_i)^T \cdot \phi(\mathbf{x}_j)$ is replaced by a kernel $K(\mathbf{x}_i, \mathbf{x}_j)$, which corresponds to the dot product of $\phi(\mathbf{x}_i)$ and $\phi(\mathbf{x}_j)$ in the new space.

$$\max_{\alpha} \sum_i \alpha_i - \frac{1}{2} \sum_{i,j} \alpha_i \alpha_j \, y_i \, y_j \, K(\mathbf{x}_i, \mathbf{x}_j), \tag{2.20}$$

subject to:

$$\sum_i \alpha_i \, y_i = 0 \text{ and } 0 \leq \alpha_i \leq C. \tag{2.21}$$

In summary, linear SVMs can be thought of as a single layer classifier and kernel SVMs can be thought of as a 2 layer neural network. However, unlike SVMs, Chapter 3 shows that deep neural networks are typically built by concatenating several nonlinear hidden layers, and thus, can extract more complex pattern from data samples.

2.3.2   RANDOM DECISION FOREST

A random decision forest [Breiman, 2001, Quinlan, 1986] is an ensemble of decision trees. As shown in Fig. 2.8a, each tree consists of split and leaf nodes. A split node performs binary classification based on the value of a particular feature of the features vector. If the value of the particular feature is less than a threshold, then the sample is assigned to the left partition, else to the right partition. Figure 2.8b shows an illustrative decision tree used to figure out whether a photo represents and indoor or an outdoor scene. If the classes are linearly separable, after $\log_2(c)$ decisions each sample class will get separated from the remaining $c - 1$ classes and reach a leaf node. For a given feature vector $\mathbf{f}$, each tree predicts independently its label and a majority voting scheme is used to predict the final label of the feature vector. It has been shown that random decision forests are fast and effective multi-class classifiers [Shotton et al., 2011].

Training

Each tree is trained on a randomly selected samples of the training data (usually $\frac{2}{3}$ samples of the training data). The remaining samples of the training data are used for validation. A subset of features is randomly selected for each split node. Then, we search for the best feature $\mathbf{f}[i]$ and an associated threshold τ_i that maximize the *information gain* of the training data after partitioning. Let $H(Q)$ be the original entropy of the training data and $H(Q|\{\mathbf{f}[i], \tau_i\})$ the entropy of Q after partitioning it into "left" and "right" partitions, Q_l and Q_r. The *information gain*, G, is given by

$$G(Q|\{\mathbf{f}[i], \tau_i\}) = H(Q) - H(Q|\{\mathbf{f}[i], \tau_i\}), \tag{2.22}$$

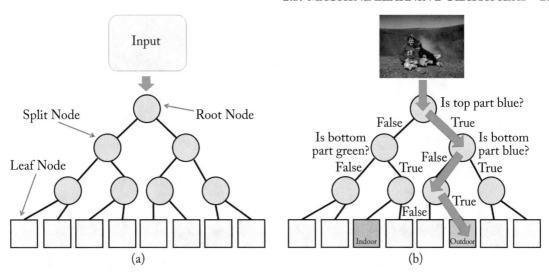

Figure 2.8: (a) A decision tree is a set of nodes and edges organized in a hierarchical fashion. The split (or internal) nodes are denoted with circles and the leaf (or terminal) nodes with squares. (b) A decision tree is a tree where each split node stores a test function which is applied to the input data. Each leaf stores the final label (here whether "indoor" or "outdoor").

where

$$H(Q|\{\mathbf{f}[i], \tau_i\}) = \frac{|Q_l|}{|Q|} H(Q_l) + \frac{|Q_r|}{|Q|} H(Q_r), \tag{2.23}$$

and $|Q_l|$ and $|Q_r|$ denote the number of data samples in the left and right partitions. The entropy of Q_l is given by

$$H(Q_l) = -\sum_{i \in Q_l} p_i \log_2 p_i, \tag{2.24}$$

where p_i is the number of samples of class i in Q_l divided by $|Q_l|$. The feature and the associated threshold which maximize the gain are selected as the splitting test for that node

$$\{\mathbf{f}_g[i], \tau_i\}^* = \arg \max_{\{\mathbf{f}_g[i], \tau_i\}} G(Q|\{\mathbf{f}_g[i], \tau_i\}). \tag{2.25}$$

Entropy and Information Gain: The entropy and information gain are two important concepts in the RDF training process. These concepts are usually discussed in information theory or probability courses and are briefly discussed below.

Information entropy is defined as a measure of the randomness in the information being processed. More precisely, the higher the entropy, the lower the information content. Mathematically, given a discrete random variable X with possible values $\{x_1, \cdots, x_n\}$ and a probability mass function $P(X)$, the entropy H (also called Shannon entropy) can be written as follows:

$$H(X) = -\sum_{i=1}^{n} P(x_i) \log_2 P(x_i). \tag{2.26}$$

For example, an action such as flipping a coin that has no affinity for "head" or "tail," provides information that is random (X with possible values of $\{$"head," "tail"$\}$). Therefore, Eq. (2.26) can be written as follows:

$$H(X) = -P(\text{"head"}) \log_2 P(\text{"head"}) - P(\text{"tail"}) \log_2 P(\text{"tail"}). \tag{2.27}$$

As shown in Fig. 2.9, this binary entropy function (Eq. (2.27)) reaches its maximum value (uncertainty is at a maximum) when the probability is $\frac{1}{2}$, meaning that $P(X = \text{"head"}) = \frac{1}{2}$ or similarly $P(X = \text{"tail"}) = \frac{1}{2}$. The entropy function reaches its minimum value (i.e., zero) when probability is 1 or 0 with complete certainty $P(X = \text{"head"} = 1)$ or $P(X = \text{"head"} = 0)$ respectively.

Information gain is defined as the change in information entropy H from a prior state to a state that takes some information (t) and can be written as follows:

$$G(Q|t) = H(Q) - H(Q|t). \tag{2.28}$$

If a partition consists of only a single class, it is considered as a leaf node. Partitions consisting of multiple classes are further partitioned until either they contain single classes or the tree reaches its maximum height. If the maximum height of the tree is reached and some of its leaf nodes contain labels from multiple classes, the empirical distribution over the classes associated with the subset of the training samples $\mathbf{v}$, which have reached that leaf, is used as its label. Thus, the probabilistic leaf predictor model for the t-th tree is $\mathbf{p}_t(c|\mathbf{v})$, where $c \in \{c_k\}$ denotes the class.

Classification

Once a set of decision trees have been trained, given a previously unseen sample $\mathbf{x}_j$, each decision tree hierarchically applies a number of predefined tests. Starting at the root, each split node applies its associated split function to $\mathbf{x}_j$. Depending on the result of the binary test the data is sent to the right or the left child. This process is repeated until the data point reaches a leaf node. Usually the leaf nodes contain a predictor (e.g., a classifier) which associates an output (e.g., a class label) to the input $\mathbf{x}_j$. In the case of forests, many tree predictors are combined together to

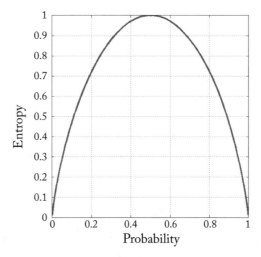

Figure 2.9: Entropy vs. probability for a two class variable.

form a single forest prediction:

$$\mathbf{p}(c|\mathbf{x}_j) = \frac{1}{T} \sum_{t=1}^{T} \mathbf{p}_t(c|\mathbf{x}_j),$$
(2.29)

where T denotes the number of decision trees in the forest.

2.4   CONCLUSION

Traditional computer vision systems consist of two steps: feature design and learning algorithm design, both of which are largely independent. Thus, computer vision problems have traditionally been approached by designing hand-engineered features such as HOG [Triggs and Dalal, 2005], SIFT [Lowe, 2004], and SURF [Bay et al., 2008] that lack in generalizing well to other domains, are time consuming, expensive, and require expert knowledge on the problem domain. These feature engineering processes are usually followed by learning algorithms such as SVM [Cortes, 1995] and RDF [Breiman, 2001, Quinlan, 1986]. However, progress in deep learning algorithms resolves all these issues, by training a deep neural network for feature extraction and classification in an end-to-end learning framework. More precisely, unlike traditional approaches, deep neural networks learn to simultaneously extract features and classify data samples. Chapter 3 will discuss deep neural networks in detail.

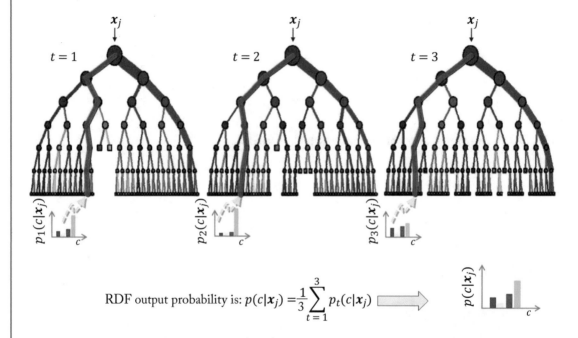

$$p(c|\mathbf{x}_j) = \frac{1}{3}\sum_{t=1}^{3} p_t(c|\mathbf{x}_j)$$

RDF output probability is: $p(c|\mathbf{x}_j) = \frac{1}{3}\sum_{t=1}^{3} p_t(c|\mathbf{x}_j)$

Figure 2.10: RDF classification for a test sample $\mathbf{x}_j$. During testing the same test sample is passed through each decision tree. At each internal node a test is applied and the test sample is sent to the appropriate child. This process is repeated until a leaf is reached. At the leaf the stored posterior $\mathbf{p}_t(c|\mathbf{x}_j)$ is read. The forest class posterior $\mathbf{p}(c|\mathbf{x}_j)$ is the average of all decision tree posteriors.

CHAPTER 3

Neural Networks Basics

3.1 INTRODUCTION

Before going into the details of the CNNs, we provide in this chapter an introduction to artificial neural networks, their computational mechanism, and their historical background. Neural networks are inspired by the working of cerebral cortex in mammals. It is important to note, however, that these models do not closely resemble the working, scale and complexity of the human brain. Artificial neural network models can be understood as a set of basic processing units, which are tightly interconnected and operate on the given inputs to process the information and generate desired outputs. Neural networks can be grouped into two generic categories based on the way the information is propagated in the network.

- **Feed-forward networks**
  The information flow in a feed-forward network happens only in one direction. If the network is considered as a graph with neurons as its nodes, the connections between the nodes are such that there are no loops or cycles in the graph. These network architectures can be referred as Directed Acyclic Graphs (DAG). Examples include MLP and CNNs, which we will discuss in details in the upcoming sections.

- **Feed-back networks**
  As the name implies, feed-back networks have connections which form directed cycles (or loops). This architecture allows them to operate on and generate sequences of arbitrary sizes. Feed-back networks exhibit memorization ability and can store information and sequence relationships in their internal memory. Examples of such architectures include Recurrent Neural Network (RNN) and Long-Short Term Memory (LSTM).

  We provide an example architecture for both feed-forward and feed-back networks in Sections 3.2 and 3.3, respectively. For feed-forward networks, we first study MLP, which is a simple case of such architectures. In Chapter 4, we will cover the CNNs in detail, which also work in a feed-forward manner. For feed-back networks, we study RNNs. Since our main focus here is on CNNs, an in-depth treatment of RNNs is out of the scope of this book. We refer interested readers to Graves et al. [2012] for RNN details.

3.2   MULTI-LAYER PERCEPTRON

3.2.1   ARCHITECTURE BASICS

Figure 3.1 shows an example of a MLP network architecture which consists of three hidden layers, sandwiched between an input and an output layer. In simplest terms, the network can be treated as a black box, which operates on a set of inputs and generates some outputs. We highlight some of the interesting aspects of this architecture in more details below.

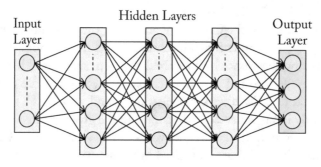

Figure 3.1: A simple feed-forward neural network with dense connections.

Layered Architecture: Neural networks comprise a hierarchy of processing levels. Each level is called a "*network layer*" and consists of a number of processing "*nodes*" (also called "neurons" or "units"). Typically, the input is fed through an *input* layer and the final layer is the *output* layer which makes predictions. The intermediate layers perform the processing and are referred to as the *hidden* layers. Due to this layered architecture, this neural network is called an MLP.

Nodes: The individual processing units in each layer are called the nodes in a neural network architecture. The nodes basically implement an "activation function" which given an input, decides whether the node will fire or not.

Dense Connections: The nodes in a neural network are interconnected and can communicate with each other. Each connection has a *weight* which specifies the strength of the connection between two nodes. For the simple case of feed-forward neural networks, the information is transferred sequentially in one direction from the input to the output layers. Therefore, each node in a layer is directly connected to all nodes in the immediate previous layer.

3.2.2   PARAMETER LEARNING

As we described in Section 3.2.1, the weights of a neural network define the connections between neurons. These weights need to be set appropriately so that a desired output can be obtained from the neural network. The weights encode the "model" generated from the training data that is used to allow the network to perform a designated task (e.g., object detection, recognition, and/or classification). In practical settings, the number of weights is huge which requires an automatic procedure to update their values appropriately for a given task. The process of automatically tuning the network parameters is called "learning" which is accomplished during the *training stage* (in contrast to the *test stage* where inference/prediction is made on "unseen data," i.e., data that the network has not "seen" during training). This process involves showing examples of the desired task to the network so that it can learn to identify the right set of relationships between the inputs and the required outputs. For example, in the paradigm of *supervised learning*, the inputs can be media (speech, images) and the outputs are the desired set of "labels" (e.g., identity of a person) which are used to tune the neural network parameters.

We now describe a basic form of learning algorithm, which is called the Delta Rule.

Delta Rule

The basic idea behind the delta rule is to learn from the mistakes of the neural network during the training phase. The delta rule was proposed by Widrow et al. [1960], which updates the network parameters (i.e., weights denoted by θ, considering 0 biases) based on the difference between the target output and the predicted output. This difference is calculated in terms of the Least Mean Square (LMS) error, which is why the delta learning rule is also referred to as the *LMS rule*. The output units are a "linear function" of the inputs denoted by x, i.e.,

$$p_i = \sum_j \theta_{ij} x_j.$$

If p_n and y_n denote the predicted and target outputs, respectively, the error can be calculated as:

$$E = \frac{1}{2} \sum_n (y_n - p_n)^2, \tag{3.1}$$

where n is the number of categories in the dataset (or the number of neurons in the output layer). The delta rule calculates the gradient of this error function (Eq. (3.1)) with respect to the parameters of the network: $\partial E / \partial \theta_{ij}$. Given the gradient, the weights are updated iteratively according to the following learning rule:

$$\theta_{ij}^{t+1} = \theta_{ij}^t + \eta \frac{\partial E}{\partial \theta_{ij}} \tag{3.2}$$

$$\theta_{ij}^{t+1} = \theta_{ij}^t + \eta (y_i - p_i) x_j, \tag{3.3}$$

where t denotes the previous iteration of the learning process. The hyper-parameter η denotes the step size of the parameter update in the direction of the calculated gradient. One can visualize that no learning happens when the gradient or the step size is zero. In other cases, the parameters are updated such that the predicted outputs get closer to the target outputs. After a number of iterations, the network training process is said to *converge* when the parameters do not change any longer as a result of the update.

If the step size is unnecessarily too small, the network will take longer to converge and the learning process will be very slow. On the other hand, taking very large steps can result in an unstable erratic behavior during the training process as a result of which the network may not converge at all. Therefore, setting the step-size to a right value is really important for network training. We will discuss different approaches to set the step size in Section 5.3 for CNN training which are equally applicable to MLP.

Generalized Delta Rule

The generalized delta rule is an extension of the delta rule. It was proposed by Rumelhart et al. [1985]. The delta rule only computes linear combinations between the input and the output pairs. This limits us to only a single-layered network because a stack of many linear layers is not better than a single linear transformation. To overcome this limitation, the generalized delta rule makes use of nonlinear activation functions at each processing unit to model nonlinear relationships between the input and output domains. It also allows us to make use of multiple hidden layers in the neural network architecture, a concept which forms the heart of deep learning.

The parameters of a multi-layered neural network are updated in the same manner as the delta rule, i.e.,

$$\theta_{ij}^{t+1} = \theta_{ij}^t + \eta \frac{\partial E}{\partial \theta_{ij}}. \tag{3.4}$$

But different to the delta rule, the errors are recursively sent backward through the multi-layered network. For this reason, the generalized delta rule is also called the "back-propagation" algorithm. Since for the case of the generalized delta rule, a neural network not only has an output layer but also intermediate hidden layers, we can separately calculate the error term (differential with respect to the desired output) for the output and hidden layers. Since the case of the **output layer** is simple, we first discuss the error computation for this layer.

Given the error function in Eq. (3.1), its gradient with respect to the parameters in the output layer L for each node i can be computed as follows:

$$\frac{\partial E}{\partial \theta_{ij}^L} = \delta_i^L x_j, \tag{3.5}$$

$$\delta_i^L = (y_i - p_i) f_i'(a_i), \tag{3.6}$$

where, $a_i = \sum_j \theta_{i,j} x_j + b_i$ is the activation which is the input to the neuron (prior to the activation function), x_j's are the outputs from the previous layer, $p_i = f(a_i)$ is the output from the neuron (prediction for the case of output layer) and $f(\cdot)$ denotes a nonlinear activation function while $f'(\cdot)$ represents its derivative. The activation function decides whether the neuron will fire or not, in response to a given input activation. Note that the nonlinear activation functions are differentiable so that the parameters of the network can be tuned using error back-propagation.

One popular activation function is the sigmoid function, given as follows:

$$p_i = f(a_i) = \frac{1}{1 + \exp(-a_i)}.$$
(3.7)

We will discuss other activation functions in detail in Section 4.2.4. The derivative of the sigmoid activation function is ideally suitable because it can be written in terms of the sigmoid function itself (i.e., p_i) and is given by:

$$f_i'(a_i) = p_i(1 - p_i).$$
(3.8)

Therefore, we can write the gradient equation for the output layer neurons as follows:

$$\frac{\partial E}{\partial \theta_{ij}^L} = (y_i - p_i)(1 - p_i)x_j p_i.$$
(3.9)

Similarly, we can calculate the error signal for the intermediate **hidden layers** in a multi-layered neural network architecture by back propagation of errors as follows:

$$\delta_i^l = f'(a_i^l) \sum_j \theta_{ij}^{l+1} \delta_j^{l+1},$$
(3.10)

where $l \in \{1 \ldots L - 1\}$ and L denotes the total number of layers in the network. The above equation applies the **chain rule** to progressively calculate the gradients of the internal parameters using the gradients of all subsequent layers. The overall update equation for the MLP parameters θ_{ij} can be written as:

$$\theta_{ij}^{t+1} = \theta_{ij}^t + \eta \delta_i^l x_j^{l-1},$$
(3.11)

where x_j^{l-1} is the output from the previous layer and t denotes the number of previous training iteration. The complete learning process usually involves a number of iterations and the parameters are continually updated until the network is optimized (i.e., after a set number of iterations or when θ_{ij}^{t+1} does not change).

> **Gradient Instability Problem:** The generalized delta rule successfully works for the case of shallow networks (ones with one or two hidden layers). However, when the networks are deep (i.e., L is large), the learning process can suffer from the vanishing or exploding gradient problems depending on the choice of the activation function (e.g., sigmoid in above example). This instability relates particularly to the initial layers in a deep network. As a result, the weights of the initial layers cannot be properly tuned. We explain this with an example below.

Consider a deep network with many layers. The outputs of each weight layer are squashed within a small range using an activation function (e.g., [0,1] for the case of the sigmoid). The gradient of the sigmoid function leads to even smaller values (see Fig. 3.2). To update the initial layer parameters, the derivatives are successively multiplied according to the chain rule (as in Eq. (3.10)). These multiplications exponentially decay the back-propagated signal. If we consider a network depth of 5, and the maximum possible gradient value for the sigmoid (i.e., 0.25), the decaying factor would be $(0.25)^5 = 0.0009$. This is called the "vanishing gradient" problem. It is easy to follow that in cases where the gradient of the activation function is large, successive multiplications can lead to the "exploding gradient" problem.

We will introduce the ReLU activation function in Chapter 4, whose gradient is equal to 1 (when a unit is "on"). Since $1^L = 1$, this avoids both the vanishing and the exploding gradient problems.

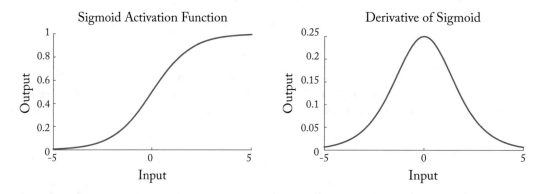

Figure 3.2: The sigmoid activation function and its derivative. Note that the range of values for the derivative is relatively small which leads to the vanishing gradient problem.

3.3   RECURRENT NEURAL NETWORKS

The feed-back networks contain loops in their network architecture, which allows them to process sequential data. In many applications, such as caption generation for an image, we want to make a prediction such that it is consistent with the previously generated outputs (e.g., already generated words in the caption). To accomplish this, the network processes each element in an input sequence in a similar fashion (while considering the previous computational state). For this reason it is also called an RNN.

Since, RNNs process information in a manner that is dependent on the previous computational states, they provide a mechanism to "remember" previous states. The memory mechanism is usually effective to remember only the short term information that is previously processed by the network. Below, we outline the architectural details of an RNN.

3.3.1 ARCHITECTURE BASICS

A simple RNN architecture is shown in Fig. 3.3. As described above, it contains a feed-back loop whose working can be visualized by unfolding the recurrent network over time (shown on the right). The unfolded version of the RNN is very similar to a feed-forward neural network described in Section 3.2. We can, therefore, understand RNN as a simple multi-layered neural network, where the information flow happens over time and different layers represent the computational output at different time instances. The RNN operates on sequences and therefore the input and consequently the output at each time instance also varies.

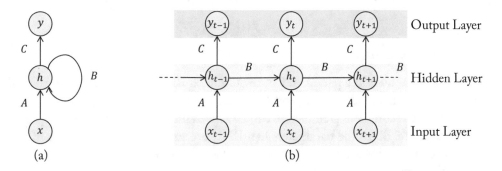

(a)   (b)

Figure 3.3: The RNN Architecture. *Left:* A simple recurrent network with a feed-back loop. *Right:* An unfolded recurrent architecture at different time-steps.

We highlight the key features of an RNN architecture below.

Variable Length Input: RNN can operate on inputs of variable length, e.g., videos with variable frame length, sentences with different number of words, 3D point clouds with variable number of points. The length of the unfolded RNN structure depends on the length of the input sequence, e.g., for a sentence consisting of 12 words, there will be a total of 12 layers in the unfolded RNN architecture. In Fig. 3.3, the input to the network at each time instance t is represented by the variable x_t.

Hidden State: The RNN holds internally the memory of the previous computation in a hidden state represented by h_t. This state can be understood as an input from the previous layer in the unfolded RNN structure. At the beginning of the sequence processing, it is initialized with a zero or a random vector. At each time step, this state is updated by considering its previous value and the current input to the network:

$$h_t = f(Ax_t + Bh_{t-1}), \tag{3.12}$$

where $f(\cdot)$ is the nonlinear activation function. The weight matrix B is called the *transition matrix* since it influences how the hidden state changes over time.

Variable Length Output: The output of RNN at each time step is denoted by y_t. The RNNs are capable of generating variable length outputs, e.g., translating a sentence in one language to another language where the output sequence lengths can be different from the input sequence length. This is possible because RNNs consider the hidden state while making predictions. The hidden state models the joint probability of the previously processed sequence which can be used to predict new outputs. As an example, given a few starting words in a sentence, the RNN can predict the next possible word in the sentence, where a special end of a sentence symbol is used to denote the end of each sentence. In this case all possible words (including the end of sentence symbol) are included in the dictionary over which the prediction is made:

$$y_t = f(Ch_t), \tag{3.13}$$

where $f(\cdot)$ is an activation function such as a softmax (Section 4.2.4).

Shared Parameters: The parameters in the unfolded RNN linking the input, the hidden state and the output (denoted by A, B, and C, respectively) are shared between all layers. This is the reason why the complete architecture can be represented by using a loop to represent its recurrent architecture. Since the parameters in a RNN are shared, the total number of tunable parameters are considerably less than an MLP, where a separate set of parameters are learned for each layer in the network. This enables efficient training and testing of the feed-back networks.

Based on the above description of RNN architecture, it can be noted that indeed the hidden state of the network provides a memory mechanism, but it is not effective when we want to remember long-term relationships in the sequences. Therefore, RNN only provide short-term memory and find difficulties in "remembering" (a few time-steps away) old information processed through it. To overcome this limitation, improved versions of recurrent networks have been introduced in the literature which include the LSTM [Hochreiter and Schmidhuber, 1997], Gated Recurrent Unit (GRU) [Cho et al., 2014], Bi-directional RNN (B-RNN) [Graves and Schmidhuber, 2005] and Neural Turing Machines (NTM) [Graves et al., 2014]. However, the details of all these network architectures and their functioning is out of the scope of this book which is focused on feed-forward architectures (particularly CNNs).

3.3.2   PARAMETER LEARNING

The parameters in a feed-back network can be learned using the generalized delta rule (back-propagation algorithm), similar to feed-forward networks. However, instead of error back-propagation through network layers as in feed-forward networks, back-propagation is performed through time in the feed-back networks. At each time instance, the output of the RNN is computed as a function of its previous and current inputs. The Back Propagation Through Time (BPTT) algorithm cannot allow the learning of long-term relationships in sequences, because of difficulties in error computations over long sequences. Specifically, when the number of iterations increases, the BPTT algorithm suffers from the vanishing or the exploding gradient problem. One way around this problem is to compute the error signal over a truncated unfolded RNN. This reduces the cost of the parameter update process for long sequences, but limits the dependence of the output at each time instance to only few previous hidden states.

3.4 LINK WITH BIOLOGICAL VISION

We think it is important to briefly discuss biological neural networks (BNNs) and their operational mechanisms in order to study their similarities and dissimilarities with artificial neural networks. As a matter of fact, artificial neural networks do not resemble their biological counterparts in terms of functioning and scale, however they are indeed motivated by the BNNs and several of the terms used to describe artificial neural networks are borrowed from the neuroscience literature. Therefore, we introduce neural networks in the brain, draw parallels between artificial and biological neurons, and provide a model of the artificial neuron based on biological vision.

3.4.1 BIOLOGICAL NEURON

The human brain contains approximately 100 billion neurons. To interpret this number, let us assume we have 100 billion one dollar bills, where each bill is only 0.11 mm thick. If we stack all these one dollar bills on top of each other, the resulting stack will be 10922.0 km high. This illustrates the scale and magnitude of the human brain.

A biological neuron is a nerve cell which processes information [Jain et al., 1996]. Each neuron is surrounded by a membrane and has a nucleus which contains genes. It has specialized projections which manage the input and output to the nerve cell. These projections are termed *dendrites* and *axons*. We describe these and other key aspects of the biological neuron below.

Dendrites: Dendrites are fibers which act as receptive lines and bring information (activations) to the cell body from other neurons. They are the inputs of the neuron.

Axons: Axons are fibers which act as transmission lines and take information away from the cell body to other neurons. They act as outputs of the neuron.

Cell body: The *cell body* (also called the *soma*) receives the incoming information through dendrites, processes it and sends it, to other neurons via axons.

Synapses: The specialized connections between axons and dendrites which allow the communication of signals are called *synapses*. The communication takes place by an electro-chemical process where the neurotransmitters (chemicals) are released at the synapse and are diffused across the synaptic gap to transmit information. There is a total of approximately 1 quadrillion (10^{15}) synapses in the human brain [Changeux and Ricoeur, 2002].

Connections: Neurons are densely inter-connected with each other. On average, each neuron receives inputs from approximately 10^5 synapses.

Neuron Firing: A neuron receives signals from connected neurons via dendrites. The cell body sums up the received signals and the neuron fires if the combined input signal exceeds a threshold. By neuron firing, we mean that it generates an output which is sent out through axons. If the combined input is below the threshold, no response signal is generated by the neuron (i.e., the neuron does not fire). The thresholding function which decides whether a neuron fires or not is called *activation function*.

Next, we describe a simple computational model which mimics the working of a biological neuron.

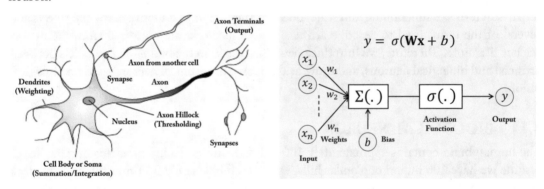

Figure 3.4: A biological neuron (*left*) and a computational model (*right*) which is used to develop artificial neural networks.

3.4.2   COMPUTATIONAL MODEL OF A NEURON

A simple mathematical model of the biological neuron known as the *Threshold Logic Unit* (TLU) was proposed by McCulloch and Pitts [1943]. It consists of a set of incoming connections which feed the unit with activations coming from other neurons. These inputs are weighted using a set of weights denoted by $\{w\}$. The processing unit then sums all the inputs and applies a nonlinear threshold function (also known as the activation function) to calculate the output. The resulting output is then transmitted to other connected neural units. We can denote the operation of a McCulloch-Pitts neuron as follows:

$$y = f\left(\sum_{i=1}^{n} w_i x_i + b\right), \tag{3.14}$$

where b is a threshold, w_i denote the synapse weight, x_i is the input to the neuron, and $f(\cdot)$ represents a nonlinear activation function. For the simplest case, f is a step function which gives 0 (i.e., neuron does not fire) when the input is below 0 (i.e., $\sum_{i=1}^{n} w_i x_i + b$ less than the firing threshold) and 1 when it is greater than 0. For other cases, the activation function can be a sigmoid, $tanh$, or an ReLU for a smooth thresholding operation (see Chapter 4).

The McCulloch-Pitts neuron is a very simple computational model. However, they have been shown to approximate complex functions quite well. McCulloch and Pitts showed that a network comprising of such neurons can perform universal computations. The universal computational ability of neural networks ensures their ability to model a very rich set of continuous functions using only a finite number of neurons. This fact is formally known as the "Universal Approximation Theorem" for neural networks. Different to McCulloch-Pitts model, state of the art neuron models also incorporate additional features such as stochastic behaviors and non-binary input and output.

3.4.3 ARTIFICIAL VS. BIOLOGICAL NEURON

Having outlined the basics of artificial and biological neuron operation, we can now draw parallels between their functioning and identify the key differences between the two.

An artificial neuron (also called a unit or a node) takes several input connections (dendrites in biological neuron) which are assigned certain weights (analogous to synapses). The unit then computes the sum of the weighted inputs and applies an activation function (analogous to the cell body in biological neuron). The result of the unit is then passed on using the output connection (axon function).

Note that the above-mentioned analogy between a biological and an artificial neuron is only valid in the loose sense. In reality, there exists a number of crucial differences in the functioning of biological neurons. As an example, biological neurons do not sum the weighted inputs, rather dendrites interact in a much complex way to combine the incoming information. Furthermore, biological neurons communicate asynchronously, different from their computational counterparts which operate synchronously. The training mechanisms in both types of neural networks are also different, while the training mechanisms in biological networks are not precisely known. The topology in biological networks are very complicated compared to the artificial networks which currently have either a feed-forward or feed-back architecture.

CHAPTER 4

Convolutional Neural Network

4.1 INTRODUCTION

We discussed neural networks in Chapter 3. CNNs are one of the most popular categories of neural networks, especially for high-dimensional data (e.g., images and videos). CNNs operate in a way that is very similar to standard neural networks. A key difference, however, is that each unit in a CNN layer is a two- (or high-) dimensional filter which is convolved with the input of that layer. This is essential for cases where we want to learn patterns from high-dimensional input media, e.g., images or videos. CNN filters incorporate spatial context by having a similar (but smaller) spatial shape as the input media, and use parameter sharing to significantly reduce the number of learn-able variables. We will describe these concepts in detail in Chapters 4, 5, and 6. However, we find it important to first give a brief historical background of CNNs.

An earliest form of CNN was the Neocognitron model proposed by Kunihiko Fukushima [Fukushima and Miyake, 1982]. It consisted of multiple layers which automatically learned a hierarchy of feature abstractions for pattern recognition. The Neocognitron was motivated by the seminal work by Hubel and Wiesel [1959] on the primary visual cortex which demonstrated that the neurons in the brain are organized in the form of layers. These layers learn to recognize visual patterns by first extracting local features and subsequently combining them to obtain higher-level representations. The network training was performed using a reinforcement learning rule. A major improvement over the Neocognitron was the LeNet model proposed by LeCun et al. [1989], where the model parameters were learned using error back-propagation. This CNN model was successfully applied to recognize handwritten digits.

CNNs are a useful class of models for both supervised and unsupervised learning paradigms. The **supervised learning** mechanism is the one where the input to the system and the desired outputs (true labels) are known and the model learns a mapping between the two. In the **unsupervised learning** mechanism, the true labels for a given set of inputs are not known and the model aims to estimate the underlying distribution of the inputs data samples. An example of a supervised learning task (image classification) is shown in Fig. 4.1. The CNN learns to map a given image to its corresponding category by detecting a number of abstract feature representations, ranging from simple to more complex ones. These discriminative features are then used within the network to predict the correct category of an input image. The neural network classifier is identical to the MLP we studied in Chapter 3. Recall that we reviewed popular hand-crafted feature representations and machine learning classifiers in Chapter 2. The function of a CNN is similar to this pipeline, with the key difference being the automatic learning of a hierarchy of useful feature representations and its integration of the classification and feature extraction stages in a single pipeline which is trainable in an end-to-end manner. This reduces the need for manual design and expert human intervention.

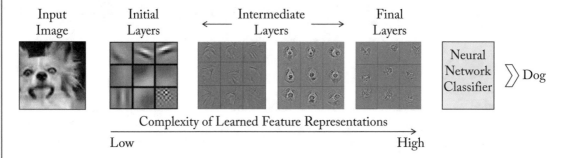

Figure 4.1: A CNN learns low-level features in the initial layers, followed by more complex intermediate and high-level feature representations which are used for a classification task. The feature visualizations are adopted from Zeiler and Fergus [2014].

4.2   NETWORK LAYERS

A CNN is composed of several basic building blocks, called the CNN layers. In this section, we study these building blocks and their function in the CNN architecture. Note that some of these layers implement basic functionalities such as normalization, pooling, convolution, and fully connected layers. These basic layers are covered first in this section to develop a basic understanding of the CNN layers. Along with such basic but fundamental building blocks, we also introduce several more complex layers later in this section which are composed of multiple building blocks (e.g., Spatial Transformer Layer and VLAD pooling layer).

4.2.1   PRE-PROCESSING

Before passing input data to the networks, the data needs to be pre-processed. The general pre-processing steps that are used consist of the following.

- **Mean-subtraction:** The input patches (belonging to both train and test sets) are zero-centered by subtracting the mean computed on the entire training set. Given N training images, each denoted by $\mathbf{x} \in \mathbb{R}^{h \times w \times c}$, we can denote the mean-subtraction step as follows:

$$\mathbf{x}' = \mathbf{x} - \hat{\mathbf{x}}, \quad \text{where} \quad \hat{\mathbf{x}} = \frac{1}{N} \sum_{i=1}^{N} \mathbf{x}_i. \tag{4.1}$$

- **Normalization:** The input data (belonging to both train and test sets) is divided with the standard deviation of each input dimension (pixels in the case of an image) calculated on the training set to normalize the standard deviation to a unit value. It can be represented as follows:

$$\mathbf{x}'' = \frac{\mathbf{x}'}{\sqrt{\frac{\sum_{i=1}^{N}(\mathbf{x}_i - \hat{\mathbf{x}})^2}{N-1}}}. \qquad (4.2)$$

- **PCA Whitening:** The aim of PCA whitening is to reduce the correlations between different data dimensions by independently normalizing them. This approach starts with the zero-centered data and calculates the covariance matrix which encodes the correlation between data dimensions. This covariance matrix is then decomposed via the Singular Value Decomposition (SVD) algorithm and the data is decorrelated by projecting it onto the eigenvectors found via SVD. Afterward, each dimension is divided by its corresponding eigenvalue to normalize all the respective dimensions in the data space.

- **Local Contrast Normalization:** This normalization scheme gets its motivation from neuroscience. As the name depicts, this approach normalizes the local contrast of the feature maps to obtain more prominent features. It first generates a local neighborhood for each pixel, e.g., for a unit radius eight neighboring pixels are selected. Afterward, the pixel is zero-centered with the mean calculated using its own and neighboring pixel values. Similarly, the pixel is also normalized with a standard deviation of its own and neighboring pixel values (only if the standard deviation is greater than one). The resulting pixel value is used for further computations.

  Another similar approach is the local response normalization [Krizhevsky et al., 2012] which normalizes the contrast of features obtained from adjacent filters in a convolution layer.

Note that PCA whitening can amplify the noise in the data and therefore recent CNN models just use a simple mean-subtraction (and optionally normalization step) for preprocessing. The scaling and shifting achieved through mean-subtraction and normalization is helpful for gradient-based learning. This is because equivalent updates are made to the network weights for all input dimensions, which enables a stable learning process. Furthermore, the local contrast normalization (LCN) and the local response normalization (LRN) are not common in the recent architectures since other approaches (e.g., batch normalization, which we will describe in Section 5.2.4) have proven to be more effective.

4.2.2 CONVOLUTIONAL LAYERS

A convolutional layer is the most important component of a CNN. It comprises a set of filters (also called convolutional kernels) which are convolved with a given input to generate an output feature map.

What is a Filter? Each filter in a convolutional layer is a grid of discrete numbers. As an example, consider a 2×2 filter shown in Fig. 4.2. The weights of each filter (the numbers in the grid) are learned during the training of CNN. This learning procedure involves a random initialization of the filter weights at the start of the training (different approaches for weight initialization will be discussed in Section 5.1). Afterward, given input-output pairs, the filter weights are tuned in a number of different iterations during the learning procedure. We will cover network training in more detail in Chapter 5.

2	0
-1	3

Figure 4.2: An example of a 2D image filter.

What is a Convolution Operation? We mentioned earlier that the convolution layer performs convolution between the filters and the input to the layer. Let's consider a 2D convolution in Fig. 4.3 to develop an insight into the layer's operation. Given a 2D input feature map and a convolution filter of matrix sizes 4×4 and 2×2, respectively, a convolution layer multiplies the 2×2 filter with a highlighted patch (also 2×2) of the input feature map and sums up all values to generate one value in the output feature map. Note that the filter slides along the width and height of the input feature map and this process continues until the filter can no longer slide further.

Remark: In the signal processing literature, there is a distinction between the terms "convolution" and "cross correlation." The operation we described above is the "correlation operation." During convolution, the only difference is that the filter is flipped along its height and width before multiplication and sum-pooling (see Fig. 4.4).

In machine learning, both operations are equivalent and there is rarely a distinction made between the two. Both terms are used interchangeably and most of the deep learning libraries implement the correlation operation in the convolution layers. The reason is that the network optimization will converge on the right filter weights for either of the two operations. If the weights of a convolutional network are replaced with the ones learned using a correlation network, the network performance will remain the same, because only the order of the operation is changed in the two networks, and their discriminative ability stays the same. In this book, we follow the machine learning convention and do not make a distinction between the two operations, i.e., a convolution layer performs the correlation operation in our case.

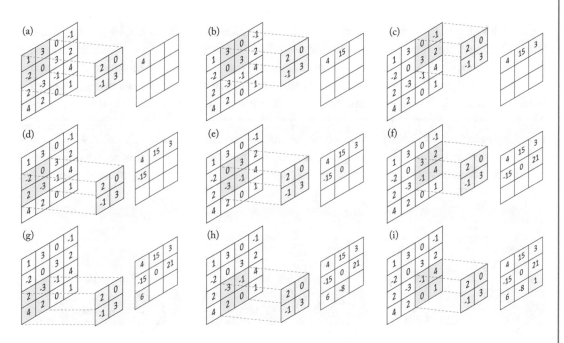

Figure 4.3: The operation of a convolution layer is illustrated in the figure above. **(a)–(i)** show the computations performed at each step, as the filter is slided onto the input feature map to compute the corresponding value in the output feature map. The 2 × 2 filter (shown in *green*) is multiplied with the same sized region (shown in *orange*) within a 4 × 4 input feature map and the resulting values are summed up to obtain a corresponding entry (shown in *blue*) in the output feature map at each convolution step.

Figure 4.4: The distinction between the correlation and convolution operations in the signal processing literature. In machine learning, this distinction is usually not important and the deep learning literature normally refers to the layers implementing the correlation operation as the convolution operation. In this book, we also follow the same naming convention that is adopted in the machine learning literature.

In the above example, in order to calculate each value of the output feature map, the filter takes a step of 1 along the horizontal or vertical position (i.e., along the column or the row of the input). This step is termed as the **stride** of the convolution filter, which can be set to a different (than 1) value if required. For example, the convolution operation with a stride of 2 is shown in Fig. 4.5. Compared to the stride of 1 in the previous example, the stride of 2 results in a smaller output feature map. This reduction in dimensions is referred to as the **sub-sampling** operation. Such a reduction in dimensions provides moderate invariance to scale and pose of the objects, which is a useful property in applications such as object recognition. We will discuss other sub-sampling mechanisms in the section where we discuss the pooling layers (Section 4.2.3).

We saw in Fig. 4.3 that the spatial size of the output feature map is reduced compared to the input feature map. Precisely, for a filter with size $f \times f$, an input feature map with size

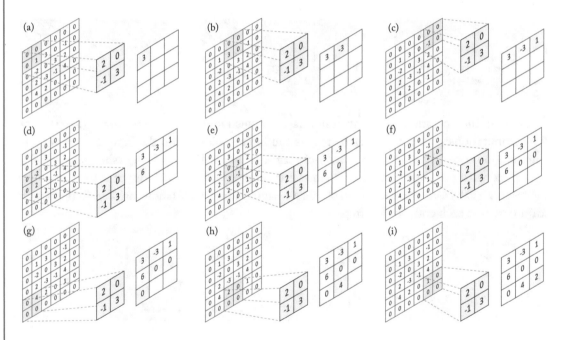

Figure 4.5: The operation of a convolution layer with a zero padding of 1 and a stride of 2 is illustrated in the figure above. **(a)–(i)** show the computations that are performed at each step, as the filter is slided onto the input feature map to compute the corresponding value of the output feature map. The 2 × 2 filter (shown in *green*) is multiplied with the same sized region (shown in *orange*) within a 6 × 6 input feature map (including zero-padding) and the resulting values are summed up to obtain a corresponding entry (shown in *blue*) in the output feature map at each convolution step.

$h \times w$ and a stride length s, the output feature dimensions are given by:

$$h' = \left\lfloor \frac{h - f + s}{s} \right\rfloor, \quad w' = \left\lfloor \frac{w - f + s}{s} \right\rfloor, \tag{4.3}$$

where, $\lfloor \cdot \rfloor$ denotes the floor operation. However, in some applications, such as image de-noising, super-resolution, or segmentation, we want to keep the spatial sizes constant (or even larger) after convolution. This is important because these applications require more dense predictions at the pixel level. Moreover, it allows us to design deeper networks (i.e., with more weight layers) by avoiding a quick collapse of the output feature dimensions. This helps in achieving better performances and higher resolution output labelings. This can be achieved by applying **zero-padding** around the input feature map. As shown in Fig. 4.5, zero padding the horizontal and vertical dimensions allows us to increase the output dimensions and therefore gives more flexibility in the architecture design. The basic idea is to increase the size of the input feature map such that an output feature map, with desired dimensions, is obtained. If p denotes the increase in the input feature map along each dimension (by padding zeros), we can represent the modified output feature map dimensions as follows:

$$h' = \left\lfloor \frac{h - f + s + p}{s} \right\rfloor, \quad w' = \left\lfloor \frac{w - f + s + p}{s} \right\rfloor. \tag{4.4}$$

In Fig. 4.5, $p = 2$ and therefore the output dimensions have been increased from 6×6 to 3×3. If the convolutional layers were to not zero-pad the inputs and apply only valid convolutions, then the spatial size of the output features will be reduced by a small factor after each convolution layer and the information at the borders will be "washed away" too quickly.

The padding convolutions are usually categorized into three types based on the involvement of zero-padding.

- **Valid Convolution** is the simplest case where no zero-padding is involved. The filter always stays within "valid" positions (i.e., no zero-padded values) in the input feature map and the output size is reduced by $f - 1$ along the height and the width.

- **Same Convolution** ensures that the output and input feature maps have equal (the "same") sizes. To achieve this, inputs are zero-padded appropriately. For example, for a stride of 1, the padding is given by $p = \left\lfloor \frac{f}{2} \right\rfloor$. This is why it is also called "half" convolution.

- **Full Convolution** applies the maximum possible padding to the input feature maps before convolution. The maximum possible padding is the one where at least one valid input value is involved in all convolution cases. Therefore, it is equivalent to padding $f - 1$ zeros for a filter size f so that at the extreme corners at least one valid value will be included in the convolutions.

Receptive Field: You would have noticed above that we used a relatively small sized kernel with respect to the input. In computer vision, the inputs are of very high dimensions (e.g., images and videos) and are required to be efficiently processed through large-scale CNN models. Therefore, instead of defining convolutional filters that are equal to the spatial size of the inputs, we define them to be of a significantly smaller size compared to the input images (e.g., in practice 3×3, 5×5, and 7×7 filters are used to process images with sizes such as 110×110, 224×224, and even larger). This design provides two key benefits: **(a)** the number of learn-able parameters are greatly reduced when smaller sized kernels are used; and **(b)** small-sized filters ensure that distinctive patterns are learned from the local regions corresponding to, e.g., different object parts in an image. The size (height and width) of the filter which defines the spatial extent of a region, which a filter can modify at each convolution step, is called the "receptive field" of the filter. Note that the receptive field specifically relates to the spatial dimensions of the input image/features. When we stack many convolution layers on top of each other, the "effective receptive field" of each layer (relative to the input of the network) becomes a function of the receptive fields of all the previous convolution layers. The effective receptive field for a stack of N convolution layers, each with a kernel size of f, is given as:

$$\text{RF}_{\text{eff}}^{n} = f + n(f - 1), \qquad n \in [1, N]. \tag{4.5}$$

As an example, if we stack two convolution layers each of kernel size 5×5 and 3×3, respectively, the receptive field of the second layer would be 3×3 but its effective receptive field with respect to the input image would be 7×7. When the stride and filter sizes of stacked convolution layers are different, the effective receptive field of each layer can be represented in a more general form as follows:

$$\text{RF}_{\text{eff}}^{n} = \text{RF}_{\text{eff}}^{n-1} + \left((f_n - 1) * \prod_{i=1}^{n-1} s_i \right), \tag{4.6}$$

where f_n denotes the filter size in the nth layer, s_i represents the stride length for each previous layer and $\text{RF}_{\text{eff}}^{n-1}$ represents the effective receptive field of the previous layer.

Extending the Receptive Field: In order to enable very deep models with a relatively reduced number of parameters, a successful strategy is to stack many convolution layers with small receptive fields (e.g., 3×3 in the VGGnet [Simonyan and Zisserman, 2014b] in Chapter 6). However, this limits the spatial context of the learned convolutional filters which only scales linearly with the number of layers. In applications such as segmentation and labeling, which require pixel-wise dense predictions, a desirable characteristic is to aggregate broader contextual information using bigger receptive fields in the convolution layer. **Dilated convolution** (or atrous convolutions [Chen et al., 2014]) is an approach which extends the receptive field size, without increasing the number of parameters [Yu and Koltun, 2015]. The central idea is that a new dilation parameter (d) is introduced, which decides on the spacing between the filter

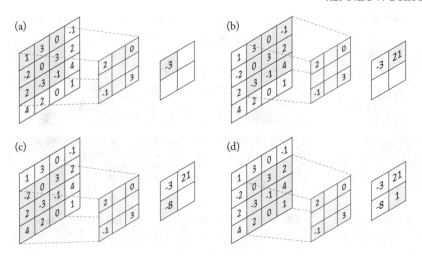

Figure 4.6: Convolution with a dilated filter where the dilation factor is $d = 2$.

weights while performing convolution. As shown in Fig. 4.6, a dilation by a factor of d means that the original filter is expanded by $d - 1$ spaces between each element and the intermediate empty locations are filled in with zeros. As a result, a filter of size $f \times f$ is enlarged to a size of: $f + (d - 1)(f - 1)$. The output dimensions corresponding to a convolution operation with a pre-defined filter size (f), zero padding (p), stride (s), dilation factor (d), an input with height (h), and width (w) is given as:

$$h' = \frac{h - f - (d - 1)(f - 1) + s + 2p}{s} \tag{4.7}$$

$$w' = \frac{w - f - (d - 1)(f - 1) + s + 2p}{s}. \tag{4.8}$$

The effective receptive field of an nth layer can be expressed as:

$$\text{RF}_{\text{eff}}^n = \text{RF}_{\text{eff}}^{n-1} + d(f - 1), \quad s.t., \quad \text{RF}_{\text{eff}}^1 = f. \tag{4.9}$$

The effect of the dilation operation can easily be understood by looking at the dilated filter for different values of parameter d. In Fig. 4.7, a stack of three convolution layers, each with different dilation parameters is shown. In the first layer, $d = 1$ and the dilated convolution is equivalent to a standard convolution. The receptive field size in this case is equal to the filter size, i.e., 3. In the second convolution layer where $d = 2$, the elements of the kernel are spread out such that there is one space between each element. This inflation of the convolution filter exponentially increases the receptive field size to 7×7. Similarly in the third layer, $d = 3$ which increases the receptive field size to 13×13 according to the relationship of Eq. (4.9). This effectively allows us to incorporate a wider context while performing convolutions. Combining multiple levels

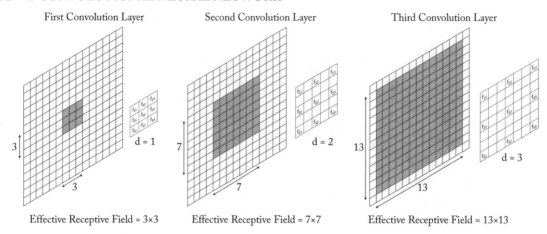

Figure 4.7: This figure shows three convolution layers with a filter of size 3×3. The first, second, and third layers have dilation factors of one, two, and three, respectively (from *left* to *right*). The effective receptive field with respect to the input image is shown in *orange* at each convolution layer. Note that an effective receptive field corresponds to the size of the region in the input image which affects each output activation in a convolution layer. At the first layer, each output activation is affected by a 3×3 region in the input image because the filter size is 3×3. In the subsequent layers, the receptive field increases due to the increasing network depth and the increasing dilation factor, both of which contribute to the incorporation of a wider context in the output feature responses.

of image context has been shown to improve the performance of classification, detection, and segmentation using deep CNNs (Chapter 7).

Hyper-parameters: The parameters of the convolution layer which need to be set by the user (based on cross-validation or experience) prior to the filter learning (such as the stride and padding) are called hyper-parameters. These hyper-parameters can be interpreted as the design choices of our network architecture based on a given application.

High Dimensional Cases: The 2D case is the simplest one, where the filter has only a single channel (represented as a matrix) which is convolved with the input feature channels to produce an output response. For higher dimensional cases, e.g., when the input to the CNN layers are tensors (e.g., 3D volumes in the case of volumetric representations), the filters are also 3D cubes which are convolved along the height, width, and depth of the input feature maps to generate a corresponding 3D output feature map. However, all the concepts that we discussed above for the 2D case still remain applicable to the processing of 3D and higher dimensional inputs (such as 3D spatio-temporal representation learning). The only difference is that the convolution operation is extended to an extra dimension, e.g., for the case of 3D, in addition to a convolution along height and width in 2D case, convolutions are performed along the depth as well. Similarly, zero-padding and striding can be performed along the depth for the 3D case.

4.2.3   POOLING LAYERS

A pooling layer operates on blocks of the input feature map and combines the feature activations. This combination operation is defined by a pooling function such as the average or the max function. Similar to the convolution layer, we need to specify the size of the pooled region and the stride. Figure 4.8 shows the max pooling operation, where the maximum activation is chosen from the selected block of values. This window is slided across the input feature maps with a step size defined by the stride (1 in the case of Fig. 4.8). If the size of the pooled region is given by $f \times f$, with a stride s, the size of the output feature map is given by:

$$h' = \left\lfloor \frac{h - f + s}{s} \right\rfloor, w' = \left\lfloor \frac{w - f + s}{s} \right\rfloor. \tag{4.10}$$

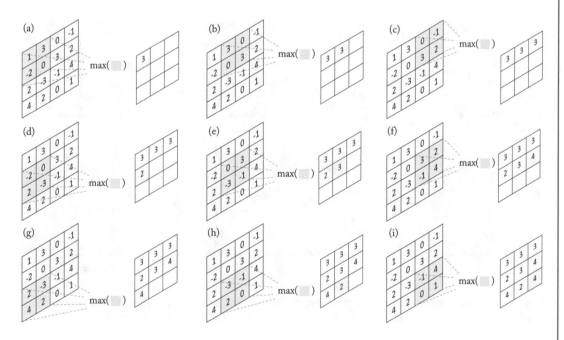

Figure 4.8: The operation of max-pooling layer when the size of the pooling region is 2×2 and the stride is 1. **(a)–(i)** shows the computations performed at each step as the pooled region in the input feature map (shown in *orange*) is slided at each step to compute the corresponding value in the output feature map (shown in *blue*).

The pooling operation effectively down-samples the input feature map. Such a down-sampling process is useful for obtaining a compact feature representation which is invariant to moderate changes in object scale, pose, and translation in an image [Goodfellow et al., 2016].

4.2.4 NONLINEARITY

The weight layers in a CNN (e.g., convolutional and fully connected layers) are often followed by a nonlinear activation (or a piece-wise linear) function. The activation function takes a real-valued input and squashes it within a small range such as $[0, 1]$ and $[-1, 1]$. The application of a nonlinear function after the weight layers is highly important, since it allows a neural network to learn nonlinear mappings. In the absence of nonlinearities, a stacked network of weight layers is equivalent to a linear mapping from the input domain to the output domain.

A nonlinear function can also be understood as a switching or a selection mechanism, which decides whether a neuron will fire or not given all of its inputs. The activation functions that are commonly used in deep networks are differentiable to enable error back propagation (Chapter 6). Below is a list of the most common activation functions that are used in deep neural networks.

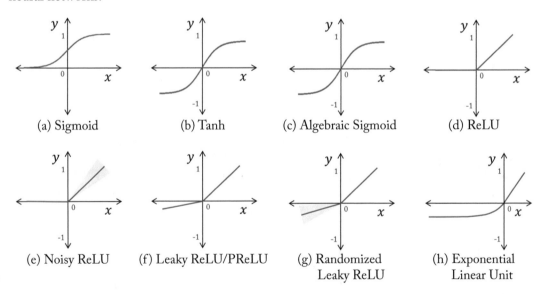

(a) Sigmoid   (b) Tanh   (c) Algebraic Sigmoid   (d) ReLU

(e) Noisy ReLU   (f) Leaky ReLU/PReLU   (g) Randomized Leaky ReLU   (h) Exponential Linear Unit

Figure 4.9: Some of the common activation functions that are used in deep neural networks.

Sigmoid (Fig. 4.9a): The sigmoid activation function takes in a real number as its input, and outputs a number in the range of $[0,1]$. It is defined as:

$$f_{sigm}(x) = \frac{1}{1 + e^{-x}}. \tag{4.11}$$

Tanh (Fig. 4.9b): The tanh activation function implements the hyperbolic tangent function to squash the input values within the range of $[-1, 1]$. It is represented as follows:

$$f_{tanh}(x) = \frac{e^x - e^{-x}}{e^x + e^{-x}}.$$

(4.12)

Algebraic Sigmoid Function (Fig. 4.9c): The algebraic sigmoid function also maps the input within the range $[-1, 1]$. It is given by:

$$f_{a-sig}(x) = \frac{x}{\sqrt{1 + x^2}}.$$

(4.13)

Rectifier Linear Unit (Fig. 4.9d): The ReLU is a simple activation function which is of a special practical importance because of its quick computation. A ReLU function maps the input to a 0 if it is negative and keeps its value unchanged if it is positive. This can be represented as follows:

$$f_{relu}(x) = \max(0, x).$$

(4.14)

The ReLU activation is motivated by the processing in the human visual cortex [Hahnloser et al., 2000]. The popularity and effectiveness of ReLU has lead to a number of its variants, which we introduce next. These variants address some of the shortcomings of the ReLU activation function, e.g., leaky ReLU does not completely reduce the negative inputs to zero.

Noisy ReLU (Fig. 4.9e): The noisy version of ReLU adds a sample drawn from a Gaussian distribution with mean zero and a variance which depends on the input value ($\sigma(x)$) in the positive input. It can be represented as follows:

$$f_{n-rel}(x) = \max(0, x + \epsilon), \quad \epsilon \sim \mathcal{N}(0, \sigma(x)).$$

(4.15)

Leaky ReLU (Fig. 4.9f): The rectifier function (Fig. 4.9d) completely switches off the output if the input is negative. A leaky ReLU function does not reduce the output to a zero value, rather it outputs a down-scaled version of the negative input. This function is represented as:

$$f_{l-rel}(x) = \begin{cases} x & if \ x > 0 \\ cx & if \ x \le 0, \end{cases}$$

(4.16)

where c is the leak factor which is a constant and typically set to a small value (e.g., 0.01).

Parametric Linear Units (Fig. 4.9f): The parametric ReLU function behaves in a similar manner as the leaky ReLU, with the only difference that the tunable leak parameter is learned during the network training. It can be expressed as follows:

$$f_{p-rel}(x) = \begin{cases} x & if \ x > 0 \\ ax & if \ x \le 0, \end{cases}$$

(4.17)

where a is the leak factor which is automatically learned during the training.

Randomized Leaky Rectifier Linear Unit (Fig. 4.9g): The randomized leaky ReLU (RReLU) randomly selects the leak factor in the leaky ReLU function from a uniform distribution. There-fore,

$$f_{r-rel}(x) = \begin{cases} x & if \ x > 0 \\ ax & if \ x \le 0 \end{cases}. \tag{4.18}$$

The factor a is randomly chosen during training and set to a mean value during the test phase to get the contribution of all samples. Thus,

$$a \sim \mathcal{U}(l, u) \qquad \qquad during \ training \tag{4.19}$$

$$a = \frac{l + u}{2} \qquad \qquad during \ testing. \tag{4.20}$$

The upper and lower limits of the uniform distribution are usually set to 8 and 3, respectively.

Exponential Linear Units (Fig. 4.9h): The exponential linear units have both positive and nega-tive values and they therefore try to push the mean activations toward zero (similar to the batch normalization). It helps in speeding up the training process while achieving a better perfor-mance.

$$f_{elu}(x) = \begin{cases} x & if \ x > 0 \\ a(e^x - 1) & if \ x \le 0. \end{cases} \tag{4.21}$$

Here, a is a non-negative hyper parameter which decides on the saturation level of the ELU in response to negative inputs.

4.2.5   FULLY CONNECTED LAYERS

Fully connected layers correspond essentially to convolution layers with filters of size 1×1. Each unit in a fully connected layer is densely connected to all the units of the previous layer. In a typ-ical CNN, full-connected layers are usually placed toward the end of the architecture. However, some successful architectures are reported in the literature which use this type of layer at an intermediate location within a CNN (e.g., NiN [Lin et al., 2013] which will be discussed in Section 6.3). Its operation can be represented as a simple matrix multiplication followed by adding a vector of bias terms and applying an element-wise nonlinear function $f(\cdot)$:

$$\mathbf{y} = f(\mathbf{W}^T \mathbf{x} + \mathbf{b}), \tag{4.22}$$

where $\mathbf{x}$ and $\mathbf{y}$ are the vector of input and output activations, respectively, $\mathbf{W}$ denotes the matrix containing the weights of the connections between the layer units, and $\mathbf{b}$ represents the bias term vector. Note that a fully connected layer is identical to a weight layer that we studied in the case of the Multi-layer Perceptron in Section 3.4.2.

4.2.6   TRANSPOSED CONVOLUTION LAYER

The normal convolution layer maps a spatially large-sized input to a relatively smaller sized output. In several cases, e.g., image super-resolution, we want to go from a spatially low-resolution feature map to a larger output feature with a higher resolution. This requirement is achieved by a transposed convolution layer, which is also called a "fractionally strided convolution layer" or the "up-sampling layer" and sometimes (incorrectly) as the deconvolution layer.[1]

One can interpret the operation of a transposed convolution layer as the equivalent of a convolution layer, but by passing through it in the opposite direction, as in a backward pass during back propagation. If the forward pass through the convolution layer gives a low-dimensional convolved output, the backward pass of the convolved output through the convolution layer should give the original high spatial dimensional input. This backward transformation layer is called the *"transposed convolution layer."* It can easily be understood in terms of standard convolution by revisiting the example of Fig. 4.3. In that example, a 2×2 filter was applied to a 4×4 input feature map with a stride of one and no zero padding to generate a 3×3 output feature map. Note that this convolution operation can be represented as a matrix multiplication, which offers a highly efficient implementation in practice. For this purpose, we can represent the 2×2 kernel as an unrolled Toeplitz matrix as follows:

$$K = \begin{bmatrix} k_{1,1} & k_{1,2} & 0 & 0 & k_{2,1} & k_{2,2} & 0 & 0 & 0 & 0 & 0 & 0 & 0 & 0 & 0 & 0 \\ 0 & k_{1,1} & k_{1,2} & 0 & 0 & k_{2,1} & k_{2,2} & 0 & 0 & 0 & 0 & 0 & 0 & 0 & 0 & 0 \\ 0 & 0 & k_{1,1} & k_{1,2} & 0 & 0 & k_{2,1} & k_{2,2} & 0 & 0 & 0 & 0 & 0 & 0 & 0 & 0 \\ 0 & 0 & 0 & 0 & k_{1,1} & k_{1,2} & 0 & 0 & k_{2,1} & k_{2,2} & 0 & 0 & 0 & 0 & 0 & 0 \\ 0 & 0 & 0 & 0 & 0 & k_{1,1} & k_{1,2} & 0 & 0 & k_{2,1} & k_{2,2} & 0 & 0 & 0 & 0 & 0 \\ 0 & 0 & 0 & 0 & 0 & 0 & k_{1,1} & k_{1,2} & 0 & 0 & k_{2,1} & k_{2,2} & 0 & 0 & 0 & 0 \\ 0 & 0 & 0 & 0 & 0 & 0 & 0 & 0 & k_{1,1} & k_{1,2} & 0 & 0 & k_{2,1} & k_{2,2} & 0 & 0 \\ 0 & 0 & 0 & 0 & 0 & 0 & 0 & 0 & 0 & k_{1,1} & k_{1,2} & 0 & 0 & k_{2,1} & k_{2,2} & 0 \\ 0 & 0 & 0 & 0 & 0 & 0 & 0 & 0 & 0 & 0 & k_{1,1} & k_{1,2} & 0 & 0 & k_{2,1} & k_{2,2} \end{bmatrix}.$$

Here, $k_{i,j}$ represents the filter element in the ith row and j^{th} column. For an input feature map X, the convolution operation can be expressed in terms of the matrix multiplication between K and the vectorized form of input, i.e., $\mathbf{x} = \text{vec}(X)$:

$$\mathbf{y} = K\mathbf{x}, \tag{4.23}$$

where $\mathbf{y}$ is the corresponding vectorized output. In the transposed convolution, we will input a 3×3 feature map to generate an output feature map of 4×4 as follows:

$$\mathbf{y} = K^T \mathbf{x}. \tag{4.24}$$

Note that the $\mathbf{x}$ and $\mathbf{y}$ in the above two equations have different dimensions.

---

[1]Note that deconvolution in signal processing literature refers to undoing the effect of the convolution operation with a filter F by applying its inverse filter F^{-1}. This deconvolution operation is usually performed in the Fourier domain. This is clearly different from the operation of a convolution transpose layer which does not use an inverse filter.

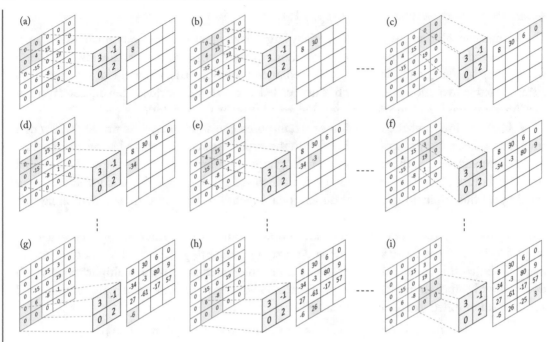

Figure 4.10: Convolution transpose operation corresponding to a forward convolution operation with a unit stride and no zero padding shown in Fig. 4.3. The input in this example has been zero-padded to obtain a 4 × 4 output. **(a)–(i)** show the computations performed at each step as the filter is slid onto the input feature map to compute the corresponding value in the output feature map. The 2 × 2 filter (shown in *green*) is multiplied with the same sized region (shown in *orange*) within a 5 × 5 input feature map (including zero-padding) and the resulting values are summed up to obtain a corresponding entry (shown in *blue*) in the output feature map at each convolution transpose step. Note that the convolution transpose operation does not invert the convolution operation (the input in Fig. 4.3 and the output here are different). However, it can be used to recover the loss in the spatial dimensions of the feature map (input size in Fig. 4.3 and output size here are the same). Furthermore, note that the filter values have been reversed for the convolution transpose operation compared to the filter used in Fig. 4.3.

The transposed convolution layers effectively up-samples the input feature maps. This can also be understood as a convolution with an input feature map which has additional rows and columns consisting of null values inserted around the actual values. The convolution with this up-sampled input will then generate the desired result. This process is shown in Figs. 4.10 and 4.11 for the outputs we obtained in the examples of Figs. 4.3 and 4.5. It is important to note that the filter entries are reversed for the convolution transpose operation. Furthermore, note that the output from the convolution transpose is equal to the size of input of the convolution operation.

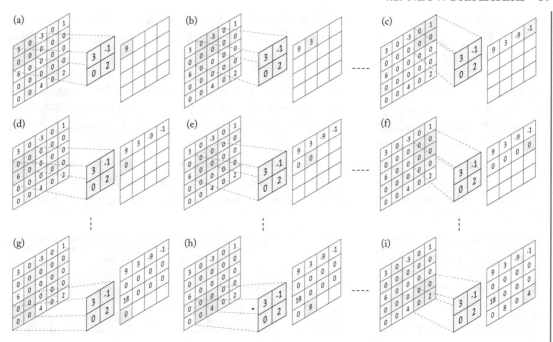

Figure 4.11: Convolution transpose operation corresponding to a forward convolution operation with a stride of 2 and unit zero padding shown in Fig. 4.5. The input in this example has been zero-padded in between the feature map values to obtain a 4 × 4 output (shown in *light blue*). **(a)–(i)** show the computations performed at each step as the filter is slided onto the input feature map to compute the corresponding value in the output feature map. The 2 × 2 filter (shown in *green*) is multiplied with the same sized region (shown in *orange*) within a 5 × 5 input feature map (including zero-padding) and the resulting values are summed up to obtain a corresponding entry (shown in *blue*) in the output feature map at each convolution transpose step. Note that the convolution transpose operation does not invert the convolution operation (input in Fig. 4.5 and output here are different). However, it can be used to recover the loss in the spatial dimensions of the feature map (input size in Fig. 4.5 and output size here are the same). Furthermore, note that the filter values have been reversed for the convolution transpose operation compared to the filter used in Fig. 4.5.

However the individual entries are different because the convolution transpose does not invert the forward convolution. We can calculate the size of the output given a kernel of size $f \times f$, stride s, padding p:

$$h' = s(\hat{h} - 1) + f - 2p + (h - f + 2p) \bmod s, \tag{4.25}$$
$$w' = s(\hat{w} - 1) + f - 2p + (w - f + 2p) \bmod s, \tag{4.26}$$

where mod denotes the modulus operation, $\hat{h}$ and $\hat{w}$ denote the input dimensions without any zero-padding, and h and w denote the spatial dimensions of the input in the equivalent forward convolution (as shown in Figs. 4.3 and 4.5).

In the example shown in Fig. 4.10, $p = 0$, $s = 1$, $f = 2$, and $\hat{h} = \hat{w} = 3$. Therefore, the spatial dimensions of the output feature map are $h' = w' = 4$. In Fig. 4.11, $s - 1$ zero values are added between each pair of input elements to extend the input to produce a spatially large output. The parameter values are $p = 1$, $s = 2$, $f = 2$, and $\hat{h} = \hat{w} = 3$ and the resulting output dimensions are again $h' = w' = 4$.

Finally, it is important to note that, from an implementation point of view, the transposed convolution operation is much faster when implemented as a matrix multiplication operation compared to the zero padding of the input feature map at intermediate locations followed by normal convolutions [Dumoulin and Visin, 2016].

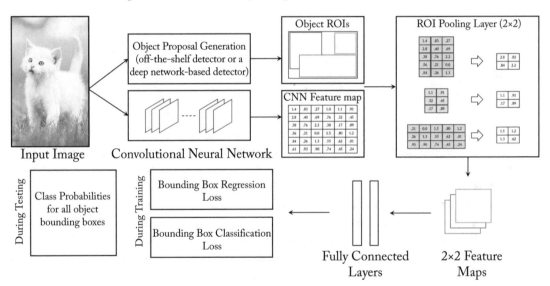

Figure 4.12: The function of a ROI pooling layer with in an object detection framework is illustrated in this figure. Note that a single feature channel, few RoI proposals (just three), and a relatively smaller output size (2 × 2) from the ROI pooling layer has been demonstrated here for the sake of clarity.

4.2.7   REGION OF INTEREST POOLING

The Region of Interest (RoI) Pooling layer is an important component of convolutional neural networks which is mostly used for object detection [Girshick, 2015] (and slightly modified versions for related tasks, e.g., instance segmentation [He et al., 2017]). In the object detection problem, the goal is to precisely locate each object in an image using a bounding box and tag it with the relevant object category. These objects can be located at any region in an image and generally vary greatly in their size, shape, appearance, and texture properties. The usual course of action with such problems is to first generate a large set of candidate object proposals with the aim to include all possible object bounding boxes that may be discovered in an image. For these initial proposals, usually off-the-shelf detectors are used such as the selective search [Uijlings et al., 2013] or the EdgeBox [Zitnick and Dollár, 2014]. Recent works have also proposed approaches to integrate the proposal generation step into a CNN (e.g., Region Proposal Network [Ren et al., 2015]). Since the valid detections are very few compared to the generated proposals (usually < 1%), the resources used to process all the negative detections are wasted.

The ROI pooling layer provides a solution to this problem by shifting the processing specific to individual bounding-boxes later in the network architecture. An input image is processed through the deep network and intermediate CNN feature maps (with reduced spatial dimensions compared to the input image) are obtained. The ROI pooling layer takes the input feature map of the complete image and the coordinates of each ROI as its input. The ROI co-ordinates can be used to roughly locate the features corresponding to a specific object. However, the features thus obtained have different spatial sizes because each ROI can be of a different dimension. Since CNN layers can only operate on fixed dimensional inputs, a ROI pooling layer converts these variable sized feature maps (corresponding to different object proposals) to a fixed sized output feature map for each object proposal, e.g., a 5×5 or a 7×7 map. The fixed size output dimensions is a hyper-parameter which is fixed during the training process. Specifically, this same-sized output is achieved by dividing each ROI into a set of cells with equal dimensions. The number of these cells is the same as the required output dimensions. Afterward, the maximum value in each cell is calculated (max-pooling) and it is assigned to the corresponding output feature map location.

By using a single set of input feature maps to generate a feature representation for each region proposal, the ROI pooling layer greatly improves the efficiency of a deep network. Thus, a CNN only needs a single pass to compute features corresponding to all the ROIs. It also makes it possible to train the network in an end-to-end manner, as a unified system. Note that the ROI pooling layer is usually plugged in the latter portion of a deep architecture to save a lot of computations which can result if the region-based processing is performed in the early layers of the network (due to the large number of proposals). An example use case of ROI pooling layer in a CNN is described in Section 7.2.1.

4.2.8   SPATIAL PYRAMID POOLING LAYER

The spatial pyramid pooling (SPP) layer [He et al., 2015b] in CNNs is inspired by the pyramid-based approaches proposed for the Bag of Visual Words (BoW) style feature encoding methods [Lazebnik et al., 2006]. The main intuition behind the SPP layer is that the interesting discriminative features can appear at a variety of scales in the convolutional feature maps. Therefore, it is useful to incorporate this information for classification purposes.

To efficiently encode this information in a single descriptor, the SPP layer divides the feature maps into three levels of spatial blocks. At the **global level**, the features corresponding to all the spatial locations are pooled together to obtain just a single vector (with a dimension equal to the number of channels of the previous layer, say n). At the **middle level**, the feature maps are divided into four (2×2) disjoint spatial blocks of equal dimensions and features within each block are pooled together to obtain a single feature vector in each of the four blocks. This n dimensional representation is concatenated for each block, resulting in a $4n$ dimensional feature vector for the middle level. **Finally**, at the local level, the feature maps are divided into 16 blocks (4×4). Features within each spatial block are pooled together to give an n dimensional feature vector. All the 16 features are concatenated to form a single $16n$ dimensional feature representation. Finally, the local, mid-level, and global feature representations are concatenated together to generate a $16n + 4n + n$ dimensional feature representation, which is forwarded to the classifier layers (or fully connected layers) for classification (see Fig. 4.13).

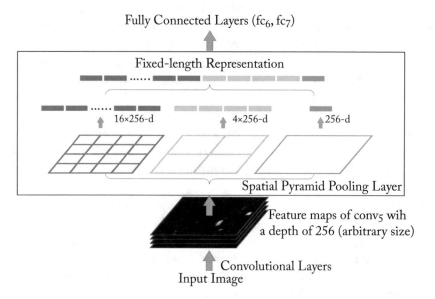

Figure 4.13: The Spatial Pyramid Pooling Layer [He et al., 2014] incorporates discriminative information at three scales which is useful for accurate classification. (Figure used with permission.)

Therefore, an SPP layer makes use of the localized pooling and the concatenation operations to generate a high-dimensional feature vector as its output. The combination of information at multiple scales helps in achieving robustness against variations in object pose, scale, and shape (deformations). Since the SPP layer output is not dependent on the length and width of the feature maps, it allows the CNN to handle input images of any size. Furthermore, it can perform a similar operation on individual object regions for the detection task. This saves a reasonable amount of time compared to the case where we input individual object proposals and obtain a feature representation for each of them.

4.2.9 VECTOR OF LOCALLY AGGREGATED DESCRIPTORS LAYER

As we saw for the case of SPP layer, the Vector of Locally Aggregated Descriptors (VLAD) layer in CNNs [Arandjelovic et al., 2016] also gets its inspiration from the VLAD pooling approach used in the BoW style models to aggregate local features [Jégou et al., 2010]. The main idea behind the VLAD layer can be explained as follows. Given a set of local descriptors $\{\mathbf{x}_i \in \mathbb{R}^D\}_{i=1}^N$, we aim to represent these local features in terms of a set of visual words $\{\mathbf{c}_i \in \mathbb{R}^D\}_{i=1}^K$ (also called "key-points" or "cluster centers"). This is achieved by finding the association of each local descriptor with all the cluster centers. The (soft) association is measured as a weighted difference between each descriptor and all the K cluster centers. This results in a $K \times D$ dimensional feature matrix F given by:

$$F(j,k) = \sum_{i=1}^N a_k(\mathbf{x}_i)(x_i(j) - c_k(j)). \tag{4.27}$$

Here, the association term a_k measures the connection between the ith local feature ($\mathbf{x}_i$) and the kth cluster center ($\mathbf{c}_k$), e.g., it will be 0 if $\mathbf{x}_i$ is furthest away from $\mathbf{c}_k$ and 1 if $\mathbf{x}_i$ is closest to $\mathbf{c}_k$. The association term is defined as follows:

$$a_k(\mathbf{x}_i) = \frac{\exp(\mathbf{w}_k^T \mathbf{x}_i + b_k)}{\sum_r \exp(\mathbf{w}_r^T \mathbf{x}_i + b_r)}, \tag{4.28}$$

where, $\mathbf{w}, b$ are the weights and biases of a fully connected layer. From an implementation point of view, the computation of the association term can be understood as passing the descriptors through a fully connected CNN layer, followed by a soft-max operation. The parameters $\mathbf{w}, b$, and $\mathbf{c}$ are learned during the training process. Note that since all the operations are differentiable, an end-to-end training is feasible. For classification purposes, the feature matrix F is first normalized column-wise using the ℓ_2 norm of each column, then converted to a vector and again ℓ_2 normalized. Figure 4.14 summarizes the operation of a VLAD layer.

4.2.10 SPATIAL TRANSFORMER LAYER

As you would have noticed for the case of the VLAD layer, the introduced layer does not involve a single operation. Instead, it involves a set of inter-connected sub-modules, each of which is implemented as an individual layer. The spatial transformer layer [Jaderberg et al., 2015] is another such example which comprises three main modules, namely **(a)** localization network, **(b)** grid generator, and **(c)** sampler. Figure 4.15 illustrates the three individual blocks and their function.

In a nutshell, the spatial transformer layer learns to focus on the interesting part of its input. This layer applies geometric transformations on the interesting parts of the input to focus

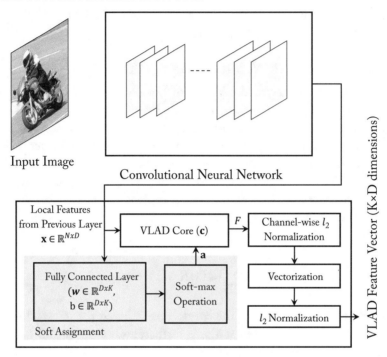

Figure 4.14: The figure shows the working of VLAD Layer [Arandjelovic et al., 2016]. It takes multiple local features from the CNN layers and aggregate them to generate a high-dimensional output feature representation.

attention and perform rectification. It can be plugged in after the input layer or any of the earlier convolutional layers which generate a relatively large-sized (height×width) output feature map.

The first module, called the **localization network**, takes the input feature maps (or the original input image) and predicts the parameters of transformation which needs to be applied. This net can be implemented as any combination of convolutional and/or fully connected layers. However, the final layer is a regression layer which generates the parameter vector θ. The dimensions of the output parameters θ depends on the kind of transformation, e.g., for an affine transformation, it is has six parameters defined as follows:

$$\theta = \begin{bmatrix} \theta_1 & \theta_2 & \theta_3 \\ \theta_4 & \theta_5 & \theta_6 \end{bmatrix}. \tag{4.29}$$

The **grid generator** generates a grid of coordinates in the input image corresponding to each pixel from the output image. This mapping is useful for the next step, where a sampling function is used to transform the input image. The **sampler** generates the output image using the grid given by the grid generator. This is achieved by using a sampling kernel which is applied at each pixel of the input image (or at each value in the input feature map). To enable end-to-end training, the sampling kernel should be differentiable with respect to the input and the grid co-ordinates (x and y coordinates). Examples of kernels include the nearest neighbor copying from the source (input) to the target (output) and the bilinear sampling kernels.

Since all the modules are fully differentiable, the spatial transformation can be learned end-to-end using a standard back-propagation algorithm. This provides a big advantage since it allows the network to automatically shift focus toward the more discriminative portions of the input image or the feature maps.

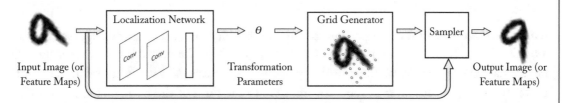

Figure 4.15: The spatial transformer layer with its three modules. The localization network predicts the transformation parameters. The grid generator identifies the points in the input domain on which a sampling kernel is applied using the sampler.

4.3   CNN LOSS FUNCTIONS

Having studied a wide variety of simple and relatively more complex CNN layers, we discuss the final layer in a CNN which is used only during the training process. This layer uses a "loss function," also called the "objective function," to estimate the quality of predictions made by the network on the training data, for which the actual labels are known. These loss functions are optimized during the learning process of a CNN, whose details will be covered in Chapter 5.

A loss function quantifies the difference between the estimated output of the model (the *prediction*) and the correct output (the *ground truth*).

The type of loss function used in our CNN model depends on our end problem. The generic set problems for which neural networks are usually used (and the associated loss functions) can be categorized into the following categories.

1. Binary Classification (SVM hinge loss, Squared hinge loss).

2. Identity Verification (Contrastive loss).

3. Multi-class Classification (Softmax loss, Expectation loss).

4. Regression (SSIM, ℓ^1 error, Euclidean loss).

Note that the loss functions which are suitable for multi-class classification tasks are also applicable to binary classification tasks. However, the case reverse is generally not true unless a multi-class problem is divided into multiple one-vs.-rest binary classification problems where a separate classifier is trained for each case using a binary classification loss. Below, we discuss the above mentioned loss functions in more detail.

4.3.1   CROSS-ENTROPY LOSS

The cross-entropy loss (also termed "log loss" and "soft-max loss") is defined as follows:

$$L(\mathbf{p}, \mathbf{y}) = -\sum_n y_n \log(p_n), \qquad n \in [1, N], \tag{4.30}$$

where $\mathbf{y}$ denotes the desired output and $\mathbf{p}$ is the probability for each output category. There is a total of N neurons in the output layer, therefore $\mathbf{p}, \mathbf{y} \in \mathbb{R}^N$. The probability of each class can be calculated using a soft-max function: $p_n = \frac{\exp(\hat{p}_n)}{\sum_k \exp(\hat{p}_k)}$, where $\hat{p}_n$ is the unnormalized output score from the previous layer in the network. Due to the form of the normalizing function in the loss, this loss is also called the soft-max loss.

It is interesting to note that optimizing the network parameters using the cross-entropy loss is equivalent to minimizing the KL-divergence between the predicted output (generated distribution, $\mathbf{p}$) and the desired output (true distribution $\mathbf{y}$). The KL-divergence between $\mathbf{p}$ and $\mathbf{y}$ can be expressed as the difference between cross-entropy (denoted by $L(\cdot)$) and the entropy (denoted by $H(\cdot)$) as follows:

$$\mathrm{KL}(\mathbf{p} \parallel \mathbf{y}) = L(\mathbf{p}, \mathbf{y}) - H(\mathbf{p}). \tag{4.31}$$

Since entropy is just a constant value, minimizing cross entropy is equivalent to minimizing the KL-divergence between the two distributions.

4.3.2   SVM HINGE LOSS

The SVM hinge loss is motivated by the error function which is normally used during the training of SVM classifier. Hinge loss maximizes the margin between the true and the negative class samples. This loss is defined as follows:

$$L(\mathbf{p}, \mathbf{y}) = \sum_n \max(0, m - (2y_n - 1)p_n), \tag{4.32}$$

where "m" is the margin which is usually set equal to a constant value of 1 and $\mathbf{p}, \mathbf{y}$ denote the predicted and desired outputs, respectively. An alternative formulation of the hinge loss is the Crammer and Singer's [Crammer and Singer, 2001] loss function given below:

$$L(\mathbf{p}, \mathbf{y}) = \max(0, m + \max_{i \neq c} p_i - p_c), \qquad c = \operatorname*{argmax}_j y_j, \tag{4.33}$$

where, p_c denotes the prediction at the correct class index c. Another similar formulation of the hinge loss was proposed by Weston and Watkins [Weston et al., 1999]:

$$L(\mathbf{p}, \mathbf{y}) = \sum_{i \neq c} \max(0, m + p_i - p_c), \qquad c = \underset{j}{\operatorname{argmax}}\, y_j. \qquad (4.34)$$

4.3.3 SQUARED HINGE LOSS

The squared hinge loss function has been shown to perform slightly better than the vanilla hinge loss function in some applications [Tang, 2013]. This loss function simply includes the square of the max function in Eqs. (4.32)–(4.34). The squared hinge loss is more sensitive to margin violations compared to the vanilla hinge loss.

4.3.4 EUCLIDEAN LOSS

The Euclidean loss (also termed the "*quadratic loss*," "*mean square error*" or "*ℓ^2 error*") is defined in terms of the squared error between the predictions ($\mathbf{p} \in \mathbb{R}^N$) and the ground truth labels ($\mathbf{y} \in \mathbb{R}^N$):

$$L(\mathbf{p}, \mathbf{y}) = \frac{1}{2N} \sum_n (p_n - y_n)^2, \qquad n \in [1, N]. \qquad (4.35)$$

4.3.5 THE ℓ^1 ERROR

The ℓ^1 loss can be used for regression problems and has been shown to outperform the Euclidean loss in some cases [Zhao et al., 2015]. It is defined as follows:

$$L(\mathbf{p}, \mathbf{y}) = \frac{1}{N} \sum_n |p_n - y_n|, \qquad n \in [1, N]. \qquad (4.36)$$

4.3.6 CONTRASTIVE LOSS

The contrastive loss is used to map similar inputs to nearby points in the feature/output space and to map the dissimilar inputs to distant points. This loss function works on the pairs of either similar or dissimilar inputs (e.g., in siamese networks [Chopra et al., 2005]). It can be represented as follows:

$$L(\mathbf{p}, y) = \frac{1}{2N} \sum_n y d^2 + (1 - y) \max(0, m - d)^2, \qquad n \in [1, N], \qquad (4.37)$$

where m is the margin and $y \in [0, 1]$ shows whether the input pairs are dissimilar or similar respectively. Here, "d" can be any valid distance measure such as the Euclidean distance:

$$d = \| f_a - f_b \|_2, \qquad (4.38)$$

where f_a and f_b are the learned representations of the two inputs in the feature space and $\| \cdot \|_2$ represents the ℓ^2 (or Euclidean) norm.

There are other variants of verification losses which extend to triplets (e.g., the triplet loss is used for triplet networks [Schroff et al., 2015] as opposed to a Siamese network).

4.3.7   EXPECTATION LOSS

The expectation loss is defined as follows:

$$L(\mathbf{p}, \mathbf{y}) = \sum_n |y_n - \frac{\exp(p_n)}{\sum_k \exp(p_k)}|, \qquad n \in [1, N]. \tag{4.39}$$

It minimizes the expected misclassification probability, which is why it is called the expectation loss. Note that the cross entropy loss also uses the soft-max function which is similar to the expectation loss. However, it directly maximizes the probability of fully correct predictions [Janocha and Czarnecki, 2017].

The expectation loss provides more robustness against outliers because the objective maximizes the expectation of true predictions. However, this loss function is seldom used in deep neural networks because it is not a convex or concave function with respect to the weights of the preceding layer. This leads to optimization issues (such as instability and slow convergence) during the learning process.

4.3.8   STRUCTURAL SIMILARITY MEASURE

For image processing problems, perceptually grounded loss functions have been used in combination with CNNs [Zhao et al., 2015]. One example of such losses is the Structural Similarity (SSIM) measure. It is defined as follows:

$$L(\mathbf{p}, \mathbf{y}) = 1 - \text{SSIM}(n), \tag{4.40}$$

where n is the center pixel of the image, $\mathbf{p}, \mathbf{y}$ denote the predicted output and the desired output, respectively, and the structural similarity for that pixel is given by:

$$\text{SSIM}(n) = \frac{2\mu_{p_n}\mu_{y_n} + C_1}{\mu_{p_n}^2 + \mu_{y_n}^2 + C_1} \cdot \frac{2\sigma_{p_n y_n} + C_2}{\sigma_{p_n}^2 + \sigma_{y_n}^2 + C_2}. \tag{4.41}$$

Here, the mean and standard deviation and covariance are represented by μ, σ and $\sigma_{p_n y_n}$, respectively. At each pixel location n, the mean and standard deviation are calculated using a Gaussian filter centered at the pixel with a standard deviation σ_G. C_1, C_2 denote the image dependent constants which provide stabilization against small denominators. Note that the calculation of SSIM at one pixel requires the neighboring pixel values in the support of the Gaussian filter. Also note that we do not calculate the SSIM measure at each pixel because it cannot be calculated straightforwardly for the pixels that are close to image boundaries.

In the following chapter, we will introduce different techniques for weight initialization and gradient-based parameter learning algorithms for deep networks.

CHAPTER 5

CNN Learning

In Chapter 4, we discussed different architecture blocks of the CNN and their operational details. Most of these CNN layers involve parameters which are required to be tuned appropriately for a given computer vision task (e.g., image classification and object detection). In this chapter, we will discuss various mechanisms and techniques that are used to set the weights in deep neural networks. We will first cover concepts such as weight initialization and network regularization in Sections 5.1 and 5.2, respectively, which helps in a successful optimization of the CNNs. Afterward, we will introduce gradient-based parameter learning for CNNs in Section 5.3, which is quite similar to the MLP parameter learning process discussed in Chapter 3. The details of neural network optimization algorithms (also called "*solvers*") will come in Section 5.4. Finally in Section 5.5, we will explain various types of approaches which are used for the calculation of the gradient during the error back-propagation process.

5.1 WEIGHT INITIALIZATION

A correct weight initialization is the key to stably train very deep networks. An ill-suited initialization can lead to the vanishing or exploding gradient problem during error back-propagation. In this section, we introduce several approaches to perform weight initialization and provide comparisons between them to illustrate their benefits and problems. Note that the discussion below pertains to the initialization of neuron weights within a network and the biases are usually set to zero at the start of the network training. If all the weights are also set to zero at the start of training, the weight updates will be identical (due to symmetric outputs) and the network will not learn anything useful. To break this symmetry between neural units, the weights are initialized randomly at the start of the training. In the following, we describe several popular approaches to network initialization.

5.1.1 GAUSSIAN RANDOM INITIALIZATION

A common approach to weight initialization in CNNs is the Gaussian random initialization technique. This approach initializes the convolutional and the fully connected layers using random matrices whose elements are sampled from a Gaussian distribution with zero mean and a small standard deviation (e.g., 0.1 and 0.01).

5.1.2 UNIFORM RANDOM INITIALIZATION

The uniform random initialization approach initializes the convolutional and the fully connected layers using random matrices whose elements are sampled from a uniform distribution (instead of a normal distribution as in the earlier case) with a zero mean and a small standard deviation (e.g., 0.1 and 0.01). The uniform and normal random initializations generally perform identically. However, the training of very deep networks becomes a problem with a random initialization of weights from a uniform or normal distribution [Simonyan and Zisserman, 2014b]. The reason is that the forward and backward propagated activations can either diminish or explode when the network is very deep (see Section 3.2.2).

5.1.3 ORTHOGONAL RANDOM INITIALIZATION

Orthogonal random initialization has also been shown to perform well in deep neural networks [Saxe et al., 2013]. Note that the Gaussian random initialization is only approximately orthogonal. For the orthogonal random initialization, a random weight matrix is decomposed by applying e.g., an SVD. The orthogonal matrix (U) is then used for the weight initialization of the CNN layers.

5.1.4 UNSUPERVISED PRE-TRAINING

One approach to avoid the gradient diminishing or exploding problem is to use layer-wise pre-training in an unsupervised fashion. However, this type of pre-training has found more success in the training of deep generative networks, e.g., Deep Belief Networks [Hinton et al., 2006] and Auto-encoders [Bengio et al., 2007]. The unsupervised pre-training can be followed by a supervised fine-tuning stage to make use of any available annotations. However, due to the new hyper-parameters, the considerable amount of effort involved in such an approach and the availability of better initialization techniques, layer-wise pre-training is seldom used now to enable the training of CNN-based very deep networks. We describe some of the more successful approaches to initialize deep CNNs next.

5.1.5 XAVIER INITIALIZATION

A random initialization of a neuron makes the variance of its output directly proportional to the number of its incoming connections (a neuron's fan-in measure). To alleviate this problem, Glorot and Bengio [2010] proposed to randomly initialize the weights with a variance measure that is dependent on the number of incoming and outgoing connections (n_{f-in} and n_{f-out} respectively) from a neuron,

$$Var(w) = \frac{2}{n_{f-in} + n_{f-out}}, \tag{5.1}$$

where w are network weights. Note that the fan-out measure is used in the variance above to balance the back-propagated signal as well. Xavier initialization works quite well in practice and leads to better convergence rates. But a number of simplistic assumptions are involved in the above initialization, among which the most prominent is that a linear relationship between the input and output of a neuron is assumed. In practice all the neurons contain a nonlinearity term which makes Xavier initialization statistically less accurate.

5.1.6 RELU AWARE SCALED INITIALIZATION

He et al. [2015a] suggested an improved version of the scaled (or Xavier) initialization noting that the neurons with a ReLU nonlinearity do not follow the assumptions made for the Xavier initialization. Precisely, since the ReLU activation reduces nearly half of the inputs to zero, therefore the variance of the distribution from which the initial weights are randomly sampled should be

$$Var(w) = \frac{2}{n_{f-in}}. \tag{5.2}$$

The ReLU aware scaled initialization works better compared to Xavier initialization for recent architectures which are based on the ReLU nonlinearity.

5.1.7 LAYER-SEQUENTIAL UNIT VARIANCE

The layer-sequential unit variance (LSUV) initialization is a simple extension of the orthonormal weight initialization in deep network layers [Mishkin and Matas, 2015]. It combines the benefits of batch-normalization and the orthonormal weight initialization to achieve an efficient training for very deep networks. It proceeds in two steps, described below.

- **Orthogonal initialization**—In the first step, all the weight layers (convolutional and fully connected) are initialized with orthogonal matrices.

- **Variance normalization**—In the second step, the method starts from the initial toward the final layers in a sequential manner and the variance of each layer output is normalized to one (unit variance). This is similar to the batch normalization layer, which normalizes the output activations for each batch to be zero centered with a unit variance. However, different from batch normalization which is applied during the training of the network, LSUV is applied while initializing the network and therefore saves the overhead of normalization for each batch during the training iterations.

5.1.8 SUPERVISED PRE-TRAINING

In practical scenarios, it is desirable to train very deep networks, but we do not have a large amount of annotated data available for many problem settings. A very successful practice in such cases is to first train the neural network on a related but different problem, where a large amount of training data is already available. Afterward, the learned model can be "adapted" to the new task by initializing with weights pre-trained on the larger dataset. This process is called *"fine-tuning"* and is a simple, yet effective, way to transfer learning from one task to another (sometimes interchangeably referred to as domain transfer or domain adaptation). As an example, in order to perform scene classification on a relatively small dataset, MIT-67, the network can be initialized with the weights learned for object classification on a much larger dataset such as ImageNet [Khan et al., 2016b].

> **Transfer Learning** is an approach to adapt and apply the knowledge acquired on another related task to the task at hand. Depending on our CNN architecture, this approach can take two forms.
>
> • *Using a Pre-trained Model:* If one wants to use an off-the-shelf CNN architecture (e.g., AlexNet, GoogleNet, ResNet, DenseNet) for a given task, an ideal choice is to adopt the available pre-trained models that are learned on huge datasets such as ImageNet (with 1.2 million images)[a] and Places205 (with 2.5 million images).[b]
>
> The pre-trained model can be tailored for a given task, e.g., by changing the dimensions of output neurons (to cater for a different number of classes), modifying the loss function and learning the final few layers from scratch (normally learning the final 2-3 layers suffices for most cases). If the dataset available for the end-task is sufficiently large, the complete model can also be fine-tuned on the new dataset. For this purpose, small learning rates are used for the initial pre-trained CNN layers, so that the learning previously acquired on the large-scale dataset (e.g., ImageNet) is not completely lost. This is essential, since it has been shown that the features learned over large-scale datasets are generic in nature and can be used for new tasks in computer vision [Azizpour et al., 2016, Sharif Razavian et al., 2014].
>
> • *Using a Custom Architecture:* If one opts for a customized CNN architecture, transfer learning can still be helpful if the target dataset is constrained in terms of size and diversity. To this end, one can first train the custom architecture on a large scale annotated dataset and then use the resulting model in the same manner as described in the bullet point above.
>
> Alongside the simple fine-tuning approach, more involved transfer learning approaches have also been proposed in the recent literature, e.g., Anderson et al. [2016] learns the way pre-trained model parameters are shifted on new datasets. The learned transformation is then applied to the network parameters and the resulting activations beside the pre-trained (non-tunable) network activations are used in the final model.

[a]Popular deep learning libraries host a wide variety of pre-trained CNN models, e.g.,
Tensorflow (https://github.com/tensorflow/models),
Torch (https://github.com/torch/torch7/wiki/ModelZoo),
Keras (https://github.com/albertomontesg/keras-model-zoo,
Caffe (https://github.com/BVLC/caffe/wiki/Model-Zoo),
MatConvNet (http://www.vlfeat.org/matconvnet/pretrained/).
[b]http://places.csail.mit.edu/downloadCNN.html

5.2   REGULARIZATION OF CNN

Since deep neural networks have a large number of parameters, they tend to over-fit on the training data during the learning process. By over-fitting, we mean that the model performs really well on the training data but it fails to generalize well to unseen data. It, therefore, results in an inferior performance on new data (usually the test set). Regularization approaches aim to avoid this problem using several intuitive ideas which we discuss below. We can categorize common regularization approaches into the following classes, based on their central idea:

- approaches which regularize the network using data level techniques
  (e.g., data augmentation);

- approaches which introduce stochastic behavior in the neural activations
  (e.g., dropout and drop connect);

- approaches which normalize batch statistics in the feature activations
  (e.g., batch normalization);

- approaches which use decision level fusion to avoid over-fitting
  (e.g., ensemble model averaging);

- approaches which introduce constraints on the network weights
  (e.g., ℓ^1 norm, ℓ^2 norm, max-norm, and elastic net constraints); and

- approaches which use guidance from a validation set to halt the learning process
  (e.g., early stopping).

Next, we discuss the above-mentioned approaches in detail.

5.2.1   DATA AUGMENTATION

Data augmentation is the easiest, and often a very effective way of enhancing the generalization power of CNN models. Especially for cases where the number of training examples is relatively low, data augmentation can enlarge the dataset (by factors of 16x, 32x, 64x, or even more) to allow a more robust training of large-scale models.

Data augmentation is performed by making several copies from a single image using straightforward operations such as rotations, cropping, flipping, scaling, translations, and shearing (see Fig. 5.1). These operations can be performed separately or combined together to form copies, which are both flipped and cropped.

Color jittering is another common way of performing data augmentation. A simple form of this operation is to perform random contrast jittering in an image. One could also find the principal color directions in the R, G, and B channels (using PCA) and then apply a random offset along these directions to change the color values of the whole image. This effectively introduces color and illumination invariance in the learned model [Krizhevsky et al., 2012].

Another approach for data augmentation is to utilize synthetic data, alongside the real data, to improve the generalization ability of the network [Rahmani and Mian, 2016, Rahmani et al., 2017, Shrivastava et al., 2016]. Since synthetic data is usually available in large quantities from rendering engines, it effectively extends the training data, which helps avoid over-fitting.

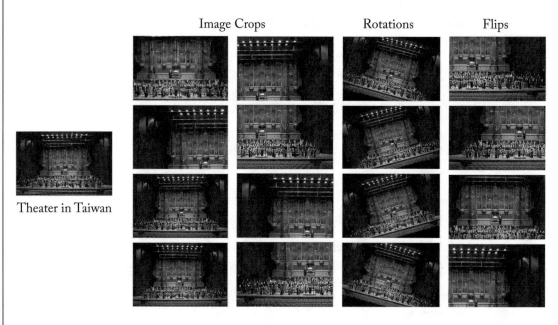

Figure 5.1: The figure shows an example of data augmentation using crops (column 1 and 2), rotations (column 3) and flips (column 4). Since the input image is quite complex (has several objects), data augmentation allows the network to figure out some possible variations of the same image, which still denote the same scene category, i.e., a theater.

5.2.2 DROPOUT

One of the most popular approaches for neural network regularization is the dropout technique [Srivastava et al., 2014]. During network training, each neuron is activated with a fixed probability (usually 0.5 or set using a validation set). This random sampling of a sub-network within the full-scale network introduces an ensemble effect during the testing phase, where the full network is used to perform prediction. Activation dropout works really well for regularization purposes and gives a significant boost in performance on unseen data in the test phase.

Let us consider a CNN that is composed of L weight layers, indexed by $l \in \{1 \ldots L\}$. Since dropout has predominantly been applied to Fully Connected (FC) layers in the literature, we consider the simpler case of FC layers here. Given output activations $\mathbf{a}_{l-1}$ from the previous layer, a FC layer performs an affine transformation followed by a element-wise nonlinearity, as follows:

$$\mathbf{a}_l = f(\mathbf{W} * \mathbf{a}_{l-1} + \mathbf{b}_l). \tag{5.3}$$

Here, $\mathbf{a}_{l-1} \in \mathbb{R}^n$ and $\mathbf{b} \in \mathbb{R}^m$ denote the activations and biases respectively. The input and output dimensions of the FC layer are denoted by n and m respectively. $\mathbf{W} \in \mathbb{R}^{m \times n}$ is the weight matrix and $f(\cdot)$ is the ReLU activation function.

The random dropout layer generates a mask $\mathbf{m} \in \mathbb{B}^m$, where each element m_i is independently sampled from a Bernoulli distribution with a probability "p" of being "on," i.e., a neuron fires:

$$m_i \sim Bernoulli(p), \qquad m_i \in \mathbf{m}. \tag{5.4}$$

This mask is used to modify the output activations $\mathbf{a}_l$:

$$\mathbf{a}_l = \mathbf{m} \circ f(\mathbf{W} * \mathbf{a}_{l-1} + \mathbf{b}_l), \tag{5.5}$$

where, "$\circ$" denotes the Hadamard product. The Hadamard product denotes a simple element wise matrix multiplication between the mask and the CNN activations.

5.2.3 DROP-CONNECT

Another similar approach to dropout is the drop-connect [Wan et al., 2013], which randomly deactivates the network weights (or connections between neurons) instead of randomly reducing the neuron activations to zero.

Similar to dropout, drop-connect performs a masking out operation on the weight matrix instead of the output activations, therefore:

$$\mathbf{a}_l = f((\mathbf{M} \circ \mathbf{W}) * \mathbf{a}_{l-1} + \mathbf{b}_l), \tag{5.6}$$
$$M_{i,j} \sim Bernoulli(p), \qquad M_{i,j} \in \mathbf{M}, \tag{5.7}$$

where "$\circ$" denotes the Hadamard product as in the case of dropout.

5.2.4   BATCH NORMALIZATION

Batch normalization [Ioffe and Szegedy, 2015] normalizes the mean and variance of the output activations from a CNN layer to follow a unit Gaussian distribution. It proves to be very useful for the efficient training of a deep network because it reduces the "internal covariance shift" of the layer activations. Internal covariance shift refers to the change in the distribution of activations of each layer as the parameters are updated during training. If the distribution, which a hidden layer of a CNN is trying to model, keeps on changing (i.e., the internal covariance shift is high), the training process will slow down and the network will take a long time to converge (simply because it is hard to reach a static target than to reach a continuously shifting target). The normalization of this distribution leads us to a consistent activation distribution during the training process, which enhances the convergence and avoids network instability issues such as the vanishing/exploding gradients and activation saturation.

Reflecting on what we have already studied in Chapter 4, this normalization step is similar to the whitening transform (applied as an input pre-processing step) which enforces the inputs to follow a unit Gaussian distribution with zero mean and unit variance. However, different to the whitening transform, batch normalization is applied to the intermediate CNN activations and can be integrated in an end-to-end network because of its differentiable computations.

The batch normalization operation can be implemented as a layer in a CNN. Given a set of activations $\{\mathbf{x}^i : i \in [1, m]\}$ (where $\mathbf{x}^i = \{x_j^i : j \in [1, n]\}$ has n dimensions) from a CNN layer corresponding to a specific input batch with m images, we can compute the first and second order statistics (mean and variance respectively) of the batch for each dimension of activations as follows:

$$\mu_{x_j} = \frac{1}{m} \sum_{i=1}^{m} x_j^i \tag{5.8}$$

$$\sigma_{x_j}^2 = \frac{1}{m} \sum_{i=1}^{m} (x_j^i - \mu_{x_j})^2, \tag{5.9}$$

where μ_{x_j} and $\sigma_{x_j}^2$ represent the mean and variance for the jth activation dimension computed over a batch, respectively. The normalized activation operation is represented as:

$$\hat{x}_j^i = \frac{x_j^i - \mu_{x_j}}{\sqrt{\sigma_{x_j}^2 + \epsilon}}. \tag{5.10}$$

Just the normalization of the activations is not sufficient, because it can alter the activations and disrupt the useful patterns that are learned by the network. Therefore, the normalized activations are rescaled and shifted to allow them to learn useful discriminative representations:

$$y_j^i = \gamma_j \hat{x}_j^i + \beta_j, \tag{5.11}$$

where γ_j and β_j are the learnable parameters which are tuned during error back-propagation.

Note that batch normalization is usually applied after the CNN weight layers, before applying the nonlinear activation function. Batch normalization is an important tool that is used in state of the art CNN architectures (examples in Chapter 6). We briefly summarize the benefits of using batch normalization below.

- In practice, the network training becomes less sensitive to hyper-parameter choices (e.g., learning rate) when batch normalization is used [Ioffe and Szegedy, 2015].

- It stabilizes the training of very deep networks and provides robustness against bad weight initializations. It also avoids the vanishing gradient problem and the saturation of activation functions (e.g., tanh and sigmoid).

- Batch normalization greatly improves the network convergence rate. This is very important because very deep network architectures can take several days (even with reasonable hardware resources) to train on large-scale datasets.

- It integrates the normalization in the network by allowing back-propagation of errors through the normalization layer, and therefore allows end-to-end training of deep networks.

- It makes the model less dependent on regularization techniques such as dropout. Therefore, recent architectures do not use dropout when batch normalization is extensively used as a regularization mechanism [He et al., 2016a].

5.2.5   ENSEMBLE MODEL AVERAGING

The ensemble averaging approach is another simple, but effective, technique where a number of models are learned instead of just a single model. Each model has different parameters due to different random initializations, different hyper-parameter choices (e.g., architecture, learning rate) and/or different sets of training inputs. The output from these multiple models is then combined to generate a final prediction score. The prediction combination approach can be a simple output averaging, a majority voting scheme or a weighted combination of all predictions. The final prediction is more accurate and less prone to over-fitting compared to each individual model in the ensemble. The committee of experts (ensemble) acts as an effective regularization mechanism which enhances the generalization power of the overall system.

5.2.6   THE ℓ^2 REGULARIZATION

The ℓ^2 regularization penalizes large values of the parameters $\mathbf{w}$ during the network training. This is achieved by adding a term with ℓ^2 norm of the parameter values weighted by a hyper-parameter λ, which decides on the strength of penalization (in practice half of the squared magnitude times λ is added to the error function to ensure a simpler derivative term). Effectively, this regularization encourages small and spread-out weight distributions over large values concentrated over only few neurons. Consider a simple network with only a single hidden layer with parameters $\mathbf{w}$ and output p_n, $n \in [1, N]$ when the output layer has N neurons. If the desired output is denoted by y_n, we can use an euclidean objective function with ℓ^2 regularization to update the parameters as follows:

$$\mathbf{w}^* = \underset{\mathbf{w}}{\mathrm{argmin}} \sum_{m=1}^{M} \sum_{n=1}^{N} (p_n - y_n)^2 + \lambda \parallel \mathbf{w} \parallel_2, \tag{5.12}$$

where M denote the number of training examples. Note that, as we will discuss later, ℓ^2 regularization performs the same operation as the weight decay technique. This approach is called "*weight decay*" because applying ℓ^2 regularization means that the weights are updated linearly (since the derivative of the regularizer term is λw for each neuron).

5.2.7 THE ℓ^1 REGULARIZATION

The ℓ^1 regularization technique is very similar to the ℓ^2 regularization, with the only difference being that the regularizer term uses the ℓ^1 norm of weights instead of an ℓ^2 norm. A hyperparameter λ is used to define the strength of regularization. For a single layered network with parameters $\mathbf{w}$, we can denote the parameter optimization process using ℓ_1 norm as follows:

$$\mathbf{w}^* = \underset{\mathbf{w}}{\mathrm{argmin}} \sum_{m=1}^{M} \sum_{n=1}^{N} (p_n - y_n)^2 + \lambda \parallel \mathbf{w} \parallel_1, \tag{5.13}$$

where N and M denote the number of output neurons and the number of training examples respectively. This effectively leads to sparse weight vectors for each neuron with most of the incoming connections having very small weights.

5.2.8 ELASTIC NET REGULARIZATION

Elastic net regularization linearly combines both ℓ^1 and ℓ^2 regularization techniques by adding a term $\lambda_1 |w| + \lambda_2 w^2$ for each weight value. This results in sparse weights and often performs better than the individual ℓ_1 and ℓ_2 regularizations, each of which is a special case of elastic net regularization. For a single-layered network with parameters $\mathbf{w}$, we can denote the parameter optimization process as follows:

$$\mathbf{w}^* = \underset{\mathbf{w}}{\mathrm{argmin}} \sum_{m=1}^{M} \sum_{n=1}^{N} (p_n - y_n)^2 + \lambda_1 \parallel \mathbf{w} \parallel_1 + \lambda_2 \parallel \mathbf{w} \parallel_2, \tag{5.14}$$

where N and M denote the number of output neurons and the number of training examples, respectively.

5.2.9 MAX-NORM CONSTRAINTS

The max-norm constraint is a form of regularization which puts an upper bound on the norm of the incoming weights of each neuron in a neural network layer. As a result, the weight vector $\mathbf{w}$ must follow the constraint $\| \mathbf{w} \|_2 < h$, where h is a hyper-parameter, whose value is usually set based on the performance of the network on a validation set. The benefit of using such a regularization is that the network parameters are guaranteed to remain in a reasonable numerical range even when high values of learning rates are used during network training. In practice, this leads to a better stability and performance [Srivastava et al., 2014].

5.2.10 EARLY STOPPING

The over-fitting problem occurs when a model performs very well on the training set but behaves poorly on unseen data. Early stopping is applied to avoid overfitting in the iterative gradient-based algorithms. This is achieved by evaluating the performance on a held-out validation set at different iterations during the training process. The training algorithm can continue to improve on the training set until the performance on the validation set also improves. Once there is a drop in the generalization ability of the learned model, the learning process can be stopped or slowed down (Fig. 5.2).

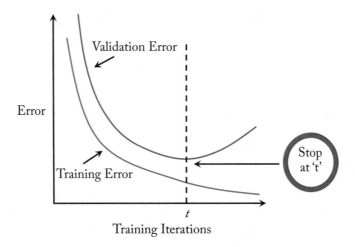

Figure 5.2: An illustration of the early stopping approach during network training.

Having discussed the concepts which enable successful training of deep neural networks (e.g., correct weight initialization and regularization techniques), we dive into the details of the network learning process. Gradient-based algorithms are the most important tool to optimally train such networks on large-scale datasets. In the following, we discuss different variants of optimizers for CNNs.

5.3   GRADIENT-BASED CNN LEARNING

The CNN learning process tunes the parameters of the network such that the input space is correctly mapped to the output space. As discussed before, at each training step, the current estimate of the output variables is matched with the desired output (often termed the "*ground-truth*" or the "*label space*"). This matching function serves as an objective function during the CNN training and it is usually called the loss function or the error function. In other words, we can say that the CNN training process involves the optimization of its parameters such that the **loss function** is minimized. The CNN parameters are the free/tunable weights in each of its layers (e.g., filter weights and biases of the convolution layers) (Chapter 4).

An intuitive, but simple, way to approach this optimization problem is by repeatedly up-dating the parameters such that the loss function **progressively** reduces to a minimum value. It is important to note here that the optimization of nonlinear models (such as CNNs) is a hard task, exacerbated by the fact that these models are mostly composed of a large number of tunable parameters. Therefore, instead of solving for a globally optimal solution, we iteratively search for the locally optimal solution at each step. Here, the gradient-based methods come as a natural choice, since we need to update the parameters in the **direction** of the steepest de-scent. The amount of parameter update, or the size of the update step is called the "**learning rate**." Each iteration which updates the parameters using the complete training set is called a "**training epoch**." We can write each training iteration at time t using the following parameter update equation:

$$\theta_t = \theta_{t-1} - \eta\,\delta_t \qquad (5.15)$$
$$s.t., \quad \delta_t = \nabla_\theta \mathcal{F}(\theta_t), \qquad (5.16)$$

where $\mathcal{F}(\cdot)$ denotes the function represented by the neural network with parameters θ, ∇ rep-resents the gradient, and η denotes the learning rate.

5.3.1   BATCH GRADIENT DESCENT

As we discussed in the previous section, gradient descent algorithms work by computing the gradient of the objective function with respect to the neural network parameters, followed by a parameter update in the direction of the steepest descent. The basic version of the gradient descent, termed "*batch gradient descent*," computes this gradient on the entire training set. It is guaranteed to converge to the global minimum for the case of convex problems. For non-convex problems, it can still attain a local minimum. However, the training sets can be very large in computer vision problems, and therefore learning via the batch gradient descent can be prohibitively slow because for each parameter update, it needs to compute the gradient on the complete training set. This leads us to the stochastic gradient descent, which effectively circumvents this problem.

5.3.2   STOCHASTIC GRADIENT DESCENT

Stochastic Gradient Descent (SGD) performs a parameter update for each set of input and output that are present in the training set. As a result, it converges much faster compared to the batch gradient descent. Furthermore, it is able to learn in an *"online manner,"* where the parameters can be tuned in the presence of new training examples. The only problem is that its convergence behavior is usually unstable, especially for relatively larger learning rates and when the training datasets contain diverse examples. When the learning rate is appropriately set, the SGD generally achieves a similar convergence behavior, compared to the batch gradient descent, for both the convex and non-convex problems.

5.3.3   MINI-BATCH GRADIENT DESCENT

Finally, the mini-batch gradient descent method is an improved form of the stochastic gradient descent approach, which provides a decent trade-off between convergence efficiency and convergence stability by dividing the training set into a number of mini-batches, each consisting of a relatively small number of training examples. The parameter update is then performed after computing the gradients on each mini-batch. Note that the training examples are usually randomly shuffled to improve homogeneity of the training set. This ensures a better convergence rate compared to the Batch Gradient Descent and a better stability compared to the Stochastic Gradient Descent [Ruder, 2016].

5.4   NEURAL NETWORK OPTIMIZERS

After a general overview of the gradient descent algorithms in Section 5.3, we can note that there are certain caveats which must be avoided during the network learning process. As an example, setting the learning rate can be a tricky endeavor in many practical problems. The training process is often highly affected by the parameter initialization. Furthermore, the vanishing and exploding gradients problems can occur especially for the case of deep networks. The training process is also susceptible to get trapped into a local minima, saddle points or a high error plateau where the gradient is approximately zero in every direction [Pascanu et al., 2014]. Note that the saddle points (also called the *"minmax points"*) are those stationary points on the surface of the function, where the partial derivative with respect to its dimensions becomes zero (Fig. 5.3). In the following discussion we outline different methods to address these limitations of the gradient descent algorithms. Since our goal is to optimize over high-dimensional parameter spaces, we will restrict our discussion to the more feasible first-order methods and will not deal with the high-order methods (Newton's method) which are ill-suited for large datasets.

5.4.1   MOMENTUM

Momentum-based optimization provides an improved version of SGD with better convergence properties. For example, the SGD can oscillate close to a local minima, resulting in an un-

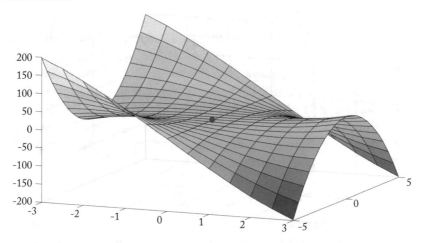

Figure 5.3: A saddle point shown as a red dot on a 3D surface. Note that the gradient is effectively zero, but it corresponds to neither a "minima" nor a "maxima" of the function.

necessarily delayed convergence. The momentum adds the gradient calculated at the previous time-step (a_{t-1}) weighted by a parameter γ to the weight update equation as follows:

$$\theta_t = \theta_{t-1} - a_t \tag{5.17}$$
$$a_t = \eta \nabla_\theta \mathcal{F}(\theta_t) + \gamma a_{t-1}, \tag{5.18}$$

where $\mathcal{F}(\cdot)$ denotes the function represented by the neural network with parameters θ, ∇ represents the gradient and η denotes the learning rate.

The momentum term has physical meanings. The dimensions whose gradients point in the same direction are magnified quickly, while those dimensions whose gradients keep on changing directions are suppressed. Essentially, the convergence speed is increased because unnecessary oscillations are avoided. This can be understood as adding more momentum to the ball so that it moves along the direction of the maximum slope. Typically, the momentum is set to 0.9 during the SGD-based learning.

5.4.2 NESTEROV MOMENTUM

The momentum term introduced in the previous section would carry the ball beyond the minimum point. Ideally, we would like the ball to slow down when the ball reaches the minimum point and the slope starts ascending. This is achieved by the Nesterov momentum [Nesterov, 1983] which computes the gradient at the next approximate point during the parameter update process, instead of the current point. This gives the algorithm the ability to "look ahead" at each iteration and plan a jump such that the learning process avoids uphill steps. The update process

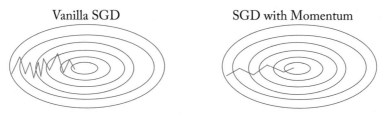

Figure 5.4: Comparison of the convergence behavior of the SGD with (*right*) and without (*left*) momentum.

can be represented as:

$$\theta_t = \theta_{t-1} - a_t \tag{5.19}$$
$$a_t = \eta \nabla_\theta \mathcal{F}(\theta_t - \gamma a_{t-1}) + \gamma a_{t-1}, \tag{5.20}$$

where $\mathcal{F}(\cdot)$ denotes the function represented by the neural network with parameters θ, ∇ represents the gradient operation, η denotes the learning rate and γ is the momentum.

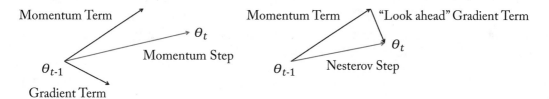

Figure 5.5: Comparison of the convergence behavior of the SGD with momentum (*left*) and the Nesterov update (*right*). While momentum update can carry the solver quickly toward a local optima, it can overshoot and miss the optimum point. A solver with Nesterov update corrects its update by looking ahead and correcting for the next gradient value.

5.4.3   ADAPTIVE GRADIENT

The momentum in the SGD refines the update direction along the slope of the error function. However, all parameters are updated at the same rate. In several cases, it is more useful to update each parameter differently, depending on its frequency in the training set or its significance for our end problem.

Adaptive Gradient (AdaGrad) algorithm [Duchi et al., 2011] provides a solution to this problem by using an adaptive learning rate for each individual parameter i. This is done at each time step t by dividing the learning rate of each parameter with the accumulation of the square of all the historical gradients for each parameter θ_i. This can be shown as follows:

$$\theta_t^i = \theta_{t-1}^i - \frac{\eta}{\sqrt{\sum_{\tau=1}^{t} {\delta_\tau^i}^2 + \epsilon}} \delta_t^i,$$ (5.21)

where δ_t^i is the gradient at time-step t with respect to the parameter θ_i and ϵ is a very small term in the denominator to avoid division by zero. The adaptation of the learning rate for each parameter removes the need to manually set the value of the learning rate. Typically, η is kept fixed to a single value (e.g., 10^{-2} or 10^{-3}) during the training phase. Note that AdaGrad works very well for sparse gradients, for which a reliable estimate of the past gradients is obtained by accumulating all of the previous time steps.

5.4.4   ADAPTIVE DELTA

Although AdaGrad eliminates the need to manually set the value of the learning rate at different epochs, it suffers from the vanishing learning rate problem. Specifically, as the number of iterations grows (t is large), the sum of the squared gradients becomes large, making the effective learning rate very small. As a result, the parameters do not change in the subsequent training iterations. Lastly, it also needs an initial learning rate to be set during the training phase.

The Adaptive Delta (AdaDelta) algorithm [Zeiler, 2012] solves both these problems by accumulating only the last k gradients in the denominator term of Eq. (5.21). Therefore, the new update step can be represented as follows:

$$\theta_t^i = \theta_{t-1}^i - \frac{\eta}{\sqrt{\sum_{\tau=t-k+1}^{t} {\delta_\tau^i}^2 + \epsilon}} \delta_t^i.$$ (5.22)

This requires the storage of the last k gradients at each iteration. In practice, it is much easier to work with a running average $E[\delta^2]_t$, which can be defined as:

$$E[\delta^2]_t = \gamma E[\delta^2]_{t-1} + (1-\gamma){\delta_t}^2.$$ (5.23)

Here, γ has a similar function to the momentum parameter. Note that the above function implements an exponentially decaying average of the squared gradients for each parameter. The new update step is:

$$\theta_t^i = \theta_{t-1}^i - \frac{\eta}{\sqrt{E[\delta^2]_t + \epsilon}} \delta_t^i,$$ (5.24)

$$\Delta\theta = -\frac{\eta}{\sqrt{E[\delta^2]_t + \epsilon}} \delta_t^i.$$ (5.25)

Note that we still did not get rid of the initial learning rate η. Zeiler [2012] noted that this can be avoided by making the units of the update step consistent by introducing a Hessian approximation in the update rule. This boils down to the following:

$$\theta_t^i = \theta_{t-1}^i - \frac{\sqrt{E[(\Delta\theta)^2]_{t-1} + \epsilon}}{\sqrt{E[\delta^2]_t + \epsilon}} \delta_t^i. \tag{5.26}$$

Note that we have considered here the local curvature of the function $\mathcal{F}$ to be approximately flat and replaced $E[(\Delta\theta)^2]_t$ (not known) with $E[(\Delta\theta)^2]_{t-1}$ (known).

5.4.5 RMSPROP

RMSprop [Tieleman and Hinton, 2012] is closely related to the AdaDelta approach, aiming to resolve the vanishing learning rate problem of AdaGrad. Similar to AdaDelta, it also calculates the running average as follows:

$$E[\delta^2]_t = \gamma E[\delta^2]_{t-1} + (1 - \gamma)\delta_t{}^2. \tag{5.27}$$

Here, a typical value of γ is 0.9. The update rule of the tunable parameters takes the following form:

$$\theta_t^i = \theta_{t-1}^i - \frac{\eta}{\sqrt{E[\delta^2]_t + \epsilon}} \delta_t^i. \tag{5.28}$$

5.4.6 ADAPTIVE MOMENT ESTIMATION

We stated that the AdaGrad solver suffers from the vanishing learning rate problem, but Ada-Grad is very useful for cases where gradients are sparse. On the other hand, RMSprop does not reduce the learning rate to a very small value at higher time steps. However on the negative side, it does not provide an optimal solution for the case of sparse gradients. The ADAptive Moment Estimation (ADAM) [Kingma and Ba, 2014] approach estimates a separate learning rate for each parameter and combines the positives of both AdaGrad and RMSprop. The main difference between Adam and its two predecessors (RMSprop and AdaDelta) is that the updates are estimated by using both the first moment and the second moment of the gradient (as in Eqs. (5.26) and (5.28)). Therefore, a running average of gradients (mean) is maintained along with a running average of the squared gradients (variance) as follows:

$$E[\delta]_t = \gamma_1 E[\delta]_{t-1} + (1 - \gamma_1)\delta_t, \tag{5.29}$$
$$E[\delta^2]_t = \gamma_2 E[\delta^2]_{t-1} + (1 - \gamma_2)\delta_t{}^2, \tag{5.30}$$

where γ_1 and γ_2 are the parameters for running averages of the mean and the variance respectively. Since the initial moment estimates are set to zero, they can remain very small even after many iterations, especially when $\gamma_{1,2} \neq 1$. To overcome this issue, the initialization bias-

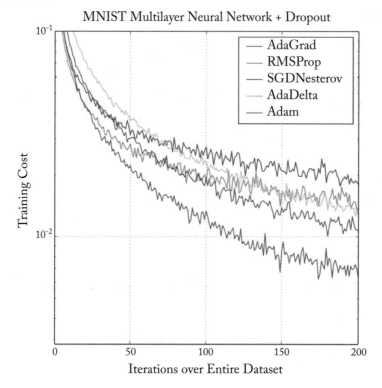

Figure 5.6: Convergence performance on the MNIST dataset using different neural network optimizers [Kingma and Ba, 2014]. (Figure used with permission.)

corrected estimates of $E[\delta]_t$ and $E[\delta^2]_t$ are obtained as follows:

$$\hat{E}[\delta]_t = \frac{E[\delta]_t}{1 - (\gamma_1)^t} \tag{5.31}$$

$$\hat{E}[\delta^2]_t = \frac{E[\delta^2]_t}{1 - (\gamma_2)^t}. \tag{5.32}$$

Very similar to what we studied in the case of AdaGrad, AdaDelta and RMSprop, the update rule for Adam is given by:

$$\theta_t^i = \theta_{t-1}^i - \frac{\eta}{\sqrt{\hat{E}[\delta^2]_t} + \epsilon} \hat{E}[\delta]_t. \tag{5.33}$$

The authors found $\gamma_1 = 0.9$, $\gamma_2 = 0.999$, $\eta = 0.001$ to be good default values of the decay (γ) and learning (η) rates during the training process.

Figure 5.6 [Kingma and Ba, 2014] illustrates the convergence performance of the discussed solvers on the MNIST dataset for handwritten digit classification. Note that the SGD with Nesterov shows a good convergence behavior, however it requires a manual tuning of the learning rate hyper-parameter. Among the solvers with an adaptive learning rate, Adam performs the best in this example (also beating the manually tuned SGD-Nesterov solver). In practice, Adam usually scales very well to large-scale problems and exhibits nice convergence properties. That is why Adam is often a default choice for many computer vision applications based on deep learning.

5.5   GRADIENT COMPUTATION IN CNNS

We have discussed a number of layers and architectures for CNNs. In Section 3.2.2, we also described the back-propagation algorithm used to train CNNs. In essence, back-propagation lies at the heart of CNN training. Error back-propagation can only happen if the CNN layers implement a differentiable operation. Therefore, it is interesting to study how the gradient can be computed for the different CNN layers. In this section, we will discuss in detail the different approaches which are used to compute the differentials of popular CNN layers.

We describe in the following the four different approaches which can be used to compute gradients.

5.5.1   ANALYTICAL DIFFERENTIATION

It involves the manual derivation of the derivatives of a function performed by a CNN layer. These derivatives are then implemented in a computer program to calculate the gradients. The gradient formulas are then used by an optimization algorithm (e.g., Stochastic Gradient Descent) to learn the optimal CNN weights.

> **Example:** Assume for a simple function, $y = f(x) = x^2$, we want to calculate the derivative analytically. By applying the differentiation formula for polynomial functions, we can find the derivative as follows:
>
> $$\frac{dy}{dx} = 2x, \tag{5.34}$$
>
> which can give us the slope at any point x.

Analytically deriving the derivatives of complex expressions is time-consuming and laborious. Furthermore, it is necessary to model the layer operation as a closed-form mathematical expression. However, it provides an accurate value for the derivative at each point.

5.5.2   NUMERICAL DIFFERENTIATION

Numerical differentiation techniques use the values of a function to estimate the numerical value of the derivative of the function at a specific point.

Example: For a given function $f(x)$, we can estimate the first-order numerical derivative at a point x by using the function values at two nearby points, i.e., $f(x)$ and $f(x + h)$, where h is a small change in x:

$$\frac{f(x + h) - f(x)}{h}. \tag{5.35}$$

The above equation estimates the first-order derivative as the slope of a line joining the two points $f(x)$ and $f(x + h)$. The above expression is called the "Newton's Difference Formula."

Numerical differentiation is useful in cases where we know little about the underline real function or when the actual function is too complex. Also, in several cases we only have access to discrete sampled data (e.g., at different time instances) and a natural choice is to estimate the derivatives without necessarily modeling the function and calculating the exact derivatives. Numerical differentiation is fairly easy to implement, compared to other approaches. However, numerical differentiation provides only an estimate of the derivative and works poorly, particularly for the calculation of higher-order derivatives.

5.5.3   SYMBOLIC DIFFERENTIATION

Symbolic differentiation uses standard differential calculus formulas to manipulate mathematical expressions using computer algorithms. Popular softwares which perform symbolic differentiation include Mathematica, Maple, and Matlab.

Example: Suppose we are given a function $f(x) = \exp(\sin(x))$, we need to calculate its 10th derivative with respect to x. An analytical solution would be cumbersome, while a numerical solution will be less accurate. In such cases, we can effectively use symbolic differentiation to get a reliable answer. The following code in Matlab (using the Symbolic Math Toolbox) gives the desired result.

```
>> syms x
>> f(x) = exp(sin(x))
>> diff(f,x,10)
256*exp(sin(x))*cos(x)² - exp(sin(x))*sin(x) -
5440*exp(sin(x))*cos(x)⁴ + 2352*exp(sin(x))*cos(x)⁶ - …
```

Symbolic differentiation, in a sense, is similar to analytical differentiation, but leveraging the power of computers to perform laborious derivations. This approach reduces the need to manually derive differentials and avoids the inaccuracies of numerical methods. However, symbolic differentiation often leads to complex and long expressions which results in slow software programs. Also, it does not scale well to higher-order derivatives (similar to numerical differentiation) due to the high complexity of the required computations. Furthermore, in neural network optimization, we need to calculate partial derivatives with respect to a large number of inputs to a layer. In such cases, symbolic differentiation is inefficient and does not scale well to large-scale networks.

5.5.4   AUTOMATIC DIFFERENTIATION

Automatic differentiation is a powerful technique which uses both numerical and symbolic techniques to estimate the differential calculation in the software domain, i.e., given a coded computer program which implements a function, automatic differentiation can be used to design another program which implements the derivative of that function. We illustrate the automatic differentiation and its relationship with the numerical and symbolic differentiation in Fig. 5.7.

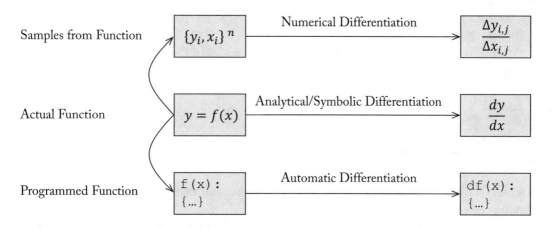

Figure 5.7: Relationships between different differentiation methods.

Every computer program is implemented using a programming language, which only supports a set of basic functions (e.g., addition, multiplication, exponentiation, logarithm and trigonometric functions). Automatic differentiation uses this modular nature of computer programs to break them into simpler elementary functions. The derivatives of these simple functions are computed symbolically and the chain rule is then applied repeatedly to compute any order of derivatives of complex programs.

Automatic differentiation provides an accurate and efficient solution to the differentiation of complex expressions. Precisely, automatic differentiation gives results which are accurate to the machine precision. The computational complexity of calculating derivatives of a function is almost the same as evaluating the original function itself. Unlike symbolic differentiation, it neither needs a closed form expression of the function nor does it suffer from expression swell which renders symbolic differentiation inefficient and difficult to code. Current state of

---
Algorithm 5.1 Forward mode of Automatic Differentiation

Input : $x, \mathcal{C}$

Output : y_n

1: $y_0 \leftarrow x$ % initialization
2: **for all** $i \in [1, n]$ **do**
3:    $y_i \leftarrow f_i^e(y_{\mathrm{Pa}(f_i^e)})$ % each function operates on its parents output in the graph
4: **end for**

Algorithm 5.2 Backward mode of Automatic Differentiation

Input : $x, \mathcal{C}$

Output : $\frac{dy_n}{dx}$

1: Perform forward mode propagation
2: **for all** $i \in [n-1, 0]$ **do**
3:    % chain rule to compute derivatives using child nodes in the graph
4:    $\dfrac{dy_n}{dy_i} \leftarrow \displaystyle\sum_{j \in \mathrm{Ch}(f_i^e)} \dfrac{dy_n}{dy_j} \dfrac{df_j^e}{dy_i}$
5: **end for**
6: $\dfrac{dy_n}{dx} \leftarrow \dfrac{dy_n}{dy_0}$

---

the art CNN libraries such as Theano and Tensorflow use automatic differentiation to compute derivatives (see Chapter 8).

Automatic differentiation is very closely related to the back-propagation algorithm we studied before in Section 3.2.2. It operates in two modes, the forward mode and the backward mode. Given a complex function, we first decompose it into a computational graph consisting of simple elementary functions which are joined with each other to compute the complex function. In the **forward** mode, given an input x, the computational graph $\mathcal{C}$ with n intermediate states (corresponding to $\{f^e\}^n$ elementary functions) can be evaluated sequentially as shown in Algorithm 5.1.

After the forward computations shown in Algorithm 5.1, the **backward** mode starts computing the derivatives toward the end and successively applies the chain rule to calculate the differential with respect to each intermediate output variable y_i, as shown in Algorithm 5.2.

A basic assumption in the automatic differentiation approach is that the expression is differentiable. If this is not the case, automatic differentiation will fail. We provide a simple example of forward and backward modes of automatic differentiation below and refer the reader to Baydin et al. [2015] for a detailed treatment of this subject in relation to machine/deep learning techniques.

Example: Consider a slightly more complex function than the previous example for symbolic differentiation,

$$y = f(x) = \exp(\sin(x) + \sin(x)^2) + \sin(\exp(x) + \exp(x)^2). \qquad (5.36)$$

We can represent its analytically or symbolically calculated differential as follows:

$$\frac{df}{dx} = \cos(\exp(2x) + \exp(x))(2\exp(2x) + \exp(x))$$
$$+ \exp(\sin(x)^2 + \sin(x))(\cos(x) + 2\cos(x)\sin(x)). \qquad (5.37)$$

But, if we are interested in calculating its derivative using automatic differentiation, the first step would be to represent the complete function in terms of basic operations (addition, exp and sin) defined as:

$$
\begin{array}{lll}
a = \sin(x) & b = a^2 & c = a + b \\
d = \exp(c) & e = \exp(x) & f = e^2 \\
g = e + f & h = \sin(g) & y = d + h.
\end{array} \qquad (5.38)
$$

The flow of computations in terms of these basic operations is illustrated in the computational graph in Fig. 5.8. Given this computational graph we can easily calculate the differential of the output with respect to each of the variables in the graph as follows:

$$
\begin{array}{lllll}
\dfrac{dy}{dd} = 1 & \dfrac{dy}{dh} = 1 & \dfrac{dy}{dc} = \dfrac{dy}{dd}\dfrac{dd}{dc} & \dfrac{dy}{dg} = \dfrac{dy}{dh}\dfrac{dh}{dg} \\[2mm]
\dfrac{dy}{db} = \dfrac{dy}{dc}\dfrac{dc}{db} & \dfrac{dy}{da} = \dfrac{dy}{dc}\dfrac{dc}{da} + \dfrac{dy}{db}\dfrac{db}{da} & \dfrac{dy}{df} = \dfrac{dy}{dg}\dfrac{dg}{df} \\[2mm]
& \dfrac{dy}{de} = \dfrac{dy}{dg}\dfrac{dg}{de} + \dfrac{dy}{df}\dfrac{df}{de} & \dfrac{dy}{dx} = \dfrac{dy}{da}\dfrac{da}{dx} + \dfrac{dy}{de}\dfrac{de}{dx}.
\end{array} \qquad (5.39)
$$

All of the above differentials can easily be computed because it is simple to compute the derivative of each basic function, e.g.,

$$\frac{dd}{dc} = \exp(c) \qquad \frac{dh}{dg} = \cos(g) \qquad \frac{dc}{db} = \frac{dc}{da} = 1 \qquad \frac{df}{de} = 2e. \quad (5.40)$$

Note that we started toward the end of the computational graph, and computed all of the intermediate differentials moving backward, until we got the differential with respect to input. The original differential expression we calculated in Eq. (5.37) was quite complex. However, once we decomposed the original expression in to simpler functions in Eq. (5.38), we note that

the complexity of the operations that are required to calculate the derivative (back-ward pass) is almost the same as the calculation of the original
expression (forward pass) according to the computational graph. Automatic
differentiation uses the forward and backward operation modes to efficiently
and precisely calculate the differentials of complex functions. As we discussed
above, the operations for the calculation of differentials in this manner have
a close resemblance to the back-propagation algorithm.

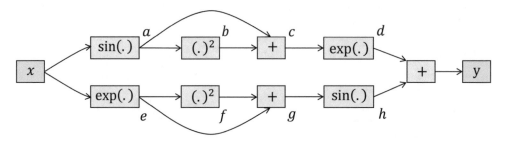

Figure 5.8: Computational graph showing the calculation of our desired function.

5.6 UNDERSTANDING CNN THROUGH VISUALIZATION

Convolutional networks are large-scale models with a huge number of parameters that are
learned in a data driven fashion. Plotting an error curve and objective function on the training and validation sets against the training iterations is one way to track the overall training
progress. However, this approach does not give an insight into the actual parameters and activations of the CNN layers. It is often useful to visualize what CNNs have learned during or after
the completion of the training process. We outline some basic approaches to visualize CNN
features and activations below. These approaches can be categorized into three types depending on the network signal that is used to obtain the visualization, i.e., weights, activations, and
gradients. We summarize some of these three types of visualization methods below.

5.6.1 VISUALIZING LEARNED WEIGHTS

One of the simplest approaches to visualize what a CNN has learned is to look at the convolution filters. For example, 9×9 and 5×5 sized convolution kernels that are learned on a
labeled shadow dataset are illustrated in Fig. 5.9. These filters correspond to the first and second
convolutional layers in a LeNet style CNN (see Chapter 6 for details on CNN architectures).

Figure 5.9: Examples of 9 × 9 (left) and 5 × 5 (right) sized convolution kernels learned for the shadow detection task. The filters illustrate the type of patterns that a particular CNN layer is looking for in the input data. (Figure adapted from Khan et al. [2014].)

5.6.2   VISUALIZING ACTIVATIONS

The feature activations from the intermediate CNN layers can also provide useful clues about the quality of learned representations.

A trivial way to visualize learned features is to plot the output feature activations corresponding to an input image. As an example, we show the output convolutional activations (or features) corresponding to sample digits 2, 5, and 0 belonging to the MNIST dataset in Fig. 5.10. Specifically, these features are the output of the first convolution layer in the LeNet architecture (see Chapter 6 for details on this architecture type).

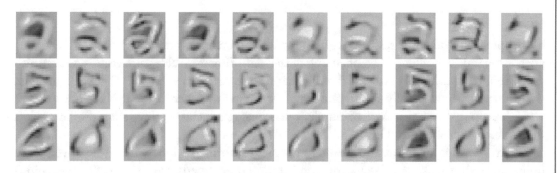

Figure 5.10: Intermediate feature representations from a CNN corresponding to example input images of handwritten digits from the MNIST dataset. Such a visualization of output activations can provide an insight about the patterns in input images that are extracted as useful features for classification.

Another approach is to obtain the feature representation from the penultimate layer of a trained CNN and visualize all the training images in a dataset as a 2D plot (e.g., using tSNE low dimensional embedding). The tSNE embedding approximately preserves the original distances in the high dimensional space between features. An example of such a visualization is shown in Fig. 5.11. This visualization can provide a holistic view and suggest the quality of learned feature representations for different classes. For instance, classes that are clustered tightly together in the feature space will be classified more accurately compared to the ones that have a widespread

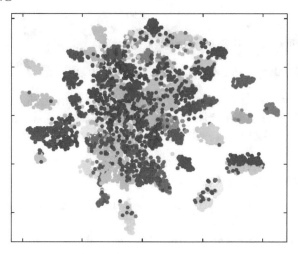

Figure 5.11: tSNE visualization of the final fully connected layer features corresponding to images from the MIT-67 indoor scene dataset. Each color represents a different class in the dataset. Note that the features belonging to the same class are clustered together. (Figure adapted from Khan et al. [2017b].)

overlapping with other classes, making it difficult to accurately model the classification boundaries. Alongside visualizing 2D embedding of the high-dimensional feature vectors, we can also visualize the input images associated with each feature vector (see Fig. 5.13). In this manner, we can observe how visually similar images are clustered together in the tSNE embedding of high-dimensional features. As an example, cellar images are clustered together on the top left in the illustration shown in Fig. 5.13.

An attention map can also provide an insight into the regions which were given more importance while making a classification decision. In other words, we can visualize the regions in an image which contributed most to the correct prediction of a category. One way to achieve this is to obtain prediction scores for individual overlapping patches with in an image and plot the final prediction score for the correct class. Examples of such a visualization is shown in Fig. 5.12. We can note that distinctive portions of the scenes played a crucial role in the correct prediction of the category for each image, e.g., a screen in an auditorium, train in a train station and bed in a bedroom.

Other interesting approaches have also been used in the literature to visualize the image parts which contribute most to the correct prediction. Zeiler and Fergus [2014] systematically occluded a square patch within an input image and plotted a heat map indicating the change in the prediction probability of the correct class. The resulting heat map indicates which regions in an input image are most important for a correct output response from the network (see Fig. 5.14a for examples). Bolei et al. [2015] first segments an input image into regions, these segments

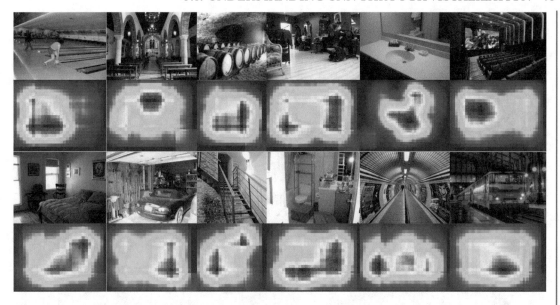

Figure 5.12: The contributions of distinctive patches with in an image toward the prediction of correct scene class are shown in the form of a heat map ("red" color denotes higher contribution). (Figure adapted from Khan et al. [2016b].)

are then iteratively dropped such that the correct class prediction is least affected. This process continues until an image with minimal scene details is left. These details are sufficient for the correct classification of the input image (see Fig. 5.14b for examples).

5.6.3   VISUALIZATIONS BASED ON GRADIENTS

Balduzzi et al. [2017] presented the idea that visualizing distributions of gradients can provide useful insight into the convergence behavior of deep neural networks. Their analysis showed that naively increasing the depth of a neural network results in the gradient shattering problem (i.e., the gradients show similar distribution as white noise). They demonstrated that the gradient distribution resembled brown noise when batch normalization and skip connections were used in a very deep network (see Fig. 5.15).

Back-propagated gradients within a CNN have been used to identify specific patterns in the input image that maximally activate a particular neuron in a CNN layer. In other words, gradients can be adjusted to generate visualizations that illustrate the patterns that a neuron has learned to look for in the input data. Zeiler and Fergus [2014] pioneered this idea and introduced a deconvolution-based approach to invert the feature representations to identify associated patterns in the input images. Yosinski et al. [2015] generated synthetic images by first selecting an ith neuron in a CNN layer. Afterward, an input image with random color values is passed

Figure 5.13: Visualization of images based on the tSNE embedding of the convolutional features from a deep network. The images belong to the MIT-67 dataset. Note that the images belonging to the same class are clustered together, e.g., all cellar images can be found in the top-left corner. (Figure adapted from Hayat et al. [2016].)

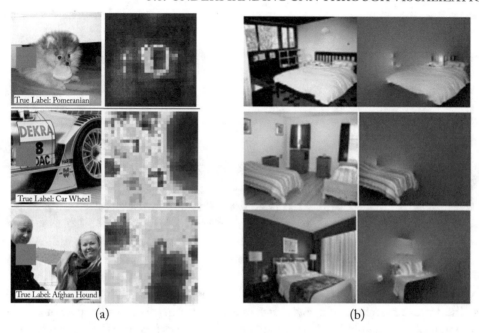

(a)   (b)

Figure 5.14: Visualization of regions which are important for the correct prediction from a deep network. (a) The grey regions in input images is sequentially occluded and the output probability of correct class is plotted as a heat map (blue regions indicate high importance for correct classification). (b) Segmented regions in an image are occluded until the minimal image details that are required for correct scene class prediction are left. As we expect, a bed is found to be the most important aspect of a bed-room scene. (Figures adapted from Bolei et al. [2015] and Zeiler and Fergus [2014], used with permission.)

through the network and the corresponding activation value for i^{th} neuron is calculated. The gradient of this activation with respect to the input image is calculated via error back propagation. This gradient basically denotes how the pixels can be changed such that the neuron gets maximally activated. The input gets iteratively modified using this information so that we obtain an image which results in a high activation for neuron i. Normally it is useful to impose a "style constraint" while modifying the input image which acts as a regularizer and enforces the input image to remain similar to the training data. Some example images thus obtained are shown in Fig. 5.16.

Mahendran and Vedaldi [2015] propose an approach to recover input images that correspond to identical high-dimensional feature representations in the second to last layer of CNN. Given an image $\mathbf{x}$, a learned CNN $\mathcal{F}$ and a high dimensional representation $\mathbf{f}$, the following loss is minimized through gradient descent optimization to find images in the input domain that

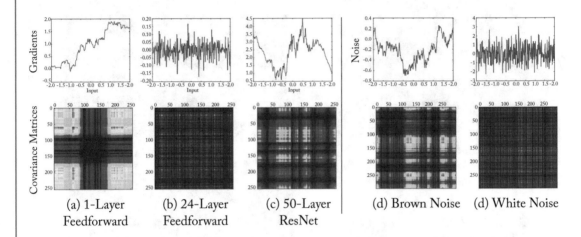

(a) 1-Layer
Feedforward

(b) 24-Layer
Feedforward

(c) 50-Layer
ResNet

(d) Brown Noise

(d) White Noise

Figure 5.15: The top row shows the gradient distributions for a range of uniformly sampled inputs. The bottom row shows the covariance matrices. The gradient for the case of a 24 layered network resemble white noise, while the gradients of high-performing ResNet resemble brown noise. Note that the ResNet used skip connections and batch normalization which results in better converegence even with much deeper network architectures. The ResNet architecture will be discussed in detail in Chapter 6. (Figure from Balduzzi et al. [2017], used with permission.)

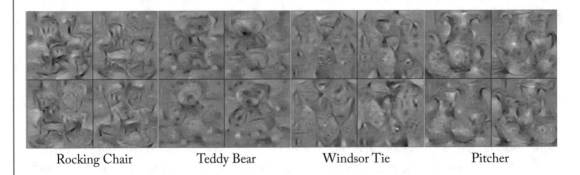

Rocking Chair   Teddy Bear   Windsor Tie   Pitcher

Figure 5.16: The figure illustrates synthetic input images that maximally activate the output neurons corresponding to different classes. As evident, the network looks for objects with similar low-level and high-level cues, e.g., edge information and holistic shape information, respectively, in order to maximally activate the relevant neuron. (Figure from Yosinski et al. [2015], used with permission.)

correspond to the same feature representation **f**:

$$\mathbf{x}^* \leftarrow \underset{\mathbf{x}}{argmin} \; \| \mathcal{F}(\mathbf{x}) - \mathbf{f} \|^2 + \mathcal{R}(\mathbf{x}).$$

Here, $\mathcal{R}$ denotes a regularizer which enforces the generated images to look natural and avoid noisy and spiky patterns that are not helpful in perceptual visualization. Figure 5.17 illustrates examples of reconstructed images obtained from the CNN features at different layers of the network. It is interesting to note that the objects vary in position, scale and deformations but the holistic characteristics remain the same. This denotes that the network has learned meaningful characteristics of the input image data.

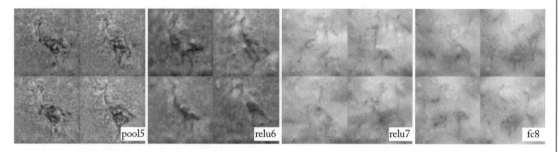

Figure 5.17: Multiple inverted images obtained from the high dimensional feature representations of a CNN. Note that the features from lower layers retain local information better than the higher ones. (Figure from Mahendran and Vedaldi [2015], used with permission.)

Up to this point, we have completed the discussion about the CNN architecture, its training process and the visualization approaches to understand the working of CNNs. Next, we will describe a number of successful CNN examples from the literature which will help us develop an insight into the state-of-the-art network topologies and their mutual pros and cons.

CHAPTER 6

Examples of CNN Architectures

We have covered the basic modules in the previous chapters which can be joined together to develop CNN-based deep learning models. Among these modules, we covered convolution, sub-sampling and several other layers which form large-scale CNN architectures. We noticed that the loss functions are used during training to measure the difference between the predicted and desired outputs from the model. We discussed modules which are used to regularize the networks and optimize their performance and convergence speeds. We also covered several gradient-based learning algorithms for successful CNN training, along with different tricks to achieve stable training of CNNs, such as weight initialization strategies. In this chapter, we introduce several successful CNN designs which are constructed using the basic building blocks that we studied in the previous chapters. Among these, we present both early architectures (which have been traditionally popular in computer vision and are rather easier to understand) and the most recent CNN models (which are relatively complex and built on top of the conventional designs). We note that there is a natural order in these architectures according to which their designs have evolved through the recent years. Therefore, we elaborate on each of these designs, while emphasizing their connections and the trend in which the designs have progressed. In the following, we begin with a simple CNN architecture, known as the LeNet.

6.1 LENET

The LeNet [LeCun et al., 1998] architecture is one of the earliest and basic forms of CNNs which was applied to handwritten digit identification. A successful variant of this architecture style is called the LeNet-5 model, because it comprises 5 weight layers in total. Specifically, it consists of two convolution layers each followed by a sub-sampling (max-pooling) layer to extract features. Afterward, a single convolution layer, followed by a set of two fully connected layers toward the end of the model to act as a classifier on the extracted features. Note that the activations after the weight layers are also squashed using a tanh nonlinearity. The model architecture used to train on the MNIST digit dataset is shown in Fig. 6.1.

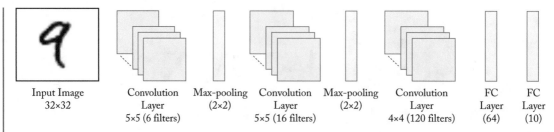

| Input Image 32×32 | Convolution Layer 5×5 (6 filters) | Max-pooling (2×2) | Convolution Layer 5×5 (16 filters) | Max-pooling (2×2) | Convolution Layer 4×4 (120 filters) | FC Layer (64) | FC Layer (10) |

Figure 6.1: The LeNet-5 Architecture.

6.2 ALEXNET

AlexNet [Krizhevsky et al., 2012] was the first large-scale CNN model which led to the resurgence of deep neural networks in computer vision (other CNN architectures before AlexNet, e.g., [Cireşan et al., 2011, LeCun et al., 1998] were relatively smaller and were not tested on large-scale datasets such as the ImageNet dataset). This architecture won the ImageNet Large-Scale Visual Recognition Challenge (ILSVRC) in 2012 by a large margin.

The main difference between the AlexNet architecture and its predecessors is the increased network depth, which leads to a significantly larger number of tunable parameters, and the used regularization tricks (such as the activation dropout [Srivastava et al., 2014] and data augmentation). It consists of a total of eight parameter layers among which the five initial layers are convolutional layers, while the later three layers are fully connected layers. The final fully connected layer (i.e., the output layer) classifies an input image into one of the thousand classes of the ImageNet dataset, and therefore contains 1,000 units. The filter sizes and the location of the max-pooling layers are shown in Fig. 6.2. Note that dropout is applied after the first two fully connected layers in the AlexNet architecture, which leads to a reduced over-fitting and a better generalization to unseen examples. Another distinguishing aspect of AlexNet is the usage of ReLU nonlinearity after every convolutional and fully connected layer, which substantially improves the training efficiency compared to the traditionally used tanh function.

Although AlexNet is relatively much smaller (in terms of the number of layers) compared to the recent state-of-the-art CNN architectures, it is interesting to note that Krizhevsky et al. [2012] had to split the training between two GPUs at the time of its first implementation. This was necessary because a single NVIDIA GTX 580 (with 3 Gb memory) could not hold the complete network which consists of around 62 million parameters. It took around six days to train the network on the complete ImageNet dataset. Note that the ImageNet training set contains 1.2 million images belonging to a thousand of different object classes.

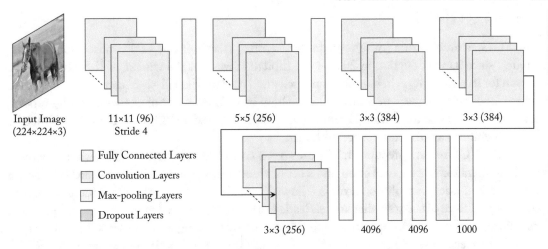

Figure 6.2: The AlexNet Architecture.

6.3   NETWORK IN NETWORK

The Network in Network (NiN) [Lin et al., 2013] architecture is a simple and lightweight CNN model which generally performs really well on small-scale datasets. It introduces two new ideas in the CNN design. **First**, it shows that incorporating fully connected layers in-between the convolutional layers results is helpful in network training. Therefore, the example architecture consists of three convolutional layers at the first, fourth, and and seventh locations (among the weight layers) with filters of size 5×5, 5×5, and 3×3, respectively. Each of these convolutional layers is followed by a pair of fully connected layers (or convolutional layers with 1×1 filter sizes) and a max-pooling layer. **Second**, this architecture utilizes a global average pooling at the end of the model as a regularizer. This pooling scheme just combines all activations within each feature map (by averaging) to obtain a single classification score which is forwarded to a soft-max loss layer. Note that a drop-out regularization block after the first two max-pooling layers also help in achieving a lower test error on a given dataset.

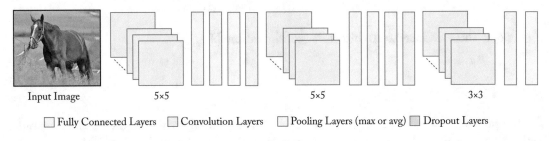

Figure 6.3: The NiN Architecture.

6.4   VGGNET

The VGGnet architecture [Simonyan and Zisserman, 2014b] is one of the most popular CNN models since its introduction in 2014, even though it was not the winner of ILSVRC'14. The reason for its popularity is in its model simplicity and the use of small-sized convolutional kernels which leads to very deep networks. The authors introduced a set of network configurations, among which the configuration D and E (commonly referred as VGGnet-16 and VGGnet-19 in the literature) are the most successful ones.

The VGGnet architecture strictly uses 3×3 convolution kernels with intermediate max-pooling layers for feature extraction and a set of three fully connected layers toward the end for classification. Each convolution layer is followed by a ReLU layer in the VGGnet architecture. The design choice of using smaller kernels leads to a relatively reduced number of parameters, and therefore an efficient training and testing. Moreover, by stacking a series of 3×3 sized kernels, the effective receptive field can be increased to larger values (e.g., 5×5 with two layers, 7×7 with three layers, and so on). Most importantly, with smaller filters, one can stack more layers resulting in deeper networks, which leads to a better performance on vision tasks. This essentially conveys the central idea of this architecture, which supports the usage of deeper networks for an improved feature learning. Figure 6.4 shows the best performing model VGGnet-16 (configuration D) which has 138 million parameters. Similar to AlexNet, it also uses activation dropouts in the first two fully connected layers to avoid over-fitting.

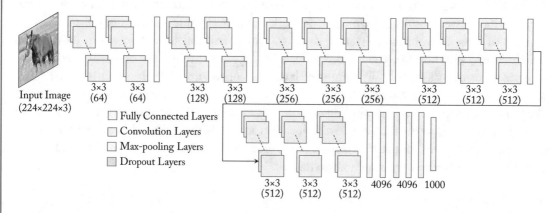

Figure 6.4: The VGGnet-16 Architecture (configuration-D).

6.5   GOOGLENET

All the previously discussed, networks consists of a sequential architecture with only a single path. Along this path, different types of layers such as the convolution, pooling, ReLU, dropout, and fully connected layers are stacked on top of each others to create an architecture of desired depth. The GoogleNet [Szegedy et al., 2015] architecture is the first popular model which uses a more complex architecture with several network branches. This model won the ILSVRC'14 competition with the best top-5 error rate of 6.7% on the classification task. Afterward, several improved and extended versions of GoogleNet have also been proposed. However, we will restrict this discussion to the ILSVRC'14 submission of the GoogleNet.

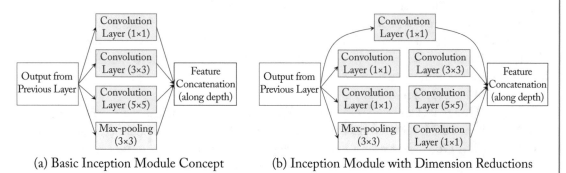

(a) Basic Inception Module Concept   (b) Inception Module with Dimension Reductions

Figure 6.5: The Inception Module.

GoogleNet consists of a total of 22 weight layers. The basic building block of the network is the *"Inception Module,"* due to which the architecture is also commonly called the *"Inception Network."* The processing of this module happens in parallel, which is in contrast to the sequential processing of previously discussed architectures. A simple (naive) version of this module in shown in Fig. 6.5a. The central idea here is to place all the basic processing blocks (which occur in a regular sequential convolutional network) in parallel and combine their output feature representations. The good thing with this design is that multiple inception modules can be stacked together to create a giant network and without the need to worry about the design of each individual layer at different stages of the network. However, as you might have noticed, the problem is that if we concatenate all the individual feature representations from each individual block along the depth dimension, it will result in a very high-dimensional feature output. To overcome this problem, the full inception module performs dimensionality reduction before passing the input feature volume (say with dimensions $h \times w \times d$) through the 3×3 and 5×5 convolution filters. This dimensionality reduction is performed by using a fully connected layer which is equivalent to a 1×1 dimensional convolution operation. As an example, if the 1×1 convolution layer has d' filters, such that $d' < d$, the output from this layer will have a smaller dimension of $h \times w \times d'$. We saw a similar fully connected layer before the convolution layer in the NiN architecture discussed earlier in Section 6.3. In both cases, such a layer leads to a better performance. You may be wondering why a fully connected layer is useful when used before the convolutional layers. The answer is that while the convolution filters operate in the spatial domain (i.e., along the height and width of the input feature channels), a fully connected layer can combine information from multiple feature channels (i.e., along the depth dimension). Such a flexible combination of information leads to not only reduced feature dimensions, but also to an enhanced performance of the inception module.

If you closely look at the inception module (Fig. 6.5), you can understand the intuition behind the combination of a set of different operations into a single block. The advantage is that the features are extracted using a range of filter sizes (e.g., $1 \times 1, 3 \times 3, 5 \times 5$) which corresponds to different receptive fields and an encoding of features at multiple levels from the input. Similarly, there is a max-pooling layer which down-samples the input to obtain a feature representation. Since all the convolution layers in the GoogleNet architecture are followed by a ReLU nonlinearity, this further enhances the capability of the network to model nonlinear relationships. In the end, these different complementary features are combined together to obtain a more useful feature representation.

In the GoogleNet architecture shown in Fig. 6.6, 9 inception modules are stacked together, which results in a 22 layer deep network (the total number of layers in the network is > 100). Similar to NiN, GoogleNet uses a global average pooling followed by a fully connected layer toward the end of the network for classification. The global average pooling layer provides faster computations with a better classification accuracy and a much reduced number of parameters. Another intuitive characteristic of the GoogleNet design is the availability of several output branches in the intermediate layers (e.g., after 4a and 4d), where classifiers are trained on the end task. This design feature avoids the vanishing gradients problem by passing strong feedback signals to the initial layers due to the classification branches extended from the initial layers. GoogleNet also uses dropout before the final fully connected layers in each output branch for regularization.

Although the GoogleNet architecture looks much more complex than its predecessors, e.g., AlexNet and VGGnet, it involves a significantly reduced number of parameters (∼6 million compared to 62 million in AlexNet and 138 million parameters in VGGnet). With a much smaller memory footprint, a better efficiency and a high accuracy, GoogleNet is one of the most intuitive CNN architectures which clearly demonstrates the importance of good design choices.

6.6   RESNET

The Residual Network [He et al., 2016a] from Microsoft won the ILSVRC 2015 challenge with a big leap in performance, reducing the top-5 error rate to 3.6% from the previous year's winning performance of 6.7% by GoogleNet [Szegedy et al., 2015]. It is worth mentioning here that the ILSVRC 2016 winners obtained an error rate of 3.0% using an ensemble of previous popular models such as the GoogleNet Inception and the Residual Network, along with their variants (e.g., Wide Residual Networks and the Inception-ResNets) [ILS].

The remarkable feature of the residual network architecture is the identity skip connections in the residual blocks, which allows to easily train very deep CNN architectures. To understand these connections, consider the residual block in Fig. 6.7. Given an input $\mathbf{x}$, the CNN weight layers implement a transformation function on this input, depicted by $F(\mathbf{x})$. In a residual block,

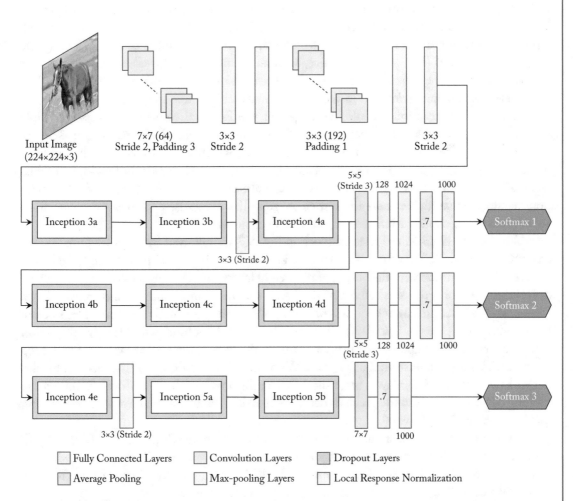

Figure 6.6: The GoogleNet Architecture. All the inception modules have the same basic architecture as described in Fig. 6.5b, however, the number of filters in each layer are different for each module. As an example, Inception 3a has 64 filters in the top-most branch (see Fig. 6.5b), 96 and 128 filters in the second branch from top, 16 and 32 filters in the third branch from top and 32 filters in the bottom branch. In contrast, Inception 4a has 192 filters in the top-most branch (in Fig. 6.5b), 96 and 208 filters in the second branch from top, 16 and 48 filters in the third branch from top and 64 filters in the bottom branch. Interested readers are referred to Table 1 in Szegedy et al. [2015] for the exact dimensions of all layers in each inception block.

the original input is added to this transformation using a direct connection from the input, which bypasses the transformation layers. This connection is called the "*skip identity connection.*" In this way, the transformation function in a residual block is split into an identity term (which represents the input) and a residual term, which helps in focusing on the transformation of the residue feature maps (Fig. 6.7). In practice, such an architecture achieves a stable learning of very deep models. The reason is that the residual feature mapping is often much simpler than the unreferenced mapping learned in the conventional architectures.

Just like the inception module in GoogleNet, the Residual Network comprises multiple residual blocks stacked on top of each others. The winning model of ILSVRC consisted of 152 weights layers (about 8× deeper than the VGGnet-19), which is shown along with a 34 layer model in Table 6.1. Figure 6.8 shows the 34 layer Residual Network as a stack of multiple residual blocks. Note that in contrast to ResNet, a very deep plain network without any residual connections achieves much higher train and test error rates. This shows that the residual connections are key to a better classification accuracy of such deep networks.

The weight layers in the residual block in Fig. 6.7 are followed by a batch normalization and a ReLU activation layer. In this design, the identity mapping has to pass through the ReLU activation after addition with the output of the weight layers. A follow-up work from the authors of Residual Networks demonstrated that this "*post-activation*" mechanism can be replaced by a "*pre-activation*" mechanism, where the batch normalization and ReLU layers are placed before the weight layers [He et al., 2016b]. This leads to a direct "unhindered" identity connection from the input to the output which further enhances the feature learning capability of very deep networks. This idea is illustrated in Fig. 6.9. With this modified design of the residual blocks, networks of a depth of 200 layers were shown to perform well without any over-fitting on the training data (in contrast to the previous design of Residual Networks which started over-fitting for the same number of layers).

Another similar network architecture is the Highway network [Srivastava et al., 2015], which adds learnable parameters to the shortcut and the main branches. This acts as a switching mechanism to control the signal flow through both the main and the shortcut branches and allows the network to decide which branch is more useful for the end-task.

6.7   RESNEXT

The ResNeXt architecture combines the strengths of GoogleNet and ResNet designs. Specifically, it utilizes skip connections which were proposed for residual networks and combines them with the multi-branch architecture in the inception module. This applies a set of transformations to the input feature maps and merges the resulting outputs together before feed-forwarding the output activations to the next module.

The ResNext block is different to the inception module in three key aspects. **First**, it contains a considerably large number of branches compared to the inception module. **Second**, in contrast to different sizes of filters in different branches of the inception architecture, the se-

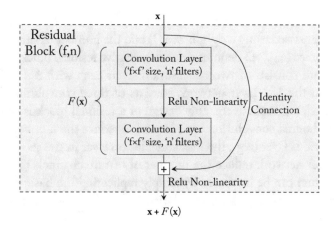

Figure 6.7: The Residual Block.

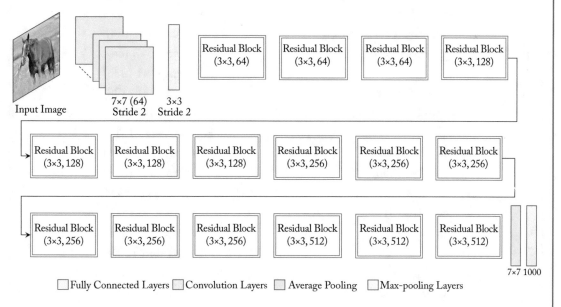

Figure 6.8: The Residual Network architecture.

Table 6.1: The ResNet Architecture for a 34-layer (*left*) and a 152-layer network (*right*). Each residual block is encompassed using a right brace (}) and the number of similar residual blocks is denoted beside each brace (e.g., ×3 denotes three consecutive residual blocks). The residual block in the 34-layer network consists of two convolution layers each with 3×3 filters. In contrast, each residual block in the 152-layer network consists of three convolution layers with 1×1, 3×3 and 1×1 filter sizes, respectively. This design of a residual block is called the "*bottleneck architecture*" because the first convolution layer is used to reduce the number of feature channels coming from the previous layer (e.g., the first convolution layer in the second group of residual blocks in the 152-layer network reduce the number of feature channels to 128). Note that the depth of the architecture can be increased by simply replicating the basic residual block which contains identity connections (Fig. 6.7). For clarity, the 34-layer network architecture has also been illustrated in Fig. 6.8.

ResNet (34 Layers)	ResNet (152 Layers)
cnv–7×7 (64), stride 2	cnv–7×7 (64), stride 2
maxpool–3×3, stride 2	maxpool–3×3, stride 2
cnv–3×3 (64) cnv–3×3 (64) } ×3	cnv–1×1 (64) cnv–3×3 (64) cnv–1×1 (256) } ×3
cnv–3×3 (128) cnv–3×3 (128) } ×4	cnv–1×1 (128) cnv–3×3 (128) cnv–1×1 (512) } ×8
cnv–3×3 (256) cnv–3×3 (256) } ×6	cnv–1×1 (256) cnv–3×3 (256) cnv–1×1 (1024) } ×36
cnv–3×3 (512) cnv–3×3 (512) } ×3	cnv–1×1 (512) cnv–3×3 (512) cnv–1×1 (2048) } ×3
avgpool	avgpool
cnv–1×1 (1000)	cnv–1×1 (1000)
softmax loss	softmax loss

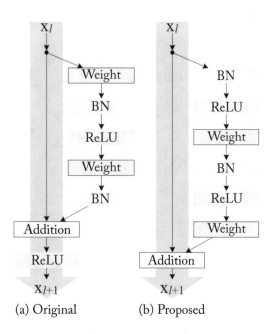

Figure 6.9: The residual block with pre-activation mechanism [He et al., 2016b]. (Figure used with permission.)

quence of transformations in each branch are identical to other branches in the ResNext module. This simplifies the hyper-parameter choices of the ResNext architecture, compared to the inception module. **Finally**, the ResNext block contains skip connections which have been found to be critical in the training of very deep networks. A comparison between a ResNet and ResNext block is shown in Fig. 6.10. Note that the multi-branch architecture, followed by the aggregation of responses, leads to an improved performance compared to ResNet. Specifically, a 101-layer ResNeXt architecture was able to achieve a better accuracy than ResNet with almost a double size (200 layers).

The overall ResNext architecture is identical to the ResNet design shown in Table 6.1. The only difference is that the residual blocks are replaced with the ResNext blocks described above. For efficiency purposes, the group of transformations in each ResNext block are implemented as *grouped convolutions*, where all the N transformation paths are joined in a single layer with a number of output channels equal to $N \times C$, when C is the number of output channels in each individual transformation layer. As an example, the first layer in a ResNext block, shown in Fig. 6.10, is implemented as a single layer with 32×4 output channels. The grouped convolutions only allow convolutions within each of the 32 groups, effectively resembling the multi-path architecture shown in the ResNext block.

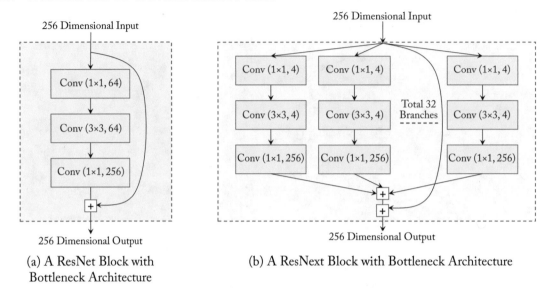

(a) A ResNet Block with Bottleneck Architecture

(b) A ResNext Block with Bottleneck Architecture

Figure 6.10: A ResNet (a) and a ResNext (b) block with roughly the same number of parameters. While the ResNet block comprises a single main branch alongside a skip connection, the ResNext block consists of a number of branches (formally termed the "*block cardinality*"), each of which implements a transformation. The proposed ResNext block has 32 branches, where each transformation is shown as the number of input channels × filter dimensions × number of output channels.

6.8   FRACTALNET

The FractalNet design is based on the observation that the residual-based learning is not the only key enabler for a successful training of very deep convolutional networks. Rather, the existence of multiple shortcut paths for (both forward and backward) information flow in a network enable a form of deep supervision, which helps during the network training. The fractal design achieves a better performance than its residual counterparts on MNIST, CIFAR-10, CIFAR-100, and SVHN datasets when no data augmentation is used during model training [Larsson et al., 2016].

The fractal design is explained in Fig. 6.11. Instead of a single main branch (as in VGG) or a two branch network where on of them is an identity connection which learns residual functions, the fractal design consists of multiple branches each of which has a different number of convolution layers. The number of convolution layers depends on the column number of the branch in the fractal block. If c represents the column number, the number of layers in the cth branch is 2^{c-1}. For example, the first column from the left has only one weight layer, the second column has two weight layers, the third has four and the fourth has eight weight layers. If C denotes the maximum number of columns in a FractalNet block, the total depth of the block will be 2^{C-1}. Note that the outputs from multiple branches are averaged together to produce a joint output.

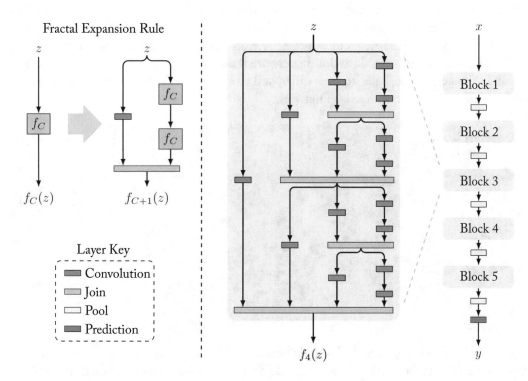

Figure 6.11: *Left:* The basic fractal design expansion rule is shown. It contains two branches for information flow. Each branch transforms the input using a single (left branch) or multiple transformations (right branch). *Right:* A FractalNet [Larsson et al., 2016] with five fractal blocks. Each block consists of C columns and H hierarchies of fractals. In the example block shown, $C = 4$ and $H = 3$. (Figure used with permission.)

In order to avoid redundant features representations and co-adaptations between the branches, FractalNet utilizes "*path-dropout*" for the regularization of the network. The path-dropout randomly ignores one of the incoming paths during the joining operation. Although this approach (called the "*local drop-path*") acts as a regularizer, multiple paths may still be available from input to output. Therefore, a second version of path-dropout (called the "*global drop-path*") was also introduced where only a single column was randomly picked in a FractalNet. Both these regularizations were alternatively applied during the network training to avoid model over-fitting.

6.9   DENSENET

The use of skip (and shortcut) connections in the previously discussed architectures, such as ResNet, FractalNet, ResNext, and Highway networks avoid the vanishing gradient problem and enable the training of very deep networks. DenseNet extends this idea by propagating the output of each layer to all subsequent layers, effectively easing the information propagation in the forward and backward directions during network training [Huang et al., 2016a]. This allows all layers in the network to "talk" to each other, and to automatically figure out the best way to combine multi-stage features in a deep network.

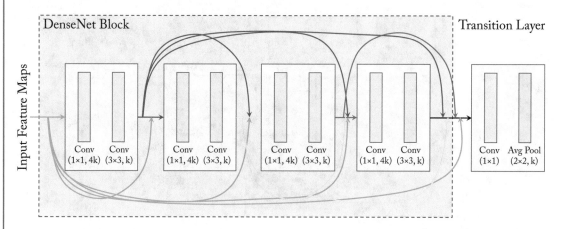

Figure 6.12: A densely connected CNN block with five layers. Note that every layer receives features from all preceding layers. A transition layer is used toward the end of each dense block to reduce the feature set dimensionality.

An example DenseNet is shown in Fig. 6.12. Since the information flow is in the forward direction, every initial layer is directly connected to all the following layers. These connections are realized by *concatenating* the feature maps of a layer with the feature maps from all the preceding layers. This is in contrast to ResNet, where skip connections are used to add the output from an initial layer before processing it through the next ResNet block (see Fig. 6.10). There are three main consequences of such direct connections in a DenseNet. **First**, the features from the initial layers are directly passed on to the later layers without any loss of information. **Second**, the number of input channels in the subsequent layers of a DenseNet increases rapidly because of the concatenation of the preceding feature maps from all preceding layers. To keep the network computations feasible, the number of output channels (also termed the "*growth rate*" in DenseNets) for each convolutional layer are relatively quite small (e.g., 6 or 12). **Third**, the concatenation of feature maps can only be performed when their spatial sizes match with each other. Therefore, a densely connected CNN consists of multiple blocks, each of which has dense connections within the layers and the pooling or strided convolution operations are performed in-between these blocks to collapse the input to a compact representation (see Fig. 6.13). The layers which reduce the size of feature representations between each pair of DenseNet blocks are called the "*transition layers*." The transition layers are implemented as a combination of batch normalization, an 1×1 convolutional layer and by a 2×2 average pooling layer.

Layers	Output Size	DenseNet-121 $(k=32)$		DenseNet-169 $(k=32)$		DenseNet-201 $(k=32)$		DenseNet-161 $(k=48)$	
Convolution	112×112	7 × 7 conv, stride 2							
Pooling	56×56	3 × 3 max pool, stride 2							
Dense Block (1)	56×56	$\begin{bmatrix} 1 \times 1 \text{ conv} \\ 3 \times 3 \text{ conv} \end{bmatrix}$	× 6	$\begin{bmatrix} 1 \times 1 \text{ conv} \\ 3 \times 3 \text{ conv} \end{bmatrix}$	× 6	$\begin{bmatrix} 1 \times 1 \text{ conv} \\ 3 \times 3 \text{ conv} \end{bmatrix}$	× 6	$\begin{bmatrix} 1 \times 1 \text{ conv} \\ 3 \times 3 \text{ conv} \end{bmatrix}$	× 6
Transition Layer (1)	56×56 / 28×28	1 × 1 conv / 2 × 2 average pool, stride 2							
Dense Block (2)	28×28	$\begin{bmatrix} 1 \times 1 \text{ conv} \\ 3 \times 3 \text{ conv} \end{bmatrix}$	× 12	$\begin{bmatrix} 1 \times 1 \text{ conv} \\ 3 \times 3 \text{ conv} \end{bmatrix}$	× 12	$\begin{bmatrix} 1 \times 1 \text{ conv} \\ 3 \times 3 \text{ conv} \end{bmatrix}$	× 12	$\begin{bmatrix} 1 \times 1 \text{ conv} \\ 3 \times 3 \text{ conv} \end{bmatrix}$	× 12
Transition Layer (2)	28×28 / 14×14	1 × 1 conv / 2 × 2 average pool, stride 2							
Dense Block (3)	14×14	$\begin{bmatrix} 1 \times 1 \text{ conv} \\ 3 \times 3 \text{ conv} \end{bmatrix}$	× 24	$\begin{bmatrix} 1 \times 1 \text{ conv} \\ 3 \times 3 \text{ conv} \end{bmatrix}$	× 32	$\begin{bmatrix} 1 \times 1 \text{ conv} \\ 3 \times 3 \text{ conv} \end{bmatrix}$	× 48	$\begin{bmatrix} 1 \times 1 \text{ conv} \\ 3 \times 3 \text{ conv} \end{bmatrix}$	× 36
Transition Layer (3)	14×14 / 7×7	1 × 1 conv / 2 × 2 average pool, stride 2							
Dense Block (4)	7×7	$\begin{bmatrix} 1 \times 1 \text{ conv} \\ 3 \times 3 \text{ conv} \end{bmatrix}$	× 16	$\begin{bmatrix} 1 \times 1 \text{ conv} \\ 3 \times 3 \text{ conv} \end{bmatrix}$	× 32	$\begin{bmatrix} 1 \times 1 \text{ conv} \\ 3 \times 3 \text{ conv} \end{bmatrix}$	× 32	$\begin{bmatrix} 1 \times 1 \text{ conv} \\ 3 \times 3 \text{ conv} \end{bmatrix}$	× 24
Classification Layer	1×1	7 × 7 global average pool / 1000D fully-connected, softmax							

Figure 6.13: **Variants of DenseNet Architectures** [Huang et al., 2016a]. In each variant, the number of dense blocks remain the same (i.e., 4), however the growth rate and the number of convolution layers are increased to design larger architectures. Each transition layer is implemented as a combination of dimensionality reduction layer (with 1×1 convolutional filters) and an average pooling layer for sub-sampling. (Table used with permission from Huang et al. [2016a].)

The concatenated feature maps from the preceding layers in a DenseNet block are not tunable. Therefore, each layer learns its own representation and concatenates it with the global information which comes from the previous network stages. This information is then provided to the next layer which can add additional information, but cannot directly alter the global information that was learned by the previous layers. This design greatly reduces the number of tunable parameters and explicitly differentiates between the global state of the network and the local contribution additions, that are made by each layer to the global state.

DenseNet borrows several design choices from the previous best approaches. For example, a pre-activation mechanism where each convolution layer is preceded by a Batch Normalization and a ReLU layer. Similarly, bottleneck layers with 1×1 filters are used to first reduce the number of input feature maps before processing them through the 3×3 filter layers. DenseNet achieves state of the art performance on a number of datasets such as MNIST, CIFAR10, and CIFAR100 with a relatively less number of parameters compared to ResNet.

CHAPTER 7

Applications of CNNs in Computer Vision

Computer vision is a very broad research area which covers a wide variety of approaches not only to process images but also to understand their contents. It is an active research field for convolutional neural network applications. The most popular of these applications include, classification, segmentation, detection, and scene understanding. Most CNN architectures have been used for computer vision problems including, supervised or unsupervised face/object classification (e.g., to identify an object or a person in a given image or to output the class label of that object), detection (e.g., annotate an image with bounding boxes around each object), segmentation (e.g., labeling pixels of an input image), and image generation (e.g., converting low-resolution images to high resolution ones). In this chapter, we describe various applications of convolutional neural networks in computer vision. Note that this chapter is not a literature review, it rather provides a description of representative works in different areas of computer vision.

7.1 IMAGE CLASSIFICATION

CNNs have been shown to be an effective tool for the task of image classification [Deng, 2014]. For instance, in the 2012 ImageNet LSVRC contest, the first large-scale CNN model, which was called AlexNet [Krizhevsky et al., 2012] (Section 6.2), achieved considerably lower error rates compared to the previous methods. ImageNet LSVRC is a challenging contest as the training set consists of about 1.2 million images belonging to 1,000 different classes, while the test set has around 150,000 images. After that, several CNN models (e.g., VGGnet, GoogleNet, ResNet, DenseNet) have been proposed to further decrease the error rate. While Chapter 6 has already introduced these state-of-the art CNN models for image classification task, we will discuss below a more recent and advanced architecture, which was proposed for 3D point cloud classification (input to the model is a raw 3D point cloud) and achieved a high classification performance.

7.1.1 POINTNET

PointNet [Qi et al., 2016] is a type of neural network which takes orderless 3D point clouds as input and well respects the permutation invariance of the input points. More precisely, PointNet approximates a set function g defined on an orderless 3D point cloud, $\{x_1, x_2, \cdots, x_n\}$, to map the point cloud to a vector:

$$g(\{x_1, x_2, \cdots, x_n\}) = \gamma(\max_{i=1\cdots n} \{h(x_i)\}), \tag{7.1}$$

where γ and h are multi-layer perceptron (mlp) networks. Thus, the set function g is invariant to the permutation of the input points and can approximate any continuous set function [Qi et al., 2016].

PointNet, shown in Fig. 7.1, can be used for classification, segmentation, and scene semantic parsing from point clouds. It directly takes an entire point cloud as input and outputs a class label to accomplish 3D object classification. For segmentation, the network returns per-point labels for all points within the input point cloud. PointNet has three main modules, which we briefly discuss below.

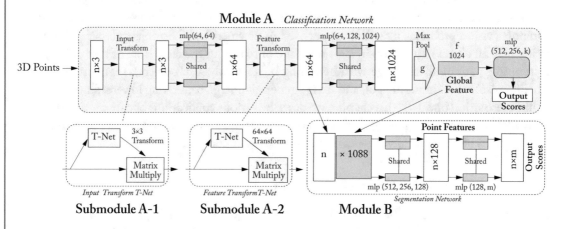

Figure 7.1: PointNet architecture: The input to classification network (Module A) are 3D point clouds. The network applies a sequence of non-linear transformations, including input and feature transformations (Submodule A-1), and then uses max-pooling to aggregate point features. The output is a classification score for C number of classes. The classification network can be extended to form the segmentation network (Module B). "mlp" stands for multi-layered perceptron and numbers in bracket are layer sizes.

Classification Network (Module A):

The first key module of PointNet is the classification network (module A), shown in Fig. 7.1. This module consists of input (Submodule A-1) and feature (Submodule A-2) transformation networks, multi-layer perceptrons (mlp) networks, and a max-pooling layer. Each point within the orderless input point cloud ($\{x_1, x_2, \cdots, x_n\}$) is first passed through two shared mlp networks (function $h(\cdot)$ in Eq. (7.1)) to transfer 3D points to a high dimensional, e.g., 1024-dimensional, feature space. Next, the max-pooling layer (function $\max(\cdot)$ in Eq. (7.1)) is used as a symmetric function to aggregate information from all the points, and to make a model invariant to input permutations. The output of the max-pooling layer ($\max_{i=1\cdots n} \{h(x_i)\}$ in Eq. (7.1)) is a vector, which represents a global shape feature of the input point cloud. This global feature is then passed through an mlp network followed by a soft-max classifier (function $\gamma(\cdot)$ in Eq. (7.1)) to assign a class label to the input point cloud.

Transformation/Alignment Network (Submodule A-1 and Submodule A-2):
The second module of PointNet is the transformation network (mini-network or T-net in Fig. 7.1), which consists of a a shared mlp network, that is applied on each point, followed by a max-pooling layer which is applied across all points and two fully connected layers. This network predicts an affine transformation to ensure that the semantic labeling of a point cloud is invariant to geometric transformations. As shown in Fig. 7.1, there are two different transformation networks, including the input (Submodule A-1) and the feature transformation (Submodule A-2) networks. The input 3D points are first passed through the input transformation network to predict a 3×3 affine transformation matrix. Then, new per-point features are computed by applying the affine transformation matrix to the input point cloud ("Matrix multiply" box in Submodule A-1).

The feature transform network is a replica of the input transform network, shown in Fig. 7.1 (Submodule A-2), and is used to predict the feature transformation matrix. However, unlike the input transformation network, the feature transformation network takes 64-dimensional points. Thus, its predicted transformation matrix has a dimension of 64×64, which is higher than the input transformation matrix (i.e., 3×3 in Submodule A-1). This contributes to the difficulty of achieving optimization. To address this problem, a regularization term is added to the soft-max loss to constrain the 64×64 feature transformation matrix to be close to an orthogonal matrix:

$$L_{reg} = \left\| I - AA^T \right\|_F^2 , \tag{7.2}$$

where A is the feature transformation matrix.

Segmentation Network (Module B):
PointNet can be extended to predict per point quantities, which rely on both the local geometry and the global semantics. The global feature computed by the classification network (Module A) is fed to the segmentation network (Module B). The segmentation network combines the global and per-point point features, and then passed them through an mlp network to extract new per-point features. These new features contain both the global and local information, which has shown to be essential for segmentation [Qi et al., 2016]. Finally, the point features are passed through a shared mlp layer to assign a label to each point.

7.2 OBJECT DETECTION AND LOCALIZATION

Recognizing objects and localizing them in images is one of the challenging problems in computer vision. Recently, several attempts have been made to tackle this problem using CNNs. In this section, we will discuss three recent CNN-based techniques, which were used for detection and localization.

7.2.1 REGION-BASED CNN

In Girshick et al. [2016], Region-based CNN (R-CNN) has been proposed for object detection. It will be good to give here the broad idea behind R-CNN, i.e., region wise feature extraction using deep CNNs and the learning of independent linear classifiers for each object class. The R-CNN object detection system consists of the following three modules.

Regional Proposals (Module A in Fig. 7.2) and Feature Extraction (Module B)
Given an image, the first module (Module A in Fig. 7.2) uses selective search [Uijlings et al., 2013] to generate category-independent region proposals, which represent the set of candidate detections available to the object detector.

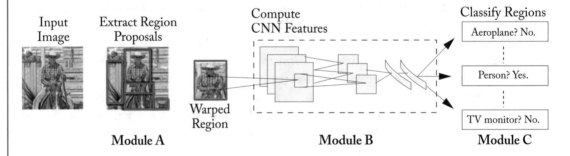

Figure 7.2: RCNN object detection system. Input to R-CNN is an RGB image. It then extracts region proposals (Module A), computes features for each proposal using a deep CNN, e.g., AlexNet (Module B), and then classifies each region using class-specific linear SVMs (Module C).

The second module (Module B in Fig. 7.2) is a deep CNN (e.g., AlexNet or VGGnet), which is used to extract a fixed-length feature vector from each region. In both cases (AlexNet or VGGnet), the feature vectors are 4096-dimensional. In order to extract features from a region of a given image, the region is first converted to make it compatible with the network input. More precisely, irrespective of the candidate region's aspect ratio or size, all pixels are converted to the required size by warping them in a tight bounding box. Next, features are computed by forward propagating a mean-subtracted RGB image through the network and reading off the output values by the last fully connected layer just before the soft-max classifier.

Training Class Specific SVMs (Module C)

After feature extraction, one linear SVM per class is learned, which is the third module of this detection system. In order to assign labels to training data, all region proposals with an overlap greater than or equal to 0.5 IoU with a ground-truth box are considered as positives for the class of that box, while the rest are considered as negatives. Since the training data is very large for the available memory, the standard hard negative mining method [Felzenszwalb et al., 2010] is used to achieve quick convergence.

Pre-training and Domain Specific Training of Feature Extractor

For the pre-training of the CNN feature extractor, a large ILSVRC2012 classification dataset with image-level annotations is used. Next, SGD training with the warped region proposals is performed for adaptation of the network to the new domain and the new task of image detection. The network architecture is kept unchanged except for a 1000-way classification layer, which is set to 20+1 for PASCAL VOC and to 200+1 for ILSVRC2013 datasets (equal to the number of classes in these datasets + background).

R-CNN Testing

At test time, a selective search is run to select 2,000 region proposals from the test image. To extract features from these regions, each one of them is warped and then forward propagated through the learned CNN feature extractor. SVM trained for each class is then used to score the feature vectors of each class. Once all these regions have been scored, a greedy non-maximum suppression is used to reject a proposal, which has an IoU overlap with a higher scoring selected region greater than a pre-specified threshold. R-CNN has been shown to improve the mean average precision (mAP) by a significant margin.

R-CNN Drawbacks

The R-CNN discussed above achieves an excellent object detection accuracy. However, it still has few drawbacks. The training of R-CNN is multi-staged. In the case of R-CNN, soft-max loss is employed to fine tune the CNN feature extractor (e.g., AlexNet, VGGnet) on object proposals. SVM are next fitted to the network's features. The role of SVMs is to perform object detection and replace the soft-max classifier. In terms of complexity in time and space, the training of this model is computationally expensive. This is because, every region proposal is required to pass through the network. For example, training VGGnet-16 on 5,000 images of the PASCAL VOC07 dataset using a GPU takes 2.5 days. In addition, the extracted features need a huge storage, i.e., hundreds of gigabytes. R-CNN is also slow in performing object detection at test time. For example, using VGGnet-16 (on a GPU) as the feature extractor in Module B, detection of an object takes around 47 seconds per image. To overcome these problems, an extension of R-CNN called the Fast R-CNN was proposed.

7.2.2 FAST R-CNN

Figure 7.3 shows the Fast R-CNN model. The input to Fast R-CNN is an entire image along with object proposals, which are extracted using the selective search algorithm [Uijlings et al., 2013]. In the first stage, convolutional feature maps (usually feature maps of the last convolutional layer) are extracted by passing the entire image through a CNN, such as AlexNet and VGGnet (Module A in Fig. 7.3). For each object proposal, a feature vector of fixed size is then extracted from the feature maps by a Region of Interest (RoI) pooling layer (Module B), which has been explained in Section 4.2.7. The role of the RoI pooling layer is to convert the features, in a valid RoI, into small feature maps of fixed size ($X \times Y$, e.g., 7×7), using max-pooling. X and Y are the layer hyper-parameters. A RoI itself is a rectangular window which is characterized by a 4-tuple that defines its top-left corner (a, b) and its height and width (x, y). The RoI layer divides the RoI rectangular area of size $x \times y$ into an $X \times Y$ grid of sub-windows, which has a size of $x/X \times y/Y$. The values in each sub-window are then max-pooled into the corresponding output grid. Note that the max-pooling operator is applied independently to each convolutional feature map. Each feature vector is then given as input to fully connected layers, which branch into two sibling output layers. One of these sibling layers (Module C in Fig. 7.3) gives estimates of the soft-max probability over object classes and a background class. The other layer (Module D in Fig. 7.3) produces four values, which redefine bounding box positions, for each of the object classes.

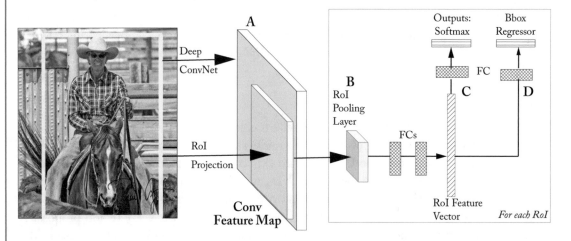

Figure 7.3: Fast R-CNN Architecture. The input to a fully convolutional network (e.g., AlexNet) is an image and RoIs (Module A). Each RoI is pooled into a fixed-size feature map (Module B) and then passed through the two fully-connected layers to form a RoI feature vector. Finally, the RoI feature vector is passed through two sibling layers, which output the soft-max probability over different classes (Module C) and bounding box positions (Module D).

Fast R-CNN Initialization and Training

Fast R-CNN is initialized from three pre-trained ImageNet models including: AlexNet [Krizhevsky et al., 2012], VGG-CNN-M-1024 [Chatfield et al., 2014], and VGGnet-16 [Simonyan and Zisserman, 2014b] models. During initialization, a Fast R-CNN model undergoes three transformations. **First**, a RoI pooling layer (Module B) replaces the last max-pooling layer to make it compatible with the network's first fully connected layer (e.g., for VGGnet-16 $X = Y = 7$). **Second**, the two sibling layers ((Module C and Module D), discussed above, replace the last fully connected layer and soft-max of the network. **Third**, the network model is tweaked to accept two data inputs, i.e., a list of images and their RoIs. Then SGD simultaneously optimizes the soft-max classifier (Module C) and the bounding-box regressor (Module D) in an end-to-end fashion by using a multi-task loss on each labeled RoI.

Detection Using Fast R-CNN

For detection, the Fast R-CNN takes as an input, an image along with a list of R object proposals to score. During testing, R is kept at around 2,000. For each test RoI (r), the class probability score for each of the K classes (module C in Fig. 7.3) and a set of refined bounding boxes are computed (module D in Fig. 7.3). Note that each of the K classes has its own refined bounding box. Next, the algorithm and the configurations from R-CNN are used to independently perform non-maximum suppression for each class. Fast R-CNN has been shown to achieve a higher detection performance (with a mAP of 66% compared to 62% for R-CNN) and computational efficiency on PASCAL VOC 2012 dataset. The training of Fast R-CNN, using VGGnet-16, was 9× faster than R-CNN and this network was found 213 × faster at test-time.

While Fast R-CNN has increased the training and testing speed of R-CNN by sharing a single CNN computation across all region proposals, its computational efficiency is bounded by the speed of the region proposal methods, which are run on CPUs. The straightforward approach to address this issue is to implement region proposal algorithms on GPUs. Another elegant way is to rely on algorithmic changes. In the following section, we discuss an architecture, known as Regional Proposal Network [Ren et al., 2015], which relies on an algorithmic change by computing nearly cost-free region proposals with CNN in an end-to-end learning fashion.

7.2.3   REGIONAL PROPOSAL NETWORK (RPN)

The Regional Proposal Network [Ren et al., 2015] (Fig. 7.4) simultaneously predicts object bounding boxes and objectness scores at each position. RPN is a fully convolutional network, which is trained in an end-to-end fashion, to produce high quality region proposals for object detection using Fast R-CNN (described in Section 7.2.2). Combining RPN with Fast R-CNN object detector results in a new model, which is called Faster R-CNN (shown in Fig. 7.5). Notably, in Faster R-CNN, the RPN shares its computation with Fast R-CNN by sharing the same convolutional layers, allowing for joint training. The former has five, while the later has

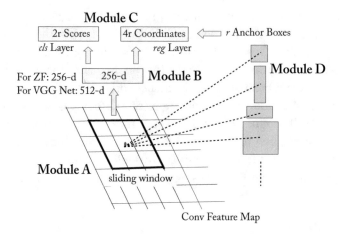

Figure 7.4: Regional proposal network (RPN) architecture, which is illustrated at a single position.

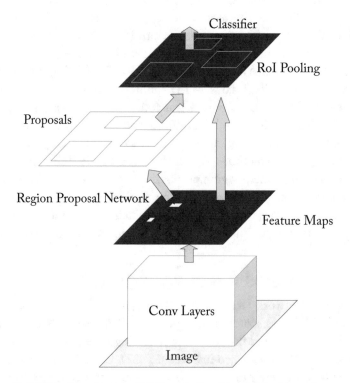

Figure 7.5: Faster R-CNN. Combining RPN with fast R-CNN object detector.

13 shareable convolutional layers. In the following, we first discuss the RPN and then Faster R-CNN, which merges RPN and Fast R-CNN into a single network.

The input to the RPN is an image (re-scaled in such a way that its smaller side is equal to 600 pixels) and the output is a set of object bounding boxes and associated objectness scores (as shown in Fig. 7.4). To generate region proposals with RPN, the image is first passed through the shareable convolutional layers. A small spatial window (e.g., 3×3) is then slid over the output feature maps of the last shared convolutional layer, e.g., conv5 for VGGnet-16 (Module A in Fig. 7.4). This sliding window at each position is then transformed to a lower-dimensional vector of size 256-d and 512-d for ZF and VGGnet-16 models (Module B in Fig. 7.4), respectively. Next, this vector is given as an input to two sibling fully connected layers, including the bounding box regression layer (*reg*) and the bounding box classification layer (*cls*) (Module C in Fig. 7.4). In summary, the above-mentioned steps (Module A, Module B, and Module C) can be implemented with a 3×3 convolutional layer followed by two sibling 1×1 convolutional layers.

Multi-scale Region Proposal Detection

Unlike image/feature pyramid-based methods, such as the spatial pyramid pooling (SPP) layer [He et al., 2015b] (discussed in Section 4.2.8), which uses time-consuming feature pyramids in convolutional feature maps, RPN uses a nearly cost-free algorithm for addressing multiple scales and aspect ratios. For this purpose, r region proposals are simultaneously predicted at the location of each sliding window. The *reg* layer (Module C in Fig. 7.4) therefore encodes the coordinates of r boxes by producing $4r$ outputs. To predict the probability of "an object" or "no object" in each proposal, the *cls* layer outputs $2r$ scores (the sum of outputs is 1 for each proposal). The r proposals are parameterized relative to anchors (i.e., r reference boxes which are centered at the sliding window as shown in Module D). These anchors are associated with three different aspect ratios and three different scales, resulting in a total of nine anchors at each sliding window.

RPN Anchors Implementation

For the anchors, 3 scales with box areas of 128^2, 256^2, and 512^2 pixels, and 3 aspect ratios of 2:1, 1:1, and 1:2 are used. When predicting large proposals, the proposed algorithm allows for the use of anchors that are larger than the receptive field. This design helps in achieving high computational efficiency, since multi-scale features are not needed.

During the training phase, all cross-boundary anchors are avoided to reduce their contribution to the loss (otherwise, the training does not converge). There are roughly $20k$ anchors, i.e., $\approx 60 \times 40 \times 9$, used for a $1,000 \times 600$ image.[1] By ignoring the cross-boundary anchors only around $6k$ anchors per image are left for training. During testing, the entire image is given as

---

[1]Since the total stride for both ZF and VGG nets on the last convolutional layer is 16 pixels.

an input to the RPN. As a result, cross boundary boxes are produced which are then clipped to the image boundary.

RPN Training

During the training of RPN, each anchor takes a binary label to indicate the presence of "an object" or "no object" in the input image. Two types of anchors take a positive label: either an anchor which has the highest IoU overlap or the IoU overlap is higher than 0.7 with ground-truth bounding box. An anchor that has an IoU ratio lower than 0.3 is assigned a negative label. In addition, the contribution of anchors which do not have a positive or negative label is not considered toward the training objective. The RPN multi-task loss function for an image is given by:

$$L(\{p_i\}, \{t_i\}) = \frac{1}{N_{cls}} \sum_i L_{cls}(p_i, p_i^*) + \lambda \frac{1}{N_{reg}} \sum_i p_i^* L_{reg}(t_i, t_i^*), \qquad (7.3)$$

where i denotes the index of an anchor, p_i represents the probability that an anchor i is an object. p_i^* stands for the ground-truth label, which is 1 for a positive anchor, and zero otherwise. Vectors t_i and t_i^* contain the four coordinates of the predicted bounding box and the ground-truth box, respectively. L_{cls} is the soft-max loss over two classes. The term $p_i^* L_{reg}$ (where L_{reg} is the regression loss) indicates the activation of the regression loss only for positive anchors, otherwise it is disabled. N_{cls}, N_{reg}, and a balancing weight λ are next used to normalize cls and reg layers.

Faster R-CNN Training: Sharing Convolutional Features for Region Proposal and Object Detection

In the previous sections, we discussed the training of the RPN network for the generation of region proposals. We did not, however, consider Fast R-CNN for region-based object detection using these proposals. In the following, we explain the training of the Faster R-CNN network, that is composed of RPN and Fast R-CNN with shared convolutional layers, as shown in Fig. 7.5.

Instead of learning the two networks (i.e., RPN and Fast R-CNN) separately, a four-step alternating optimization approach is used to share convolutional layers between these two models. **Step 1:** The RPN is trained using the previously stated strategy. **Step 2:** The proposals produced by step 1 are used to train a separate Fast R-CNN detection network. The two networks do not share convolutional layers at this stage. **Step 3:** The Fast R-CNN network initializes the training of RPN and the layers specific to RPN are fine-tuned, while keeping the shared convolutional layers fixed. At this point, the two networks share convolutional layers. **Step 4:** The fc layers of the Fast R-CNN are fine-tuned by keeping the shared convolutional layers fixed. As such, a unified network, which is called Faster R-CNN, is formed by using both of these models, which share the same convolutional layers. The Faster R-CNN model has been shown to achieve competitive detection results, with mAP of 59.9%, on PASCAL VOC 2007 dataset.

7.3   SEMANTIC SEGMENTATION

CNNs can also be adapted to perform dense predictions for per-pixel tasks such as semantic segmentation. In this section, we discuss three representative semantic segmentation algorithms which use CNN architectures.

7.3.1   FULLY CONVOLUTIONAL NETWORK (FCN)

In this section, we will briefly describe the Fully Convolutional Network (FCN) [Long et al., 2015], shown in Fig. 7.6, for semantic segmentation.

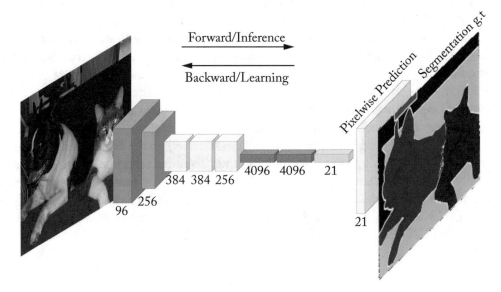

Figure 7.6: FCN architecture. The first seven layers are adopted from AlexNet. Convolutional layers, shown in orange, have been changed from fully connected (*fc*6 and *fc*7 in AlexNet) to convolutional layers (*conv*6 and *conv*7 in FCN). The next convolutional layer (shown in green) is added on top of *conv*7 to produce 21 coarse output feature maps (21 denotes the number of classes + background in the PASCAL VOC dataset). The last layer (yellow) is the transposed convolutional layer, that up-samples the coarse output feature maps produced by *conv*8 layer.

Typical classification networks (discussed in Chapter 6) take fixed-size images as input and produce non-spatial output maps, that are fed to a soft-max layer to perform classification. The spatial information is lost, because these networks use fixed dimension fully connected layers in their architecture. However, these fully connected layers can also be viewed as convolution layers with large kernels, which cover their entire input space. For example, a fully-connected layer with 4,096 units that takes a volume of size $13 \times 13 \times 256$ as input, can be equivalently expressed as a convolutional layer with 4,096 kernels of size 13×13. Hence, the dimension of the output will be $1 \times 1 \times 4{,}096$, which results in an identical output as the initial fully-connected layer. Based on this reinterpretation, the convolutionalized networks can take **(1) input images of any size** and produce **(2) spatial output maps**. These two aspects make the fully convolutional models a natural choice for semantic segmentation.

FCN for semantic segmentation [Long et al., 2015] is built by first converting typical classification networks, (e.g., AlexNet, VGGnet-16) into fully convolutional networks and, then, appending a transposed convolution layer (discussed in Section 4.2.6) to the end of the convolutionalized networks. The transposed convolution layer is used for up-sampling the coarse output feature maps produced by the last layer of the convolutionalized networks. More precisely, given a classification network, e.g., AlexNet, the last three fully-connected layers (4,096-D *fc6*, 4,096-D *fc7*, and 1,000-D *fc8*) are converted to three convolutional layers (*conv6*: consisting of 4,096 filters with size 13×13, *conv7*: consisting of 4,096 filters with size 1×1, and *conv8*: consisting of 21^2 filters with size 1×1) for semantic segmentation on PASCAL VOC dataset. However, forward passing an $H \times W \times 3$ input image through this modified network produces output feature maps with a spatial size of $\frac{H}{32} \times \frac{W}{32}$ which is 32× smaller than the spatial size of the original input image. Thus, these coarse output feature maps are fed to the transposed convolution layer[3] to produce a dense prediction of the input image.

However, a large pixel stride, (e.g., 32 for the AlexNet) at the transposed convolution layer limits the level of details in the up-sampled output. To address this issue, FCN is extended to new fully convolutional networks, i.e., FCN-16s and FCN-8s by combining coarse features with fine ones that are extracted from the shallower layers. The architecture of these two FCNs are shown in the second and third rows of Fig. 7.7, respectively. The FCN-32s in this figure is identical to the FCN discussed above (and shown in Fig. 7.6), except that their architectures are different.[4]

FCN-16s

As shown in the second row of Fig. 7.7, FCN-16s combines predictions from the final convolutional layer and the *pool4* layer, at stride 16. Thus, the network predicts finer details compared to FCN-32s, while retaining high-level semantic information. More precisely, the class scores computed on top of *conv7* layer are passed through a transposed convolutional layer (i.e., 2× up-sampling layer) to produce class scores for each of the PASCAL VOC classes (including background). Next, a 1×1 convolutional layer with a channel dimension of 21 is added on top of *pool4* layer to predict new scores for each of the PASCAL classes. Finally, these 2 stride 16 predicted scores are summed up and fed to another transposed convolutional layer (i.e., 16× up-sampling layer) to produce prediction maps with the same size as the input image. FCN-16s

---

[2]Equal to the number of classes in the PASCAL VOC dataset plus the background class.
[3]The 32 pixel stride is used to output a dense prediction at the same scale as the input image.
[4]The original FCN shown in Fig. 7.6 initialized with AlexNet model and the extended FCN shown in Fig. 7.7 initialized with VGGnet-16 model.

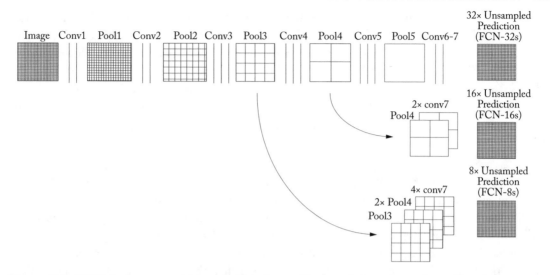

Figure 7.7: FCN learns to combine shallow layer (fine) and deep layer (coarse) information. The first row shows FCN-32s, which up-samples predictions back to pixels in a single step. The second row illustrates FCN-16s, which combines predictions from both the final and the *pool*4 layer. The third row shows FCN-8s, which provides further precision by considering additional predictions from *pool*3 layer.

improved the performance of FCN-32s on the PASCAL VOC 2011 dataset by 3 mean IoU and achieved 62.4 mean IoU.

FCN-8s

In order to obtain more accurate prediction maps, FCN-8s combines predictions from the final convolutional layer and shallower layers, i.e., *pool*3 and *pool*4 layers. The third row of Fig. 7.7 shows the architecture of the FCN-8s network. First, a 1×1 convolutional layer with channel dimension of 21 is added on top of *pool*3 layer to predict new scores at stride 8 for each of the PASCAL VOC classes. Then, the summed predicted scores at stride 16 (second row in Fig. 7.7) is passed through a transposed convolutional layer (i.e., 2× up-sampling layer) to produce new prediction scores at stride 8. These two predicted scores at stride 8 are summed up and then fed to another transposed convolutional layer (i.e., 8× up-sampling layer) to produce prediction maps with the same size as the input image. FCN-8s improved the performance of FCN-18s by a small mean IoU and achieved 62.7 mean IoU on the PASCAL VOC 2011.

FCN Fine-tuning

Since training from scratch is not feasible due to the large number of training parameters and the small number of training samples, fine-tuning using back-propagation through the entire network is done to train FCN for segmentation. It is important to note that FCN uses whole image training instead of patch-wise training, where the network is learned from batches of random patches (i.e., small image regions surrounding the objects of interest). Fine-tuning of the coarse FCN-32s version, takes three GPU days, and about one day on GPU each for the FCN-16s and FCN-8s [Long et al., 2015]. FCN has been tested on PASCAL VOC, NYUDv2, and SIFT Flow datasets for the task of segmentation. It has been shown to achieve superior performance compared to other reported methods.

FCN Drawbacks

FCN discussed above has few limitations. The **first** issue is related to a single transposed convolutional layer of FCN, which cannot accurately capture the detailed structures of objects. While FCN-16s and FCN-8s attempt to avoid this issue by combining coarse (deep layer) information with fine (shallower layers) information, the detailed structure of objects are still lost or smoothed in many cases. The **second** issue is related to the scale, i.e., fixed-size receptive field of FCN. This causes the objects that are larger or smaller than the receptive field to be mislabeled. To overcome these challenges, Deep Deconvolution Network (DDN) has been proposed, which is discussed in the following section.

7.3.2   DEEP DECONVOLUTION NETWORK (DDN)

DDN [Noh et al., 2015] consists of convolution (Module A shown in Fig. 7.8) and deconvolution networks (Module B). The convolution network acts as a feature extractor and converts the input image to a multi-dimensional feature representation. On the other hand, the deconvolution network is a shape generator, that uses these extracted feature maps and produces class score prediction maps at the output with a spatial size of the input image. These class score prediction maps represent the probability that each pixel belongs to different classes.

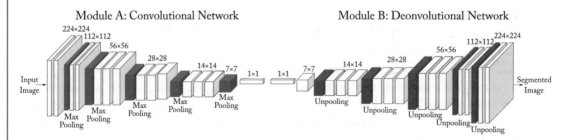

Figure 7.8: Overall architecture of deep deconvolution network. A multilayer deconvolution network is put on top of the convolution network to accurately perform image segmentation. Given a feature representation from the convolution network (Module A), dense class score prediction maps are constructed through multiple un-pooling and transposed convolution layers (Module B).

DDN uses convolutionalized VGGnet-16 network for the convolutional part. More precisely, the last fully connected layer of VGGnet-16 is removed and the last two fully connected layers are converted to convolutional layers (similar to FCN). The deconvolution part is the reciprocal of the convolution network. Unlike FCN-32s, which uses a single transposed convolutional layer, the deconvolution network of DDN uses a sequence of un-pooling and transposed convolution layers to generate class prediction maps with the same spatial size as the input image. In contrast to the convolution part of the model, which decreases the spatial size of the output feature maps through feed-forwarding, its counterpart increases the size by combining the transposed convolution and un-pooling layers.

Un-pooling Layer

The un-pooling layers of the deconvolution network of DDN perform the reverse operation of the max-pooling layers of the convolution network. To be able to perform reverse max-pooling, the max-pooling layers save the locations of the maximum activations in their "switch variables," i.e., essentially the argmax of the max-pooling operation. The un-pooling layers then employ these switch variables to place the activations back to their original pooled locations.

DDN Training

To train this very deep network with relatively small training examples, the following strategies are adopted. **First**, every convolutional and transposed convolutional layer is followed by a batch normalization layer (discussed in Section 5.2.4), which has been found to be critical for DDN optimization. **Second**, unlike FCN which performs image-level segmentation, DDN uses instance-wise segmentation, in order to handle objects in various scales and decrease the training complexity. For this purpose, a two-stage training approach is used.

In the **first phase**, DDN is trained with easy samples. To generate the training samples for this phase, ground-truth bounding box annotations of objects are used to crop each object so that the object is centered at the cropped bounding box. In the **subsequent phase**, the learned model from the first phase is fine-tuned with more challenging samples. Thus, each object proposal contributes to the training samples. Specifically, the candidate object proposals, which sufficiently overlap with the ground-truth segmented regions (≥ 0.5 in IoU) are selected for training. To include context, post-processing is also adopted in this phase.

DDN Inference

Since DDN uses instance-wise segmentation, an algorithm is required to aggregate the output score prediction maps of individual object proposals within an image. DDN uses the pixel-wise maximum of the output prediction maps for this purpose. More precisely, the output prediction maps of each object proposal ($g_i \in \mathrm{R}^{W \times H \times C}$, where C is the number of classes and i, W and H denote the index, height and width of the object proposal, respectively) are first superimposed on the image space with zero padding outside g_i. Then, the pixel-wise prediction map of the entire image is computed as follows:

$$P(x, y, c) = \max_i G_i(x, y, c), \forall i, \tag{7.4}$$

where G_i is the prediction map corresponding to g_i in the image space with zero padding outside g_i. Next, a soft-max loss is applied to the aggregated prediction maps, P in Eq. (7.4), to obtain class probability maps (O) in the entire image space. The final pixel-wise labeled image is computed by applying the fully connected CRF [Krähenbühl and Koltun, 2011] to the output class probability maps O.

> **Conditional Random Field (CRF):** CRF is a class of statistical modeling technique, which are categorized as the sequential version of logistic regression. In contrast to logistic regression, which is a log linear classification model, CRFs are log linear models for sequential labeling.
>
> The CRF is defined as the conditional probabilities of X and Y, represented as $P(Y|X)$, where X denotes a multi-dimensional input, i.e., features, and Y denotes a multi-dimensional output, i.e., labels. The probabilities can be modeled in two different ways, i.e., unary potential and pairwise potential. Unary potential is used to model the probabilities that a given pixel or a patch belongs to each particular category, while pairwise potential is defined to model the relation between two different pixels and patches of an image. In fully connected CRF, e.g., Krähenbühl and Koltun [2011], the latter approach is explored to establish pairwise potential on all pixel pairs in a given image, thus resulting into refined segmentation and labeling. For more details on CRF, the readers are referred to Krähenbühl and Koltun [2011].

DDN Testing

For each testing image, approximately 2,000 object proposals are generated using edge-box algorithm [Zitnick and Dollár, 2014]. Next, the best 50 proposals with the highest objectness scores are selected. These object proposals are then used to compute instance-wise segmentations, which are then aggregated, using the algorithm discussed above, to obtain the semantic segmentation for the whole image. DDN has been shown to achieve an outstanding performance of 72.5% on PASCAL VOC 2012 dataset compared to other reported methods.

DDN Drawbacks

DDN discussed above has a couple of limitations. **First**, DDN uses multiple transposed convolutional layers in its architecture, which requires additional memory and time. **Second**, training DDN is tricky and requires a large corpus of training data to learn the transposed convolutional layers. **Third**, DDN deals with objects at multiple scales by performing instant-wise segmentation. Therefore, it requires feed-forwarding all object proposals through the DDN, which is a time-consuming process. To overcome these challenges, DeepLab model has been proposed, which is discussed in the following section.

7.3.3   DEEPLAB

In DeepLab [Chen et al., 2014], the task of semantic segmentation has been addressed by employing convolutional layers with up-sampled filters, which are called *atrous* convolution (or dilated convolution as discussed in Chapter4).

Recall that forward passing an input image through the typical convolution classification networks reduces the spatial scale of the output feature maps, typically by a factor of 32. However, for dense predictions tasks, e.g., semantic segmentation, a stride of 32 pixels limits the level of details in the up-sampled output maps. One partial solution is to append multiple transposed convolutional layers as in FCN-8s and DDN, to the top of the convolutionalized classification networks to produce output maps with the same size of the input image. However, this approach is too costly.[5] Another critical limitation of these convolutionalized classification networks is that they have a predefined fixed-size receptive field. For example, FCN and all its variants (i.e., FCN-16s and FCN-8s) use VGNNnet-16 with fixed-size 3×3 filters. Therefore, an object with a substantially smaller or larger spatial size than the receptive field is problematic.[6]

DeepLab uses *atrous* convolution in its architecture to simultaneously address these two issues. As discussed in Chapter 4, atrous convolution allows to explicitly control the spatial size of the output feature maps that are computed within convolution networks. It also extends the receptive field, without increasing the number of parameters. Thus, it can effectively incorporate a wider image context while performing convolutions. For example, to increase the spatial size of the output feature maps in the convolutionalized VGGnet-16 network[7] by a factor of 2, one could set the stride of the last max-pooling layer (*pool5*) to 1, and then substitute the subsequent convolutional layer (*conv6*, which is the convolutionalized version of *fc6*) with the atrous convolutional layers with a sampling factor $d = 2$. This modification also extends the filter size of 3×3 to 5×5, and therefore enlarges the receptive field of the filters.

DeepLab-LargeFOV Architecture

DeepLab-LargeFOV is a CNN with an atrous convolutional layer which has a large receptive field. Specifically, DeepLab-LargeFOV is built by converting the first two fully-connected layers of VGGnet-16 (i.e., *fc6* and *fc7*) to convolutional layers (i.e., *conv6* and *conv7*) and then appending a 1×1 convolution layer (i.e., *conv8*) with 21 channels at the end of the convolutionalized networks for semantic segmentation on PASCAL VOC dataset. The stride of the last two max-pooling layers (i.e., *pool4* and *pool5*) is changed to 1,[8] and the convolutional filter of

---

[5]Training these networks requires relatively more training data, time, and memory.

[6]Label prediction for large objects are obtained from only local information. Thus, the pixels which belong to the same large object may have inconsistent labels. Moreover, the pixels which belong to small objects may be classified as background.

[7]A convolutionalized VGGnet-16 is obtained by converting all the fully-connected layers to convolution layers.

[8]The stride of *pool4* and *pool5* layers in the original VGGnet-16 is 2.

*conv*6 layer is replaced with an atrous convolution of kernel size 3×3 and an atrous sampling factor $d = 12$. Therefore, the spatial size of the output class score prediction maps is increased by a factor of 4. Finally, a fast bilinear interpolation layer[9] (i.e., 8× up-sampling) is employed to recover the output prediction maps at the original image size.

Atrous Spatial Pyramid Pooling (ASPP)

In order to capture objects and context at multiple scales, DeepLab employs multiple parallel atrous convolutional layers (discussed in Section 4.2.2) with different sampling factors d, which is inspired by the success of the Spatial Pyramid Pooling (SPP) layer discussed in Section 4.2.8. Specifically, DeepLab with atrous Spatial Pyramid Pooling layer (called DeepLab-ASPP) is built by employing 4 parallel *conv*6 − *conv*7 − *conv*8 branches with 3×3 filters and different atrous factors ($d = \{6, 12, 18, 24\}$) in the *conv*6 layers, as shown in Fig. 7.9. The output prediction maps from all four parallel branches are aggregated to generate the final class score maps. Next, a fast bilinear interpolation layer is employed to recover the output prediction maps with the original image size.

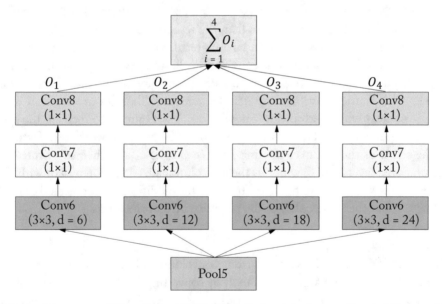

Figure 7.9: Architecture of DeepLab-ASPP (DeepLab with Atrous Spatial Pyramid Pooling layer). *pool*5 denotes the output of the last pooling layer of VGGnet-16.

---

[9]Instead of using transposed convolutional layers as in FCN and DDN, DeepLab uses a fast bilinear interpolation layer without training its parameters. This is because, unlike FCN and DDN, the output class score prediction maps of DeepLab (i.e., the output maps of *conv*8 layer) are quite smooth and thus a single up-sampling step can efficiently recover the output prediction maps with the same size as the input image

DeepLab Inference and Training

The output prediction maps of the bilinear interpolation layer can only predict the presence and rough position of objects, but the boundaries of objects cannot be recovered. DeepLab handles this issue by combining the fully connected CRF [Krähenbühl and Koltun, 2011] with the output class prediction maps of the bilinear interpolation layer. The same approach is also used in DDN. During training, the Deep Convolutional Neural Network (DCNN) and the CRF training stages are decoupled. Specifically, a cross validation of the fully connected CRF is performed after the fine-tuning of the convolutionalized VGGnet-16 network.

DeepLab Testing

DeepLab has been tested on the PASCAL VOC 2012 validation set and has been shown to achieve state-of-the-art performance of 71.6% mean IoU compared to other reported methods including fully convolutional networks. Moreover, DeepLab with atrous Spatial Pyramid Pooling layer (DeepLab-ASPP) achieved about 2% higher accuracy than DeepLab-LargeFOV. Experimental results show that DeepLab based on ResNet-101 delivers better segmentation results compared to Deep Lab employing VGGnet-16.

7.4   SCENE UNDERSTANDING

In computer vision, the recognition of single or isolated objects in a scene has achieved significant success. However, developing a higher level of visual scene understanding requires more complex reasoning about individual objects, their 3D layout and mutual relationships [Khan, 2016, Li et al., 2009]. In this section, we will discuss how CNNs have been used in the area of scene understanding.

7.4.1   DEEPCONTEXT

DeepContext [Zhang et al., 2016] presents an approach to embed 3D context into the topology of a neural network, trained to perform holistic scene understanding. Given an input RGB-D image, the network can simultaneously make global predictions (e.g., scene category and 3D scene layout) as well as local decisions (e.g., the position and category of each constituent object in the 3D space). This method works by first learning a set of scene templates from the training data, which encodes the possible locations of single or multiple instances of objects belonging to a specific category. Four different scene templates, including sleeping area, lounging area, office area, and a table and chair sets are used. Given this contextual scene representation, DeepContext matches an input volumetric representation of an RGBD image with one of the scene templates using a CNN (Module B, Fig. 7.10). Afterward, the input scene is aligned with the scene template using a transformation network (Module C, Fig. 7.10). The aligned volumetric input is fed to a deep CNN with two main branches; **one** works on the complete 3D input and obtains a global feature representation while the **second** works on the local object level and predicts the location and existence of each potential object in the aligned template (Module D, Fig. 7.10).

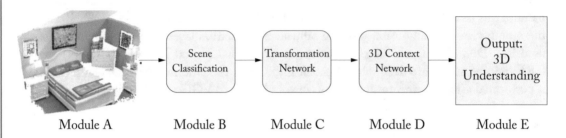

| Module A | Module B | Module C | Module D | Module E |

Figure 7.10: The block diagram for DeepContext processing pipeline. Given a 3D volumetric input (module A), the transformation network (module C) aligns the input data with its corresponding scene template (estimated by module B). Using this roughly aligned scene, the 3D context network (module D) estimates the existence of an object and adjusts the object location based on local object features and holistic scene features, to understand a 3D scene.

The DeepContext algorithm follows a hierarchical process for scene understanding which is discussed below.

Learning Scene Templates
The layouts of the scene templates (e.g., office, sleeping area) are learned from the SUN RGB-D dataset [Song et al., 2015], which comes with 3D object bounding box annotations. Each template represents a scene context by summarizing the bounding box locations and the category information of the objects that are present in the training set. As an initial step, all the clean examples of each scene template (i.e., sleeping area, lounging area, office area and a table and chair sets) are identified. Next, a major object is manually identified in each scene template (e.g., a bed in the sleeping area) and its position is used to align all the scenes belonging to a specific category. This rough alignment is used to find the most frequent locations for each object (also called "anchor positions") by performing k-means clustering and choosing the top k centers for each object. Note that the object set includes not only the regular objects (e.g., bed, desk) but also the scene elements which define the room layout (e.g., walls, floor and ceiling).

The clean dataset of the scene categories used to learn the scene templates, is also used in subsequent processing stages, such as scene classification, scene alignment, and 3D object detection. We will discuss these stages below.

Scene Classification (Module B, Fig. 7.10)
A global CNN is trained to classify an input image to one of the scene templates. Its architecture is exactly same as the global scene pathway in Fig. 7.11. Note that the input to the network is a 3D volumetric representation of the input RGB-D images, which is obtained using the Truncated Signed Distance Function (TSDF) [Song and Xiao, 2016]. This first representation is

processed using three processing blocks, each consisting of a 3D convolution layer, a 3D pooling layer, and a ReLU nonlinearity. The output is an intermediate "spatial feature" representation corresponding to a grid of 3D spatial locations in the input. It is further processed by two fully connected layers to obtain a "global feature" which is used to predict the scene category. Note that both the local spatial feature and the global scene-level feature is later used in the 3D context network.

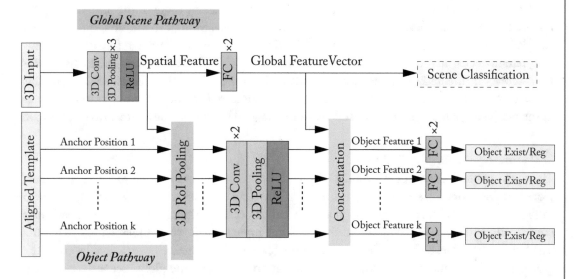

Figure 7.11: Deep 3D Context network (Module D, Fig. 7.10) architecture. The network consists of two channels for global scene-level recognition and local object-level detection. The scene pathway is supervised with the scene classification task during pre-training only (Module B). The object pathway performs object detection, i.e., predicts the existence/non-existence of an object and regresses its location. Note that the object pathway brings in both local and global features from the scene pathway.

3D Transformation Network (Module C, Fig. 7.10)

Once the corresponding scene template category has been identified, a 3D transformation network estimates a global transformation which aligns the input scene to the corresponding scene-template. The transformation is calculated in two steps: a rotation followed by a translation. Both these transformation steps are implemented individually as classification problems, for which CNNs are well suited.

For the **rotation**, only the rotation about the vertical-axis (yaw) is predicted since the gravity direction is known for each scene in the SUN RGB-D dataset. Since an exact estimation of the rotation along the vertical axis is not required, the 360° angular range is divided into 36 regions, each encompassing 10°. A 3D CNN is trained to predict the angle of rotation along the vertical axis. The CNN has the same architecture as the one used in Module B (scene classification), however, its output layer has 36 units which predicts one of the 36 regions denoting the y-axis rotation.

Once the rotation has been applied, another 3D CNN is used to estimate the **translation** that is required to align the major object (e.g., bed, desk) in the input scene and the identified scene template. Again, the CNN has essentially the same architecture as Module B, however, the last layer is replaced by a soft-max layer with 726 units. Each value of the output units denotes a translation in a discretized space of $11 \times 11 \times 6$ values. Similar to rotation, the estimated translation is also a rough match due to the discretized set of values. Note that for such problems (i.e., parameter estimation), regression is a natural choice since it avoids errors due to discretization. However, the authors could not successfully train a CNN with a regression loss for this problem. Since the context network regresses the locations of each detected object in the scenes in the next stage, a rough alignment suffices at this stage. We explain the context network below.

3D Context Network (Fig. 7.11)

The context neural network performs 3D object detection and layout estimation. A separate network is trained for each scene template category. This network has two main branches, as shown in Fig. 7.11: a global scene level branch and a local object level branch. Both network pathways encode different levels of details about the 3D scene input, which are complementary in nature. The local object-level branch is dependent on the features from the initial and final layers of the global scene-level branch. To avoid any optimization problems, the global scene-level branch is initialized with the weights of the converged scene classification network (Module B) (since both have the same architecture). Each category-specific context network is then trained separately using only the data from that specific scene template. During this training procedure, the scene-level branch is fine-tuned while the object-level branch is trained from scratch.

The object-level branch operates on the spatial feature from the global scene-level branch. The spatial feature is the output activation map after the initial set of three processing layers, each consisting of a 3D convolution, pooling, and ReLU layers. This feature map is used to calculate object-level features (corresponding to anchor positions) at a $6 \times 6 \times 6$ resolution using the 3D Region of Interest (RoI) pooling. The 3D RoI pooling is identical to its 2D counterpart described in Section 4.2.7, with only an extra depth dimension. The pooled feature is then processed through 3D convolution and fully connected layers to predict the object existence and its location (3D bounding box). The object location is regressed using the R-CNN localization loss to minimize the offset between the ground-truth and the predicted bounding boxes (Section 7.2.1).

Hybrid Data for Pre-training

Due to the lack of huge amount of RGB-D training data for scene understanding, this approach uses an augmented dataset for training. In contrast to the simple data augmentation approaches we discussed in Section 5.2.1, the proposed approach is more involved. Specifically, a hybrid training set is generated by replacing the annotated objects from the SUN RGB-D dataset with the same category CAD models. The resulting hybrid set is 1,000 times bigger than the original RGBD training set. For the training of 3D context network (scene pathway), the models are trained on this large hybrid dataset first, followed by a fine-tuning on the real RGB-D depth maps to ensure that the training converges. For the alignment network, the pre-trained scene pathway from the 3D context network is used for the initialization. Therefore, the alignment network also benefits from the hybrid data.

The DeepContext model has been evaluated on the SUN RGB-D dataset and has been shown to model scene contexts adequately.

7.4.2   LEARNING RICH FEATURES FROM RGB-D IMAGES

The object and scene level reasoning system presented in the previous section was trained end-to-end on 3D images. Here, we present an RGB-D- (2.5D instead of 3D) based approach [Gupta et al., 2014] which performs object detection, object instance segmentation, and semantic segmentation, as shown in Fig. 7.12. This approach is not end-to-end trainable, it rather extends the pre-trained CNN on color images to depth images by introducing a new depth encoding method. This framework is interesting, since it demonstrates how pre-trained networks can be effectively used to transfer learning from domains where large quantities of data is available to the ones where labeled data is scarce, and even for new data modalities (e.g., depth in this case). In the following sections, we briefly discuss the processing pipeline (summarized in Fig. 7.12).

Encoding Depth Images for Feature Learning
Instead of directly training a CNN on the depth images, Gupta et al. [2014] propose to encode the depth information using three geometric features calculated at each pixel location. These include: the horizontal disparity, the height above the ground, and the angle between the surface normals at a given pixel and the estimated gravity direction. This encoding is termed as the HHA encoding (first letter of each geometric feature). For the training dataset, all these channels are mapped to a constant range of 0–255.

The HHA encoding and color images are then fed to the deep network to learn more discriminative feature representations on top of the geometric features based on raw depth information. Since the NYU-Depth dataset used in this work, consisted of only 400 images, an explicit encoding of the geometric properties of the data made a big difference to the network, which usually requires much larger amounts of data to automatically learn the best feature representations. Furthermore, the training dataset was extended by rendering synthetic CAD models in the NYU-Depth dataset scenes. This is consistent with the data augmentation approach that we discussed for the case of DeepContext [Zhang et al., 2016].

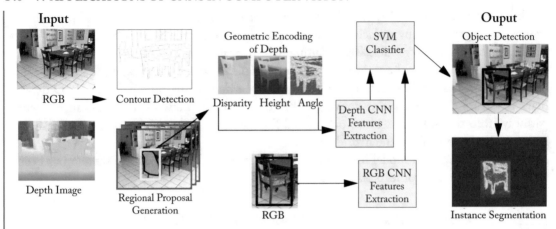

Figure 7.12: The input to this framework is a RGB and a depth image. First, object proposals are generated using the contour information. The color and the encoded depth image are passed through separately trained CNNs to obtain features which are then classified into object categories using the SVM classifiers. After detection, a Random Forest classifier is used to identify foreground object segmentation within each valid detection.

CNN Fine-tuning for Feature Learning

Since the main goal of this work is object detection, it is useful to work on the object proposals. The region proposals are obtained using an improved version of Multiscale Combinatorial Grouping (MCG) [Arbeláez et al., 2014] approach which incorporated additional geometric features based on the depth information. The regions proposals which have a high overlap with the ground-truth object bounding box are first used to train a deep CNN model for classification. Similar to R-CNN, the pre-trained AlexNet [Krizhevsky et al., 2012] is fine-tuned for this object classification task. Once the network is fine-tuned, object specific linear classifiers (SVMs) are trained using the intermediate CNN features for the object detection task.

Instance Segmentation

Once the object detections are available, the pixels belonging to each object instance are labeled. This problem is tackled by predicting the *foreground* or *background* label for each pixel within a valid detection. For this purpose, a random forest classifier is used to provide the pixel level labelings. This classifier is trained on the local hand-crafted features whose details are available in Gupta et al. [2013]. Since these predictions are calculated roughly for individual pixels, they can be noisy. To smooth the initial predictions of the random forest classifier, these predictions are averaged on each super-pixel. Note that subsequent works on instance segmentation (e.g., He et al. [2017]) have incorporated a similar pipeline (i.e., first detecting object bounding boxes and then predicting the foreground mask to label the individual object instance). However, in contrast to Gupta et al. [2014], He et al. [2017] use an end to end trainable CNN model which avoids manual parameter selection and a series of isolated processing steps toward the final goal. As a result, He et al. [2017] achieve highly accurate segmentations compared to the non-end-to-end trainable approaches.

Another limitation of this approach is the separate processing of both color and depth images. As we discussed in Chapter 6, AlexNet has a huge number of parameters, and learning two separate set of parameters for both modalities doubles the parameter space. Moreover, since both images belong to the same scene, we expect to learn better cross-modality relationships if both modalities are considered jointly. One approach to learn a shared set of parameters in such cases is to stack the two modalities in the form of a multichannel input (e.g., six channels) and perform a joint training over both modalities [Khan et al., 2017c, Zagoruyko and Komodakis, 2015].

7.4.3 POINTNET FOR SCENE UNDERSTANDING

PointNet (discussed in Section 7.1.1) has also been used for scene understanding by assigning a semantically meaningful category label to each pixel in an image (Module B in Figure 7.1). While we have discussed the details of PointNet before, it is interesting to note its similarity with the Context Network in DeepContext (Section 7.4.1 and Figure 7.11). Both these networks learn an initial representation, shared among the global (scene classification) and the local (semantic segmentation or object detection) tasks. Afterward, the global and local branches split up, and the scene context is added in the local branch by copying the high-level features from the global branch to the local one. One can notice that the incorporation of both the global and local contexts are essential for a successful semantic labeling scheme. Other recent works in scene segmentation are also built on similar ideas, i.e., better integration of scene context using for example a pyramid-based feature description [Zhao et al., 2017], dilated convolutions [Yu and Koltun, 2015], or a CRF model [Khan et al., 2016a, Zheng et al., 2015].

7.5 IMAGE GENERATION

Recent advances in image modeling with neural networks, such as Generative Adversarial Networks (GANs) [Goodfellow et al., 2014], have made it feasible to generate photo-realistic images, which can capture the high-level structure of the natural training data [van den Oord et al., 2016]. GANs are one type of generative networks, which can learn to produce realistic-looking images in an unsupervised manner. In recent years, a number of GAN-based image generation methods have emerged which work quite well. One such promising approach is Deep Convolutional Generative Adversarial Networks (DCGANs) [Radford et al., 2015], which generates photo-realistic images by passing random noise through a deep convolutional network. Another interesting approach is Super-Resolution Generative Adversarial Networks (SRGAN) [Ledig et al., 2016], which generates high-resolution images from low-resolution counterparts. In this section, we shall first briefly discuss GANs and then extend our discussion to DCGANs and SRGAN.

7.5.1   GENERATIVE ADVERSARIAL NETWORKS (GANS)

GANs were first introduced by Goodfellow et al. [2014]. The main idea behind a GAN is to have two competing neural network models (shown in Fig. 7.13). The first model is called *generator*, which takes noise as input and generates samples. The other neural network, called *discriminator*, receives samples from both the generator (i.e., fake data) and the training data (i.e., real data), and discriminates between the two sources. These two networks undergo a continuous learning process, where the generator learns to produce more realistic samples, and the discriminator learns to get better at distinguishing generated data from real data. These two networks are trained simultaneously with the aim that this training will drive the generated samples to be indistinguishable from real data. One of the advantages of GANs is that they can back-propagate the gradient information from the discriminator back to the generator network. The generator, therefore, knows how to adapt its parameters in order to produce output data that can fool the discriminator.

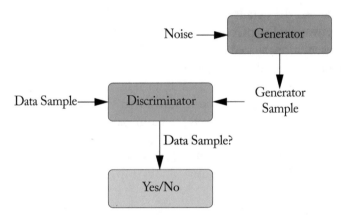

Figure 7.13: Generative Adversarial Networks Overview. Generator takes the noise as an input and generates samples. The discriminator distinguishes between the generator samples and the training data.

GANs Taining

The training of GANs involves the computation of two loss functions, one for the generator and one for the discriminator. The loss function for the generator ensures that it produces better data samples, while the loss function for the discriminator ensures that it distinguishes between the generated and real samples. We now briefly discuss these loss functions. For more details, the readers are referred to Goodfellow [2016].

Discriminator Loss Function

The discriminator's loss function $J^{(D)}$ is represented by:

$$J^{(D)}(\theta^{(D)}, \theta^{(G)}) = -\frac{1}{2}\mathbb{E}_{x \sim p_{data}}[\log D(x)] - \frac{1}{2}\mathbb{E}_{z \sim p_{(z)}}[\log(1 - D(G(z)))], \qquad (7.5)$$

which is the cross entropy loss function. In this equation, $\theta^{(D)}$ and $\theta^{(G)}$ are the parameters of the discriminator and the generator networks, respectively. p_{data} denotes the distribution of real data, x is a sample from p_{data}, $p_{(z)}$ is the distribution of the generator, z is a sample from $p_{(z)}$, $G(z)$ is the generator network and D is the discriminator network. One can note from Eq. (7.5) that the discriminator is trained as a binary classifier (with sigmoid output) on two mini-batches of data. One of the them is from the data set containing real data samples with label 1 assigned to all examples, and the other from the generator (i.e., fake data) with label 0 for all the examples.

> **Cross-entropy:** The cross-entropy loss function for the binary classification task is defined as follows:
>
> $$H((x_1, y_1), D) = -y_1 \log D(x_1) - (1 - y_1) \log(1 - D(x_1)), \qquad (7.6)$$
>
> where x_1 and $y_1 \in [-1 \ \ 1]$ denote a sample from a probability distribution function D and its desired output, respectively. After summing over m data samples, Eq. (7.5) can be written as follows:
>
> $$H((x_i, y_i)_{i=1}^{m}, D) = -\sum_{i=1}^{m} y_i \log D(x_i) - \sum_{i=1}^{m}(1 - y_i) \log(1 - D(x_i)).$$
>
> $$(7.7)$$
>
> In the case of GANs, data samples come from two sources, the discriminator's distribution $x_i \sim p_{data}$ or the generator's distribution $x_i = G(z)$, where $z \sim p_{(z)}$. Let's assume that the number of samples from both distributions is equal. By writing Eq. (7.7) probabilistically, i.e., replacing the sums with expectations, the label y_i with $\frac{1}{2}$ (because the number of samples from both generator and discriminator distributions is equal), and the $\log(1 - D(x_i))$ with $\log(1 - D(G(z)))$, we get the same loss function as Eq. (7.5), for the discriminator.

Generator Loss Function

The discriminator, discussed above, distinguishes between the two classes, i.e., the real and the fake data, and therefore needs the cross entropy function, which is the best option for such tasks. However, in the case of the generator, the following three types of loss functions can be used.

- **The minimax Loss function:** The minimax loss[10] is the simplest version of the loss function, which is represented as follows:

$$J^{(G)} = -J^{(D)} = \frac{1}{2}\mathbb{E}_{x \sim p_{data}}[\log D(x)] + \frac{1}{2}\mathbb{E}_{z \sim p_{(z)}}[\log(1 - D(G(z)))]. \qquad (7.8)$$

The minimax version has been found to be less useful due to the gradient saturation problem. The latter occurs due to the poor design of the generator's loss function. Specifically, as shown in Fig. 7.14, when the generator samples are successfully rejected by the discriminator with high confidence[11] (i.e., $D(G(z))$ is close to zero), the generator's gradient vanishes and thus, the generator's network cannot learn anything.

- **Heuristic, non-saturation loss function:** The heuristic version is represented as follows:

$$J^{(G)} = -\frac{1}{2}\mathbb{E}_z[\log D(G(z))]. \qquad (7.9)$$

This version of the loss function is based on the concept that the gradient of the generator is only dependent on the second term in Eq. (7.5). Therefore, as opposed to the minimax function, where the signs of $J^{(D)}$ are changed, in this case the target is changed, i.e., $\log D(G(z))$ is used instead of $\log(1 - D(G(z)))$. The advantage of this strategy is that the generator gets a strong gradient signal at the start of the training process (as shown in Fig. 7.14), which helps it in attaining a fast improvement to generate better data, e.g., images.

- **Maximum Likelihood loss function:** As the name indicates, this version of the loss function is motivated by the concept of maximum likelihood (a well-known approach in machine learning) and can be written as follows:

$$J^{(G)} = -\frac{1}{2}\mathbb{E}_z[\exp(\sigma^{-1}(D(G(z))))], \qquad (7.10)$$

where σ is the logistic sigmoid function. Like the minimax loss function, the maximum likelihood loss also suffers from the gradient vanishing problem when $D(G(z))$ is close to zero, as shown in Fig. 7.14. Moreover, unlike the minimax and the heuristic loss functions, the maximum likelihood loss, as a function of $D(G(z))$, has a very high variance, which is problematic. This is because most of the gradient comes from a very small number of the generator's samples that are most likely to be real rather than fake.

---

[10]In the minimax game, there are two players (e.g., generator and discriminator) and in all states the reward of player 1 is the negative of reward of player 2. Specifically, the discriminator minimizes a cross-entropy, but the generator maximizes the same cross-entropy.

[11]At the start of the training, the generator likely produces random samples, which are quite different from the real samples, so the discriminator can easily classify the real and fake samples.

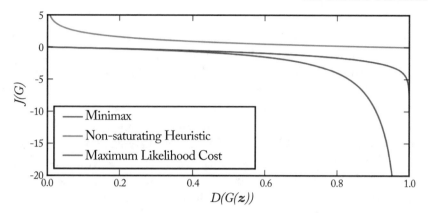

Figure 7.14: The loss response curves as functions of $D(G(z))$ for three different variants of the GAN generator's loss functions.

To summarize, one can note that all three generator loss functions do not depend on the real data (x in Eq. (7.5)). This is advantageous, because the generator cannot copy input data x, which helps in avoiding the over-fitting problem in the generator. With this brief overview of generative adversarial models and their loss functions, we will now summarize the different steps that are involved in GANs training.

1. sampling a mini-batch of m samples from the real dataset p_{data};

2. sampling a mini-batch of m samples from the generator $p_{(z)}$ (i.e., fake samples);

3. learning the discriminator by minimizing its loss function in Eq. (7.5);

4. sampling a mini-batch of m samples from the generator $p_{(z)}$ (i.e., fake sample); and

5. learning the generator by minimizing its loss function in Eq. (7.9).

These steps are repeated until convergence occurs or until the iteration is terminated. With this brief overview of generative adversarial networks, we will now discuss two representative applications of GANs, known as DCGANs [Radford et al., 2015] and SRGAN [Ledig et al., 2016].

7.5.2 DEEP CONVOLUTIONAL GENERATIVE ADVERSARIAL NETWORKS (DCGANS)

DCGANs [Radford et al., 2015] are the first GAN models, which can generate realistic images from random input samples. In the following, we shall discuss the architecture and the training of DCGANs.

Architecture of DCGANs

DCGANs provide a family of CNN architectures, which can be used in the generator and the discriminator parts of GANs. The overall architecture is the same as the baseline GAN architecture, which is shown in Fig. 7.13. However, the architecture of both the generator (shown in Fig. 7.15) and the discriminator (shown in Fig. 7.16) is borrowed from the all-convolutional network [Springenberg, 2015], meaning that these models do not contain any pooling or un-pooling layers. In addition, the generator uses transposed convolution to increase the representation's spatial size, as illustrated in Fig. 7.15. Unlike the generator, the discriminator uses convolution to squeeze the representation's spatial size for the classification task (Fig. 7.16). For both networks, a stride greater than 1 (usually 2) is used in the convolutional and transposed convolutional layers. Batch normalization is used in all layers of both the discriminator and the generator models of DCGANs with the exception of the first layer of the discriminator and the last layer of the generator. This is done to ensure that DGCAN learns the correct scale of the data distribution and its mean. DCGANs use the ReLU activation in all transposed convolutional layers except the output layer, which uses tanh activation function. It is because a bounded activation function such as tanh, allows the generator to speed-up the learning process and cover the color space of the samples from the training distribution. For the discriminator model, leaky ReLU (discussed in Section 4.2.4) was found to be better than ReLU. DCGANs use the Adam optimizer (discussed in Section 5.4.6) rather than SGD with momentum.

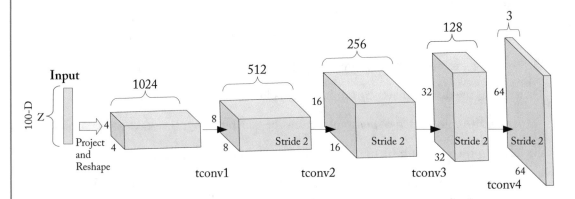

Figure 7.15: Example DCGAN generator's architecture for Large-scale Scene Understanding (LSUN) dataset [Song and Xiao, 2015]. A 100-dimensional uniform distribution z is projected and then reshaped to a $4 \times 4 \times 1,024$ tensor, where 1,024 is the number of feature maps. Next, the tensor is passed through a sequence of transposed convolutional layers (i.e., *tconv*1 − *tconv*2 − *tconv*3 − *tconv*4) to generate a $64 \times 64 \times 3$ realistic image.

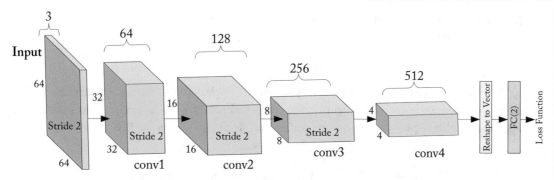

Figure 7.16: Example DCGAN discriminator's architecture for LSUN dataset [Song and Xiao, 2015]. An 64 × 64 RGB input image is passed through a sequence of convolutional layers (i.e., *conv*1 − *conv*2 − *conv*3 − *conv*4) followed by a fully-connected layer with 2 outputs.

DCGANs as a Feature Extractor

DCGANs uses ImageNet as a dataset of natural images for unsupervised training to evaluate the quality of the features learned by DCGAN. For this purpose, DCGANs is first trained on ImageNet dataset. Note that the image labels are not required during training (unsupervised learning). Also, it is important to note that all the training and test images are scaled to the range of [-1, 1], i.e., the range of tanh activation function. No other pre-processing is done. Then, for each training image in a supervised dataset (e.g., CIFAR-10 dataset), the output feature maps from all the convolutional layers of the discriminator are max-pooled to produce a 4 × 4 spatial grid for each layer. These spatial grids are then flattened and concatenated to form a high dimensional feature representation of the image. Finally, an ℓ_2 regularized linear SVM is trained on the high dimensional feature representation of all the training images in the supervised dataset. It is interesting to note that although DCGAN is not trained on the supervised dataset, it outperforms all K-means-based methods. DCGANs can also be used for image generation. For example, experiments show that the output of the last layer in the generator network of DCGAN trained on LSUN dataset [Song and Xiao, 2015] produces really cool bedroom images.

7.5.3   SUPER RESOLUTION GENERATIVE ADVERSARIAL NETWORK (SRGAN)

In Ledig et al. [2016], a generative adversarial network for single SRGAN is presented, where the input to the network is a low-resolution (LR) image and the output is its high-resolution (HR) counterpart. Unlike existing optimization-based super resolution techniques, which rely on the minimization of the Mean Squared Error (MSE) as loss function, this technique proposes the perceptual loss function for the generator. The latter is comprised of two losses which are called "content loss" and "adversarial loss." In the following, we will briefly discuss these loss functions, followed by the architecture of SRGAN.

Content Loss

The MSE loss function smooths images by suppressing the high-frequency contents, which results in perceptually unsatisfied solutions [Ledig et al., 2016]. To overcome this problem, a content loss function that is motivated by perceptual similarity is used in SRGAN:

$$l_{Con}^{SR} = \frac{1}{WH} \sum_{x=1}^{W} \sum_{y=1}^{H} (\phi(I^{HR})_{x,y} - \phi(G_{\theta_G}(I^{LR}))_{x,y})^2, \tag{7.11}$$

where I^{LR} and I^{HR} are the LR and HR images, $\phi(\cdot)$ is the output feature map produced by a convolutional layer of VGGnet-19, W and H are the width and the height of the feature map, respectively. In summary, Eq. (7.11) computes the Euclidean distance between the output feature maps (i.e., the output of a convolutional layer of the pre-trained VGGnet-19) of the generated image ($G_{\theta_G}(I^{LR})$) and the real high resolution image I^{HR}. Note that the pre-trained VGGnet-19 is only used as a feature extractor (i.e., its weight parameters are not changed during the training of SRGAN).

Adversarial Loss

The adversarial loss is the same as the heuristic loss function in the baseline GAN (Eq. (7.9)), and is defined as follows:

$$l_{Adv}^{SR} = -\log D_{\theta_D}(G_{\theta_G}(I^{LR})), \tag{7.12}$$

where $D_{\theta_D}(G_{\theta_G}(I^{LR}))$ is the probability that the image produced by the generator, $G_{\theta_G}(I^{LR})$, is a HR image (i.e., real image).

Perceptual Loss Function as the Generator Loss

The perceptual loss function, which is used as the generator loss in SRGAN, is calculated as the weighted sum of the content loss and the adversarial loss, discussed above and is given by:

$$l^{SR} = l_{Con/i,j}^{SR} + 10^{-3} l_{Adv}^{SR}, \tag{7.13}$$

where $l_{Con/i,j}^{SR}$ represents the content loss, while l_{Gen}^{SR} is the adversarial loss.

Discriminator Loss

The discriminator loss is the cross-entropy loss function (Eq. (7.5)), which is trained as a binary classifier (HR or LR class) with a sigmoid output.

SRGAN Architecture

Similar to the baseline GAN [Goodfellow et al., 2014], SRGAN has two key components: the discriminator and the generator. We will now briefly discuss the architecture of these two SRGAN components.

Discriminator Network of SRGAN

The discriminator network of SRGAN, shown in Fig. 7.17, is inspired by the architecture of DCGAN (discussed in Section 7.5.2). The network consists of eight convolutional layers with 3×3 convolution kernels followed by two fully connected layers, and a sigmoid function to perform binary classification.

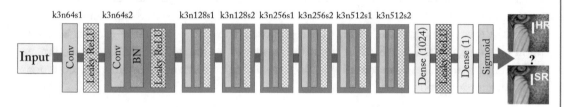

Figure 7.17: Architecture of the discriminator network of SRGAN. k, n, and s represent the kernel size, number of feature maps, and stride for each convolutional layer.

Generator Network of SRGAN

The generator component of the SRGAN, shown in Fig. 7.18, is inspired by the deep residual network (discussed in Section 6.6) and the architecture of DCGAN (discussed in Section 7.5.2). As suggested by DCGAN [Radford et al., 2015], a leaky ReLU activation function is used in all layers. Moreover, batch normalization is used after all convolutional layers with the exception of the first convolutional layer.

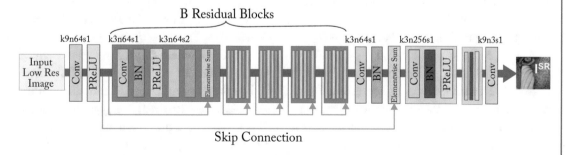

Figure 7.18: Architecture of the generator network of SRGAN. Similar to the discriminator network, k, n, and s represent the kernel size, number of feature maps, and stride for each convolutional layer.

In summary, SRGAN is able to estimate high resolution images with photo-realistic textures from heavily down-sampled images. It achieved a very good performance on three publicly available datasets including Set5, Set14, and BSD100.

7.6   VIDEO-BASED ACTION RECOGNITION

Human action recognition in videos is a challenging research problem, which has received a significant amount of attention in the computer vision community [Donahue et al., 2015, Karpathy et al., 2014, Rahmani and Bennamoun, 2017, Rahmani and Mian, 2016, Rahmani et al., 2017, Simonyan and Zisserman, 2014a]. Action recognition aims to enable computers to automatically recognize human actions from real world videos. Compared to the single-image classification, the temporal extent of action videos provides an additional information for action recognition. Inspired by this, several approaches have been proposed to extend state-of-the-art image classification CNNs (e.g., VGGnet, ResNet) for action recognition from video data. In this section, we shall briefly discuss three representative CNN-based architectures used for video-based human action recognition task.

7.6.1   ACTION RECOGNITION FROM STILL VIDEO FRAMES

CNNs have so far achieved promising image recognition results. Inspired by this, an extensive evaluation of CNNs for extending the connectivity of a CNN to the temporal domain for the task of large-scale action recognition is provided in Karpathy et al. [2014]. We shall now discuss different architectures for encoding temporal variations of action videos.

Single Frame Architecture

We discuss a single-frame baseline architecture, shown in Fig. 7.19a, to analyze the contribution of the static appearance to the classification accuracy. The single frame model is similar to the AlexNet [Krizhevsky et al., 2012], which won the ImageNet challenge. However, instead of accepting the original input of size $224 \times 224 \times 3$, the network takes $170 \times 170 \times 3$ sized image. This network has the following configuration: $Covn(96, 11, 3) - N - P - Conv(256, 5, 1) - N - P - Conv(384, 3, 1) - Conv(384, 3, 1) - Conv(256, 3, 1) - P - FC(4096) - FC(4096)$, where $Conv(f, s, t)$ represents a convolutional layer, which has filters f of spatial size $s \times s$ and an input stride t. A fully connected layer, with n nodes, is represented by $FC(n)$. For the pooling layers P and all the normalization layers N the architectural details described in Krizhevsky et al. [2012] are used along with the following parameters: $k = 2; n = 5; \alpha = 10^{-4}; \beta = 0.5$, where the constants k, n, α, and β are hyper-parameters. A softmax layer is connected to the last fully connected layer with dense connections.

Given an entire action video, the video-level prediction is produced by forward propagating each frame individually through the network and then averaging individual frame predictions over the durations of the video.

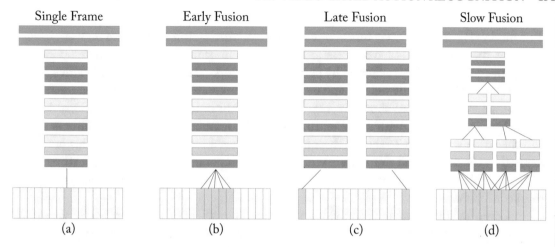

Figure 7.19: Approaches for fusing information over the temporal dimension through the network. (a) Single Frame, (b) Early Fusion, (c) Late Fusion, and (d) Slow Fusion. In the Slow Fusion Model (d), the depicted columns share parameters. The pink, green, and blue boxes denote convolutional, normalization and pooling layers, respectively.

Early Fusion Architecture

We now discuss the Early Fusion model (Fig. 7.19b). This model captures an entire time window information and combines it across at a pixel level. To achieve this, the filters on the first *Conv* layer in the single frame network (described above) are modified. The new filters have a size of $11 \times 11 \times 3 \times T$ pixels, where T defines the temporal extent and is set to 10. This direct and early connectivity to the pixel data helps this model to accurately detect the speed and the direction of the local motion.

For a given entire video, 20 randomly selected sample clips are individually passed through the network and their class predictions are then averaged to produce video-level action class prediction.

Late Fusion Architecture

The late fusion model (Fig. 7.19c) consists of two separate single frame networks (described above) with shared parameters up to the last *Conv* layer, *Conv*(256, 3, 1). The outputs of the last *Conv* layer of these two separate single frame networks are then merged in the first fully connected layer. Global motion characteristics are computed by the first fully connected layer by comparing the output of both single-frame networks. These two separate single frame networks are placed at a distance of 15 frames apart. More precisely, the input to the first and the second single frame networks is the i-th frame and $i + 15$-th frame, respectively.

Slow Fusion Architecture

This model (Fig. 7.19d) slowly fuses the temporal information throughout the network in such way that the higher layers have access to more global information in both the temporal and the spatial domains. This is achieved by performing a temporal convolution along with a spatial convolution to calculate the weights and by extending the connectivity of all convolutional layers in time. More precisely, as shown in Fig. 7.19d, every filter in the first convolutional layer is applied on an input clip, with a size of 10 frames. The temporal extent of each filter is $T = 4$ and the stride is equal to 2. Thus, 4 responses are produced for each video clip. This process is iterated by the second and third layers with filters of temporal extent $T = 2$ and a stride equal to 2. Therefore, the information across all the input frames (a total of 10) can be accessed by the third convolutional layer.

Given an entire human action video, video-level classification is performed by passing 20 randomly selected sample clips through the network and then averaging individual clip predictions over the durations of the video.

Multi-resolution Architecture

In order to speed-up the above mentioned models while retaining their accuracy, the multi-resolution architecture has been proposed in Karpathy et al. [2014]. The multi-resolution model consists of two separate networks (i.e., fovea and context networks) over two spatial resolutions, as shown in Fig 7.20. The architecture of the fovea and context networks is similar to the single-frame architecture discussed above. However, instead of accepting the original input of size 170 × 170 × 3, these networks take 89 × 89 × 3 sized images. More precisely, the input to the fovea model is the center region of size 89 × 89 at the original spatial resolution, while for the context stream the down-sampled frames at half the original resolution are used. The total dimensionality of the inputs is therefore halved. Moreover, the last pooling layer is removed from both the fovea and context networks and the activation outputs of both networks are concatenated and fed into the first fully connected layer.

Model Comparison

All models were trained on the Sport-1M dataset [Simonyan and Zisserman, 2014a], which consists of 200,000 test videos. The results showed that the variation among different CNN architectures (e.g., Single Frame, Multi-resolution, Early, Late, and Slow Fusion) is surprisingly insignificant. Moreover, the results were significantly worse than the state-of-the-art hand-crafted shallow models. One reason is that these models cannot capture the motion information in many cases. For example, the Slow Fusion model is expected to implicitly learn the spatio-temporal features in its first layers, which is a difficult task [Simonyan and Zisserman, 2014a]. To resolve this issue, two-stream CNNs [Simonyan and Zisserman, 2014a] model was proposed to explicitly take into account both spatial and temporal information in a single end-to-end learning framework.

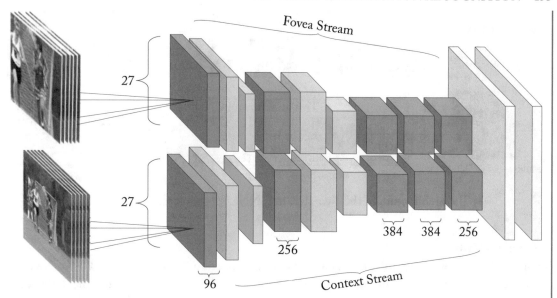

Figure 7.20: Multi-resolution architecture. Input frames are passed through two separate streams: a context stream which models the low-resolution image and a fovea stream which processes the high-resolution center crop image. The pink, green, and blue boxes denote convolutional, normalization, and pooling layers, respectively. Both streams converge to two fully connected layers (yellow boxes).

7.6.2   TWO-STREAM CNNS

The two-stream CNNs model [Simonyan and Zisserman, 2014a] (shown in Fig. 7.21) uses two separate spatial and temporal CNNs, which are then combined by late fusion. The spatial network performs action recognition from single video frames, while the temporal network is learned to recognize action from motion, i.e., dense optical flow. The idea behind this two-stream model is related to the fact that the human visual cortex contains two pathways for object and motion recognition, i.e., the ventral stream performs object recognition and the dorsal stream recognizes motion.

Spatial Stream CNN

The spatial stream CNN model is similar to the single frame model in Section 7.6.1. Given an action video, each video frame is individually passed through the spatial model shown in Fig. 7.21 and an action label is assigned to each frame. Note that the label of all frames belonging to a given action video is the same as the label of the action video.

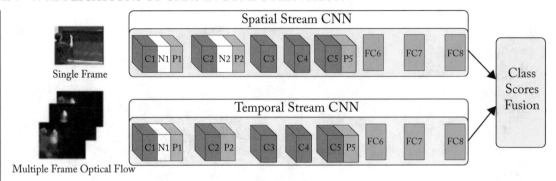

Figure 7.21: The architecture of the two-stream CNNs for action classification.

Temporal Stream CNN

Unlike the motion-aware CNN models introduced in Section 7.6.1 (e.g., Slow Fusion), which use stacked single video frames as input, temporal stream CNN takes stacked optical flow displacement fields between several consecutive frames as input to explicitly learn the temporal feature. In the following, three variations of the optical flow-based input are explained.

- **Optical flow stacking:** The input of the temporal stream CNN is formed by stacking the dense optical flow of L consecutive frames (shown in Fig. 7.22). The optical flow at point (u, v) in frame t is a 2D displacement vector (i.e., horizontal and vertical displacement), which moves the point to the corresponding point in the next frame $t + 1$. Note that the horizontal and vertical components of the dense optical flow of a frame can be seen as image channels. Thus, the stacked dense optical flow of L consecutive frames forms an input image of $2L$ channels, which are fed to the temporal stream CNN as input.

- **Trajectory stacking:** Unlike the optical flow stacking method which samples the displacement vectors at the same location in L consecutive frames, the trajectory stacking method represents motion in an input image of $2L$ channels by sampling L 2D points along the motion trajectories [Wang et al., 2011a], as shown in Fig. 7.22.

- **Bi-directional optical flow stacking:** Both optical flow and trajectory stacking methods operate on the forward optical flow. The bi-directional optical flow stacking method extends these methods by computing both forward and backward displacement optical flow fields. More precisely, motion information is encoded in an input image of $2L$ channels by stacking $\frac{L}{2}$ forward optical flows between frames t and $t + \frac{L}{2}$ and $\frac{L}{2}$ backward optical flows between frames $t - \frac{L}{2}$ and t.

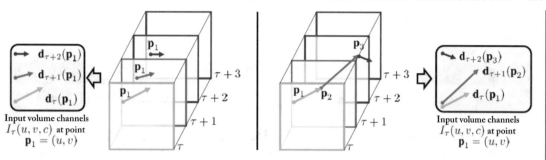

Figure 7.22: *Left:* optical flow stacking method; *right:* trajectory stacking method.

Architecture

The architecture of the two-stream CNNs model is shown in Fig. 7.21. The architecture of the spatial and temporal CNN models is similar, except that the second normalization layer is removed from the temporal CNN to reduce memory consumption. As shown in this figure, a class score fusion is added to the end of the model to combine the softmax scores of both the spatial and temporal models by late fusion. Different approaches can be used for class score fusion. However, experimental results showed that training a linear SVM classifier on stacked ℓ_2-normalized softmax scores outperforms simple averaging.

7.6.3   LONG-TERM RECURRENT CONVOLUTIONAL NETWORK (LRCN)

Unlike the methods in Section 7.6.1 and Section 7.6.2 which learn CNN filters based on a stack of a fixed number of input frames, Long-term Recurrent Convolutional Network (LRCN) [Donahue et al., 2015] is not constrained to fixed length input frames and, thus, could learn to recognize more complex action video. As shown in Fig. 7.23, in LRCN, individual video frames are first passed through CNN models with shared parameters and then connected to a single-layer LSTM network (described in Chapter 3). More precisely, the LRCN model combines a deep hierarchical visual feature extractor, which is a CNN feature extractor, with an LSTM that can learn to recognize the temporal variations in an end-to-end fashion.

In this chapter, we discussed representative works, which use CNNs in computer vision. In Table 7.1, we provide an overview of some of the other important CNN applications and the most representative recent works, which have not been covered in detail in this book. In the following chapter, we will discuss some prominent tools and libraries of CNN.

Table 7.1: Few recent/most representative applications of CNN, not discussed in this book (*Continues.*)

Applications	Paper Title
Image captioning	• Deep Visual-Semantic Alignments for Generating Image Descriptions [Karpathy and Fei-Fei, 2015] • DenseCap: Fully Convolutional Localization Networks for Dense Captioning [Johnson et al., 2016]
3D reconstruction from a 2D image	• Large Pose 3D Face Reconstruction from a Single Image via Direct Volumetric CNN Regression [Jackson et al., 2017] • Semantic Scene Completion from a Single Depth Image [Song et al. 2017]
Contour/ edge detection	• DeepContour: A Deep Convolutional Feature Learned by Positive Sharing Loss for Contour Detection [Shen et al., 2015b] • Edge Detection Using Convolutional Neural Network [Wang, 2016]
Text detection and recognition	• Reading Text in the Wild with Convolutional Neural Networks [Jaderberg et al., 2016] • End-to-End Text Recognition with Convolutional Neural Networks [Wang et al., 2012]
Octree representation for shape analysis	• O-CNN: Octree-based Convolutional Neural Networks for 3D Shape Analysis [Wang et al., 2017] • OctNet: Learning Deep 3D Representations at High Resolutions [Riegler et al., 2016]
Face recognition	• DeepFace: Closing the Gap to Human-Level Performance in Face Verification [Taigman et al., 2014] • FaceNet: A Unified Embedding for Face Recognition and Clustering [Schroff et al., 2015]
Depth estimation	• Learning Depth from Single Monocular Images Using Deep Convolutional Neural Fields [Liu et al., 2016] • Deep Convolutional Neural Fields for Depth Estimation from a Single Image [Liu et al., 2015]
Pose estimation	• PoseNet: A Convolutional Network for Real-Time 6-DOF Camera Relocalization [Kendall et al., 2015] • DeepPose: Human Pose Estimation via Deep Neural Networks [Toshev and Szegedy, 2014]

Table 7.1: (*Continued.*) Few recent/most representative applications of CNN, not discussed in this book

Tracking	• Hedged Deep Tracking [Qi et al., 2016b] • Hierarchical Convolutional Features for Visual Tracking [Ma et al., 2015]
Shadow detection	• Automatic Shadow Detection and Removal from a Single Image [Khan et al., 2016a] • Shadow Optimization from Structured Deep Edge Detection [Shen et al., 2015a]
Video summarization	• Highlight Detection with Pairwise Deep Ranking for First-Person Video Summarization [Yao et al., 2016] • Large-Scale Video Summarization Using Web-Image Priors [Khosla et al., 2013]
Visual question answering	• Multi-level Attention Networks for Visual Question Answering [Yu et al., 2017] • Image Captioning and Visual Question Answering Based on Attributes and External Knowledge [Wu et al., 2017]
Event detection	• DevNet: A Deep Event Network for multimedia event detection and evidence recounting [Gan et al., 2015] • A Discriminative CNN Video Representation for Event Detection [Xu et al., 2015]
Image retrieval	• Collaborative Index Embedding for Image Retrieval [Zhou et al., 2017] • Deep Semantic Ranking Based Hashing for Multi-Label Image Retrieval [Zhao et al., 2015a]
Person re-identification	• Recurrent Convolutional Network for Video-Based Person Reidentification [McLaughlin et al., 2016] • An Improved Deep Learning Architecture for Person Re-Identification [Ahmed et al., 2015]
Change detection	• Forest Change Detection in Incomplete Satellite Images with Deep Neural Networks [Khan et al., 2017c] • Detecting Change for Multi-View, Long-Term Surface Inspection [Stent et al., 2015]

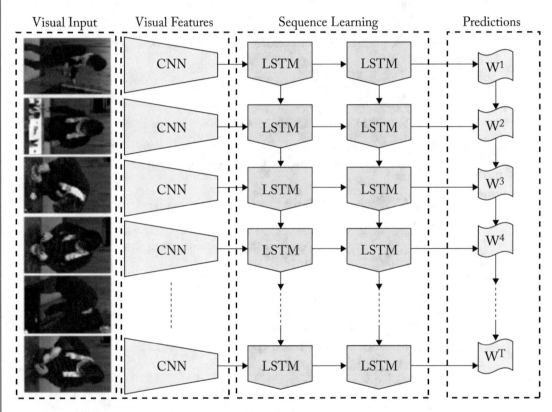

Figure 7.23: The architecture of the LRCN.

CHAPTER 8

Deep Learning Tools and Libraries

There have been a lot of interest from academics (e.g., The University of California Berkeley, New York University, The University of Toronto, The University of Montreal) and industry groups (e.g., Google, Facebook, Microsoft) to develop deep learning frameworks. It is mainly due to their popularity in many applications domains over the last few years. The key motivation for developing these libraries is to provide an efficient and friendly development environment for researchers to design and implement deep neural networks. Some of the widely used deep learning frameworks are: Caffe, TensorFlow, MatConvNet, Torch7, Theano, Keras, Lasange, Marvin, Chainer, DeepLearning4J, and MXNet.[1] Many of these libraries are well supported, with dozens of active contributors and large user bases. Because of strong CUDA backends, many of these frameworks are very fast in training deep networks with billions of parameters. Based on the number of users in the Google groups and the number of contributors for each of the frameworks in their corresponding GitHub repositories, we selected ten widely developed and supported deep learning frameworks including Caffe, TensorFlow, MatConvNet, Torch7, Theano, Keras, Lasagne, Marvin, Chainer, and PyTorch for further discussions.

8.1 CAFFE

Caffe is a fully open-source deep learning framework and perhaps the first industry-grade deep learning framework, due to its excellent CNN implementation at the time. It was developed by the Berkeley Vision and Learning Center (BVLC), as well as community contributors. It is highly popular within the computer vision community. The code is written in C++, with CUDA used for GPU computation, and has Python, MATLAB, and commandline interfaces for training and deployment purposes. Caffe stores and communicates data using blobs, which are 4-dimensional arrays. It provides a complete set of layer types including: convolution, pooling, inner products, nonlinearities like rectified linear and logistic, local response normalization, element-wise operations, and different types of losses, such as soft-max and hinge. The learned

---

[1]For a more complete list of Deep Learning frameworks, see http://deeplearning.net/software_links/.

models can be saved to disk as Google Protocol Buffers,[2] which have many advantages such as minimal-size binary strings when serialized, efficient serialization, easier to use programmatically, and a human-readable text format compatible with the binary version, over XML for serializing structured data. Large-scale data is stored in LevelDB2 databases. There are also pre-trained models for the state-of-the-art networks which allows reproducible research. We refer the readers to the official website[3] to learn more about the Caffe framework.

However, its support for recurrent networks and language modeling is poor in general. Moreover, it can only be used for image-based application, while not for other deep learning applications such as text or speech. Another draw back is that the user needs to manually define gradient formula for back propagation. As we will discuss further, more recent libraries offer automatic gradient computations which makes it easy to define new layers and modules.

Following the footsteps of Caffe, Facebook also developed Caffe2, a new lightweight, modular deep learning framework which is built on the original Caffe and make improvements on Caffe, particularly a modern computation graph design, supporting large-scale distributed training, flexibility to port to multiple platforms with ease, and minimalist modularity.

8.2   TENSORFLOW

TensorFlow was originally developed by the Google Brain team. TensorFlow is written with a Python API over a C/C++ engine for numerical computation using data flow graphs. Multiple APIs have been provided. The complete programming control is provided with the lowest level APIs, called TensorFlow Core. Machine learning researchers and others who need fine levels of control over their models are recommended to use the TensorFlow Core. The higher level APIs are built on top of TensorFlow Core and they are easier to learn and use, compared to the TensorFlow Core.

TensorFlow offers automatic differentiation capabilities, which simplify the process of defining new operations in the network. It uses data flow graphs to perform numerical computations. The graph nodes represent mathematical operations and the edges represent tensors. TensorFlow supports multiple backends, CPU or GPU on desktop, server or mobile platforms. It has well-supported bindings to Python and C++. TensorFlow also has tools to support reinforcement learning. For more details, we suggest the readers to visit the TensorFlow website.[4]

8.3   MATCONVNET

This is a MATLAB toolbox for the implementation of convolutional neural networks. It was developed by the Oxford Visual Geometry Group, as an educational and research platform. Un-

---

[2]Google Protocol Buffers are a way of efficiently encoding structured data. It is smaller, faster and simpler than XML. It is useful in developing programs to communicate with each others over a wire or for storing data. First, a user-defined data structure is built, and then, a special generated source code is used to easily write and read the structured data to and from a variety of data streams and using a variety of languages.

[3]http://caffe.berkeleyvision.org/

[4]https://www.tensorflow.org/

like most existing deep network frameworks which hide the neural network layers behind a wall of a compiled code, MatConvNet layers can be implemented directly in MATLAB, which is one of the most popular development environments in computer vision research and in many other areas. Thus, layers can easily be modified, extended, or integrated with new ones. However, many of its CNN building blocks, such as convolution, normalization, and pooling, use optimized CPU and GPU implementations written in C++ and CUDA. The implementation of the CNN computations in this library are inspired by the Caffe framework.

Unlike most existing deep learning frameworks, MatConvNet is simple to compile and install. The implementation is fully self-contained, requiring only MATLAB and a compatible C++ compiler. However, MatConvNet does not support recurrent networks. It has a few number of state-of-the-art pre-trained models. In order to learn more about this framework, we refer the readers to the official website.[5]

8.4   TORCH7

Torch7 is a scientific computing framework which provides a wide support for machine learning algorithms, especially deep neural networks. It provides a MATLAB-like environment and has strong CUDA and CPU backends. Torch7 is built using Lua that runs on Lua (JIT) compiler. The Lua scripting language was chosen to provide three main advantages: **(1)** Lua is easy for the development of numerical algorithms, **(2)** Lua can easily be embedded in a C application, and provides a great C API, and **(3)** Lua is the fastest interpreted language (also the fastest Just In Time (JIT) compiler). Lua is implemented as a library, written in C.

Torch7 relies on its Tensor class to provide an efficient multi-dimensional array type. Torch7 has C, C++, and Lua interfaces for model learning and deployment purposes. It also has an easy to use multi-GPU support which makes it powerful for the learning of deep models. Torch7 has a large community of developers and is being actively used within large organizations such as, New York University, Facebook AI lab, Google DeepMind, and Twitter. Unlike most existing frameworks, Torch7 offers a rich set of RNNs. However, unlike TensorFlow, Torch7 has the GPU and automatic differentiation support in two separate libraries, cutorch and autograd, that makes Torch7 a little less slick and a little harder to learn. The tutorials and demos provided in the Torch7 official website[6] help the readers to better understand this framework. Torch7 is probably the fastest deep learning platform available.

8.5   THEANO

Theano is a Python library and an optimizing compiler which efficiently defines, optimizes, and evaluates mathematical expressions involving multi-dimensional arrays. Theano was primarily developed by a machine learning group at the University of Montreal. It combines computer

---

[5]http://www.vlfeat.org/matconvnet/
[6]http://torch.ch/docs/getting-started.html

algebra system with an optimizing compiler that is useful for tasks in which complicated mathematical expressions are evaluated repeatedly, and evaluation speed is critical. Theano provides different implementations for the convolution operation, such as an FFT-based implementation [Mathieu et al., 2014], and an implementation based on the open-source code of image classification network in Krizhevsky et al. [2012]. Several libraries, such as Pylearn2, Keras, and Lasagne, have been developed on top of Theano providing building blocks for fast experimentation of well-known models. Theano uses symbolic graph for programming a network. Its symbolic API supports looping control, which makes the implementation of RNNs easy and efficient.

Theano has implementations for most state-of-the-art networks, either in the form of a higher-level framework, such as Blocksa and Keras, or in pure Theano. However, Theano is somewhat low-level and large models have long compilation times. For more information, we refer the authors to the official website.[7] However, Theano will no longer be developed (implementing new features) after 2018.

8.6 KERAS

Keras is an open-source high-level neural networks API, written in Python, and capable of running on top of TensorFlow and Theano. Thus, Keras benefits from the advantages of both and provides a higher-level and more intuitive set of abstractions, which make it easy to configure neural networks, regardless of the back-end scientific computing library. The primary motivation behind Keras is to enable fast experimentation with deep neural networks and to go from idea to results as quickly as possible. The library consists of numerous implementations of neural network building blocks and tools to make working with image and text data easier. For instance, Fig. 8.1 shows a Keras code, compared with the code needed to program in Tensorflow, to achieve the same purpose. As shown in this figure, a neural network can be built in just few lines of code. For more examples, please visit the Keras official website.[8]

Keras offers two types of deep neural networks including sequence-based networks (where the inputs flow linearly through the network) and graph-based networks (where the inputs can skip certain layers). Thus, implementing more complex network architectures such as GoogLeNet and SqueezeNet is easy. However, Keras does not provide most state-of-the-art pre-trained models.

8.7 LASAGNE

Lasagne[9] is a lightweight python library to construct and train networks in Theano. Unlike Keras, Lasange was developed to be a light wrapper around Theano. Lasange supports a wide

---

[7]http://deeplearning.net/software/theano/
[8]https://keras.io/
[9]https://github.com/Lasagne/Lasagne

```
import tensorflow as tf

input_data = [[0., 0.], [0., 1.], [1., 0.], [1., 1.]]  # XOR input
output_data = [[0.], [1.], [1.], [0.]]  # XOR output

n_input = tf.placeholder(tf.float32, shape=[None, 2], name="n_input")
n_output = tf.placeholder(tf.float32, shape=[None, 1], name="n_output")

hidden_nodes = 5

b_hidden = tf.Variable(tf.random_normal([hidden_nodes]), name="hidden_bias")
W_hidden = tf.Variable(tf.random_normal([2, hidden_nodes]), name="hidden_weights")
hidden = tf.sigmoid(tf.matmul(n_input, W_hidden) + b_hidden)

W_output = tf.Variable(tf.random_normal([hidden_nodes, 1]), name="output_weights")  # output layer's weight matrix
output = tf.sigmoid(tf.matmul(hidden, W_output))  # calc output layer's activation

cross_entropy = tf.square(n_output - output)  # simpler, but also works

loss = tf.reduce_mean(cross_entropy)  # mean the cross_entropy
optimizer = tf.train.AdamOptimizer(0.01)  # take a gradient descent for optimizing with a "stepsize" of 0.1
train = optimizer.minimize(loss)  # let the optimizer train

init = tf.initialize_all_variables()

sess = tf.Session()  # create the session and therefore the graph
sess.run(init)  # initialize all variables

for epoch in xrange(0, 2001):
    # run the training operation
    cvalues = sess.run([train, loss, W_hidden, b_hidden, W_output],
                        feed_dict={n_input: input_data, n_output: output_data})

    if epoch % 200 == 0:
        print("")
        print("step: {:>3}".format(epoch))
        print("loss: {}".format(cvalues[1]))

print("")
print("input: {} | output: {}".format(input_data[0], sess.run(output, feed_dict={n_input: [input_data[0]]})))
print("input: {} | output: {}".format(input_data[1], sess.run(output, feed_dict={n_input: [input_data[1]]})))
print("input: {} | output: {}".format(input_data[2], sess.run(output, feed_dict={n_input: [input_data[2]]})))
print("input: {} | output: {}".format(input_data[3], sess.run(output, feed_dict={n_input: [input_data[3]]})))
```

(a) TensorFlow

```
import numpy as np
from keras.models import Sequential
from keras.layers.core import Activation, Dense
from keras.optimizers import SGD

X = np.array([[0,0],[0,1],[1,0],[1,1]], "float32")
y = np.array([[0],[1],[1],[0]], "float32")

model = Sequential()
model.add(Dense(2, input_dim=2, activation='sigmoid'))
model.add(Dense(1, activation='sigmoid'))

sgd = SGD(lr=0.1, decay=1e-6, momentum=0.9, nesterov=True)
model.compile(loss='mean_squared_error', optimizer=sgd)

history = model.fit(X, y, nb_epoch=10000, batch_size=4, verbose=0)

print model.predict(X)
```

(b) Keras

Figure 8.1: This figure illustrates the difference in the size of the code for (a) TensorFlow and (b) Keras to achieve the same purpose.

range of deep models including feed-forward networks, such as Convolutional Neural Networks (CNNs), recurrent networks, such as LSTM, and any combination of feed-forward and recurrent networks. It allows architectures of multiple inputs and multiple outputs, including auxiliary classifiers. Defining cost functions is easy and there is no need to derive gradients due to Theano's symbolic differentiation.

8.8 MARVIN

Marvin[10] was developed by researchers from Princeton University's Vision Group. It is a GPU-only neural network framework, written in C++, and made with simplicity, hackability, speed, memory consumption, and high-dimensional data in mind. Marvin implementation consists of two files, namely *marvin.hpp* and *marvin.cu*. It supports multi-GPU, receptive field calculations and filter visualization. Marvin can easily be installed on different operating systems including Windows, Linux, Mac, and all other platforms that CUDNN supports.

Marvin does not provide most state-of-the-art pre-trained models. It, however, provides a script to convert Caffe models into a format that works in Marvin. Moreover, Marvin does not provide a good documentation, which makes the building of new models difficult.

8.9 CHAINER

Chainer is an open-source neural network framework with a Python API. It was developed at Preferred Networks, a machine-learning startup based in Tokyo. Unlike existing deep learning frameworks, which use the define-and-run approach, Chainer was designed on the principle of define-by-run.

In the define-and-run-based frameworks, as shown in Fig. 8.2, models are built in two phases, namely define and run. In the Define phase, a computational graph is constructed. More precisely, the Define phase is the instantiation of a neural network object based on a model definition, which specifies the inter-layer connections, initial weights, and activation functions, such as Protobuf for Caffe. In the Run phase, given a set of training examples, the model is trained by minimizing the loss function using optimization algorithms, such as SGD. However, the define-and-run-based frameworks have three major problems, namely **(1)** inefficient memory usage, especially for RNN models; **(2)** limited extensibility; and **(3)** the inner workings of the neural network are not accessible to the user, e.g., for the debugging of the models.

Chainer overcomes these drawbacks by providing an easier and more straightforward way to implement the more complex deep learning architectures. Unlike other frameworks, Chainer does not fix a model's computational graph before the model is trained. Instead, the computational graph is implicitly memorized when the forward computation for the training data set takes place as shown in Fig. 8.2. Thus, Chainer allows to modify networks during runtime, and

---

[10]http://marvin.is/

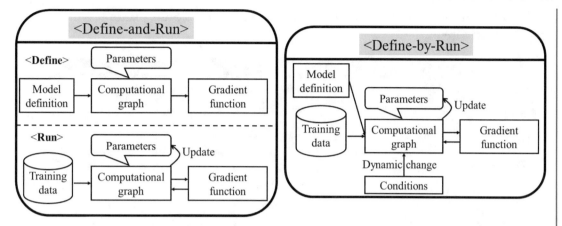

Figure 8.2: Unlike define-and-run-based frameworks, Chainer is a define-by-run framework, which does not fix a model's computational graph before the model is trained.

use arbitrary control flow statements. The Chainer official website[11] provides several examples and more details about Chainer core Concept.

8.10 PYTORCH

PyTorch is an open source machine learning library for Python. It was developed by Facebook's artificial intelligence research group. Unlike Torch which is written in Lua (a relatively unpopular programming language), PyTorch leverages the rising popularity of Python. Since its introduction, PyTorch has quickly become the favorite among machine-learning researchers because it allows certain complex architectures to be built easily.

PyTorch is mainly influenced by Chainer. Particularly, PyTorch allows to modify networks during runtime, i.e., define-by-run framework. The tutorials and demos provided in the PyTorch official website[12] help the readers to better understand this framework.

[11]https://github.com/chainer/chainer
[12]http://pytorch.org/tutorials/

Table 8.1: Comparison of deep learning framework in terms of creator, platform, language, and provided interface

Software	Creator	Platform	Core Language	Interface
Caffe	Berkeley Vision and Learning Center (BVLC)	Linux, Mac OS X, Windows	C++	Python, MATLAB
TensorFlow	Google Brain team	Linux, Mac OS X Windows	C++, Python	Python, C/ C++, Java, Go
MatConvNet	Oxford Visual Geometry Group (VGG)	Linux, Mac OS X, Windows	MATLAB, C++	MATLAB
Torch7	Ronan Collobert, Koray Kavukcuoglu, Clement Farabet, Soumith Chintala	Linux, Mac OS X, Windows, Android, iOS	C, Lua	Lua, LuaJIT, C, utility library for C++
Theano	Monteral University	Cross-platform	Python	Python
Keras	Francois Chollet	Linux, Mac OS X, Windows	Python	Python
Lasagne	Saunder Dieleman and others	Linux, Mac OS X, Windows	Python	Python
Marvin	Jianxiong Xiao, Shuran Song, Daniel Suo, Fisher Yu	Linux, Mac OS X, Windows	C++	C++
Chainer	Seiya Tokui, Kenta Oono, Shohei Hido, Justin Clayton	Linux, Mac OS X,	Python	Python
PyTorch	Adam Paszke, Sam Gross, Soumith Chintala, Gregory Chanan	Linux, Mac OS X, Windows	Python, C, CUDA	Python

Table 8.2: Comparison of deep learning framework in terms of OpenMP, OpenCL, and Cuda support, number of available pre-trained models, RNNs, CNNs, and RBM/DBNs

Software	OpenMP Support	OpenCL Support	CUDA Support	Pretrained Models	RNNs	CNNs	RBM/DBNs
Caffe	No	Yes	Yes	Yes	Yes	Yes	Yes
TensorFlow	No	On roadmap	Yes	Yes	Yes	Yes	Yes
MatConvNet	Yes	No	Yes	A few	No	Yes	No
Torch7	Yes	Third party implementations	Yes	Yes	Yes	Yes	Yes
Theano	Yes	If using Theano as backend	Under development	Yes	Yes	Yes	Yes
Keras	Yes	Under development for the Theano backend, on roadmap for the TensorFlo backend	Yes	A few	Yes	Yes	Yes
Lasagne	No	Yes	Yes	Yes	Yes	Yes	Yes
Marvin	Yes	Yes	Yes	A few	Yes	Yes	No
Chainer	Yes	No	Yes	A few	Yes	Yes	No
PyTorch	Yes	No	Yes	Yes	Yes	Yes	Yes

CHAPTER 9

Conclusion

BOOK SUMMARY

The application of deep learning algorithms, especially CNNs, to computer vision problems have seen a rapid progress. This has led to highly robust, efficient, and flexible vision systems. This book aimed to introduce different aspects of CNNs in computer vision problems. The first part of this book (Chapter 1 and Chapter 2) introduced computer vision and machine learning subjects, and reviewed the traditional feature representation and classification methods. We then briefly covered two generic categories of deep neural networks, namely the feed-forward and the feed-back networks, their respective computational mechanisms and historical background in Chapter 3. Chapter 4 provided a broad survey of the recent advances in CNNs, including state-of-the-art layers, weight initialization techniques, regularization approaches, and several loss functions. Chapter 5 reviewed popular gradient-based learning algorithms followed by gradient-based optimization methodologies. Chapter 6 introduced the most popular CNN architectures which were mainly developed for object detection and classification tasks. A wide range of CNN applications in computer vision tasks, including image classification, object detection, object tracking, pose estimation, action recognition, and scene labeling have been discussed in Chapter 7. Finally, several widely used deep learning libraries have been presented in Chapter 8 to help the readers to understand the main features of these frameworks.

FUTURE RESEARCH DIRECTIONS

While Convolutional Neural Networks (CNNs) have achieved great performances in experimental evaluations, there are still several challenges which we believe deserve further investigation.

First, deep neural networks require massive amounts of data and computing power to be trained. However, the manual collection of large-scale labeled datasets is a daunting task. The requirement of large amounts of labeled data can be relaxed by extracting hierarchical features through unsupervised learning techniques. Meanwhile, to speed up the learning process, the development of effective and scalable parallel learning algorithms warrants further investigation. In several application domains, there exists a long tail distribution of object classes, where enough training examples are not available for the less frequent ones. In such scenarios, deep networks need to be adapted appropriately to overcome the class-imbalance problem [Khan et al., 2017a].

Second, the memory required to store the huge amounts of parameters is another challenge in deep neural networks, including CNNs. At testing time, these deep models have a high memory footprint, which makes them unsuitable for mobile and other hand-held devices that have limited resources. Thus, it is important to investigate how to decrease the complexity of deep neural networks without the loss of accuracy.

Third, selecting suitable model hyper-parameters (e.g., learning rate, number of layers, kernel size, number of feature maps, stride, pooling size, and pooling regions) requires considerable skill and experience. These hyper-parameters have a significant impact on the accuracy of deep models. Without an automated hyper-parameter tuning method, one needs to make manual adjustments to the hyper-parameters using many training runs to achieve the optimal values. Some recent works [He et al., 2016a, Huang et al., 2016b] have tried optimization techniques for hyper-parameter selection and have shown that there is room to improve current optimization techniques for learning deep CNN architectures.

Fourth, although deep CNNs have demonstrated an impressive performance on a variety of applications, they still lack solid mathematical and theoretical foundations. There is little insight into the behavior of these complex neural networks, or how they achieve such good performance. As a result, it might be difficult to improve their performance, and thus, the development of better models is restricted to trial-and-error. Therefore, attempting to see what features have been learned, and to understand what computations are performed at each layer in deep CNNs is an increasingly popular direction of research [Mahendran and Vedaldi, 2015, 2016, Zeiler and Fergus, 2014].

Fifth, several machine learning algorithms, including state-of-the-art CNNs are vulnerable to adversarial examples. Adversarial examples have intentionally been designed to cause the learned model to make a mistake. For example, by adding a small perturbation to an image of a "panda" in a way that is undetectable to the human eye, the resultant image is recognized as a "gibbon" with high confidence (Fig. 9.1). Thus, sophisticated attackers could trick neural networks. For example, one could target autonomous vehicles by using stickers to design an adversarial *stop* sign that the vehicle would interpret as a *yield* sign [Papernot et al., 2017]. Therefore, coming up with sophisticated defense strategies is a vital part of many machine learning algorithms, including CNNs.

Finally, a major shortcoming of convolutional networks is the inability to work on arbitrary shaped inputs, e.g., cyclic and acyclic graphs. Furthermore, there does not exist a principled way to incorporate structured losses in the deep network formulation. Such losses are essential for structured prediction tasks such as the body pose estimation and semantic segmentation. There have recently been some efforts toward the extension of CNNs to arbitrarily shaped graph structures [Defferrard et al., 2016, Kipf and Welling, 2016]. However, this area has numerous promising applications and needs further technical breakthroughs to enable fast and scalable architectures that are suitable for graphs.

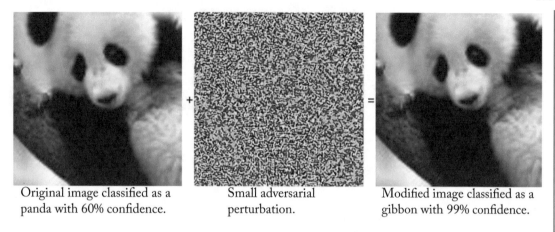

Original image classified as a panda with 60% confidence.

Small adversarial perturbation.

Modified image classified as a gibbon with 99% confidence.

Figure 9.1: Adversarial example: by mathematically manipulating a "panda" image in a way that is undetectable to the human eye (e.g., adding a small perturbation), the learned neural networks can be tricked into misclassifying objects by sophisticated attackers.

In conclusion, we hope that this book not only provides a better understanding of CNNs for computer vision tasks, but also facilitates future research activities and application developments in the field of computer vision and CNNs.

Bibliography

ILSVRC 2016 Results. http://image-net.org/challenges/LSVRC/2016/results 106

A. Alahi, R. Ortiz, and P. Vandergheynst. Freak: Fast retina keypoint. In *IEEE Conference on Computer Vision and Pattern Recognition*, pages 510–517, 2012. DOI: 10.1109/cvpr.2012.6247715. 14

Ark Anderson, Kyle Shaffer, Artem Yankov, Court D. Corley, and Nathan O. Hodas. Beyond fine tuning: A modular approach to learning on small data. *arXiv preprint arXiv:1611.01714*, 2016. 72

Relja Arandjelovic, Petr Gronat, Akihiko Torii, Tomas Pajdla, and Josef Sivic. Netvlad: CNN architecture for weakly supervised place recognition. In *Proc. of the IEEE Conference on Computer Vision and Pattern Recognition*, pages 5297–5307, 2016. DOI: 10.1109/cvpr.2016.572. 63, 64

Pablo Arbeláez, Jordi Pont-Tuset, Jonathan T. Barron, Ferran Marques, and Jitendra Malik. Multiscale combinatorial grouping. In *Proc. of the IEEE Conference on Computer Vision and Pattern Recognition*, pages 328–335, 2014. DOI: 10.1109/cvpr.2014.49. 140

Hossein Azizpour, Ali Sharif Razavian, Josephine Sullivan, Atsuto Maki, and Stefan Carlsson. Factors of transferability for a generic convnet representation. *IEEE Transactions on Pattern Analysis and Machine Intelligence*, 38(9):1790–1802, 2016. DOI: 10.1109/tpami.2015.2500224. 72

David Balduzzi, Marcus Frean, Lennox Leary, J. P. Lewis, Kurt Wan-Duo Ma, and Brian McWilliams. The shattered gradients problem: If resnets are the answer, then what is the question? *arXiv preprint arXiv:1702.08591*, 2017. 95, 98

Herbert Bay, Andreas Ess, Tinne Tuytelaars, and Luc Van Gool. Speeded-up robust features (surf). *Computer Vision and Image Understanding*, 110(3):346–359, 2008. DOI: 10.1016/j.cviu.2007.09.014. 7, 11, 14, 19, 29

Atilim Gunes Baydin, Barak A. Pearlmutter, Alexey Andreyevich Radul, and Jeffrey Mark Siskind. Automatic differentiation in machine learning: A survey. *arXiv preprint arXiv:1502.05767*, 2015. 90

N. Bayramoglu and A. Alatan. Shape index sift: Range image recognition using local features. In *20th International Conference on Pattern Recognition*, pages 352–355, 2010. DOI: 10.1109/icpr.2010.95. 13

Yoshua Bengio, Pascal Lamblin, Dan Popovici, Hugo Larochelle, et al. Greedy layer-wise training of deep networks. *Advances in Neural Information Processing Systems*, 19:153, 2007. 70

Zhou Bolei, Aditya Khosla, Agata Lapedriza, Aude Oliva, and Antonio Torralba. Object detectors emerge in deep scene CNNs. In *International Conference on Learning Representations*, 2015. 94, 97

Leo Breiman. Random forests. *Machine Learning*, 45(1):5–32, 2001. DOI: 10.1023/A:1010933404324. 7, 11, 22, 26, 29

M. Brown and D. Lowe. Invariant features from interest point groups. In *Proc. of the British Machine Vision Conference*, pages 23.1–23.10, 2002. DOI: 10.5244/c.16.23. 20

M. Calonder, V. Lepetit, C. Strecha, and P. Fua. BRIEF: Binary robust independent elementary features. In *11th European Conference on Computer Vision*, pages 778–792, 2010. DOI: 10.1007/978-3-642-15561-1_56. 14

Jean-Pierre Changeux and Paul Ricoeur. *What Makes Us Think?: A Neuroscientist and a Philosopher Argue About Ethics, Human Nature, and the Brain*. Princeton University Press, 2002. 40

Ken Chatfield, Karen Simonyan, Andrea Vedaldi, and Andrew Zisserman. Return of the devil in the details: Delving deep into convolutional nets. *arXiv preprint arXiv:1405.3531*, 2014. DOI: 10.5244/c.28.6. 123

Liang-Chieh Chen, George Papandreou, Iasonas Kokkinos, Kevin Murphy, and Alan L. Yuille. Semantic image segmentation with deep convolutional nets and fully connected CRFs. *arXiv preprint arXiv:1412.7062*, 2014. 50, 133

Kyunghyun Cho, Bart Van Merriënboer, Dzmitry Bahdanau, and Yoshua Bengio. On the properties of neural machine translation: Encoder-decoder approaches. *arXiv preprint arXiv:1409.1259*, 2014. DOI: 10.3115/v1/w14-4012. 38

Sumit Chopra, Raia Hadsell, and Yann LeCun. Learning a similarity metric discriminatively, with application to face verification. In *Computer Vision and Pattern Recognition, (CVPR). IEEE Computer Society Conference on*, volume 1, pages 539–546, 2005. DOI: 10.1109/cvpr.2005.202. 67

Dan C. Cireşan, Ueli Meier, Jonathan Masci, Luca M. Gambardella, and Jürgen Schmidhuber. High-performance neural networks for visual object classification. *arXiv preprint arXiv:1102.0183*, 2011. 102

Corinna Cortes. Support-vector networks. *Machine Learning*, 20(3):273–297, 1995. DOI: 10.1007/bf00994018. 7, 11, 22, 29

Koby Crammer and Yoram Singer. On the algorithmic implementation of multiclass kernel-based vector machines. *Journal of Machine Learning Research*, 2:265–292, 2001. 66

Michaël Defferrard, Xavier Bresson, and Pierre Vandergheynst. Convolutional neural networks on graphs with fast localized spectral filtering. In *Advances in Neural Information Processing Systems*, pages 3844–3852, 2016. 170

Li Deng. A tutorial survey of architectures, algorithms, and applications for deep learning. *APSIPA Transactions on Signal and Information Processing*, 3:e2, 2014. DOI: 10.1017/atsip.2014.4. 117

Jeff Donahue, Lisa Anne Hendricks, Sergio Guadarrama, Marcus Rohrbach, Subhashini Venugopalan, Kate Saenko, and Trevor Darrell. Long-term recurrent convolutional networks for visual recognition and description. *IEEE Conference on Computer Vision and Pattern Recognition (CVPR)*, pages 2625–2634, 2015. DOI: 10.1109/cvpr.2015.7298878. 150, 155

John Duchi, Elad Hazan, and Yoram Singer. Adaptive subgradient methods for online learning and stochastic optimization. *Journal of Machine Learning Research*, 12:2121–2159, 2011. 83

Vincent Dumoulin and Francesco Visin. A guide to convolution arithmetic for deep learning. *arXiv preprint arXiv:1603.07285*, 2016. 60

Pedro F. Felzenszwalb, Ross B. Girshick, David McAllester, and Deva Ramanan. Object detection with discriminatively trained part-based models. *IEEE Transactions on Pattern Analysis and Machine Intelligence*, 32(9):1627–1645, 2010. DOI: 10.1109/tpami.2009.167. 121

R. A. Fisher. The use of multiple measurements in taxonomic problems. *Annals of Eugenics*, 7(7):179–188, 1936. DOI: 10.1111/j.1469-1809.1936.tb02137.x. 22

Yoav Freund and Robert E. Schapire. A decision-theoretic generalization of online learning and an application to boosting. *Journal of Computer and System Sciences*, 55(1):119–139, 1997. DOI: 10.1006/jcss.1997.1504. 22

Jerome H. Friedman. Greedy function approximation: A gradient boosting machine. *Annals of Statistics*, 29:1189–1232, 2000. 22

Kunihiko Fukushima and Sei Miyake. Neocognitron: A self-organizing neural network model for a mechanism of visual pattern recognition. In *Competition and Cooperation in Neural Nets*, pages 267–285. Springer, 1982. DOI: 10.1007/978-3-642-46466-9_18. 43

Ross Girshick. Fast R-CNN. In *Proc. of the IEEE International Conference on Computer Vision*, pages 1440–1448, 2015. DOI: 10.1109/iccv.2015.169. 60

Ross Girshick, Jeff Donahue, Trevor Darrell, and Jitendra Malik. Region-based convolutional networks for accurate object detection and segmentation. *IEEE Transactions on Pattern Analysis and Machine Intelligence*, 38(1):142–158, 2016. DOI: 10.1109/tpami.2015.2437384. 120

Xavier Glorot and Yoshua Bengio. Understanding the difficulty of training deep feedforward neural networks. In *Aistats*, 9:249–256, 2010. 70

Ian Goodfellow. Nips 2016 tutorial: Generative adversarial networks. *arXiv preprint arXiv:1701.00160*, 2016. 142

Ian Goodfellow, Jean Pouget-Abadie, Mehdi Mirza, Bing Xu, David Warde-Farley, Sherjil Ozair, Aaron Courville, and Yoshua Bengio. Generative adversarial nets. In *Advances in Neural Information Processing Systems*, pages 2672–2680, 2014. 141, 142, 149

Ian Goodfellow, Yoshua Bengio, and Aaron Courville. *Deep Learning*. MIT Press, 2016. http://www.deeplearningbook.org 54

Alex Graves and Jürgen Schmidhuber. Framewise phoneme classification with bidirectional LSTM and other neural network architectures. *Neural Networks*, 18(5):602–610, 2005. DOI: 10.1016/j.neunet.2005.06.042. 38

Alex Graves, Greg Wayne, and Ivo Danihelka. Neural turing machines. *arXiv preprint arXiv:1410.5401*, 2014. 38

Alex Graves et al. *Supervised Sequence Labelling with Recurrent Neural Networks*, volume 385. Springer, 2012. DOI: 10.1007/978-3-642-24797-2. 31

Saurabh Gupta, Pablo Arbelaez, and Jitendra Malik. Perceptual organization and recognition of indoor scenes from RGB-D images. In *Proc. of the IEEE Conference on Computer Vision and Pattern Recognition*, pages 564–571, 2013. DOI: 10.1109/cvpr.2013.79. 140

Saurabh Gupta, Ross Girshick, Pablo Arbeláez, and Jitendra Malik. Learning rich features from RGB-D images for object detection and segmentation. In *European Conference on Computer Vision*, pages 345–360. Springer, 2014. DOI: 10.1007/978-3-319-10584-0_23. 139, 141

Richard H. R. Hahnloser, Rahul Sarpeshkar, Misha A. Mahowald, Rodney J. Douglas, and H. Sebastian Seung. Digital selection and analogue amplification coexist in a cortex-inspired silicon circuit. *Nature*, 405(6789):947, 2000. DOI: 10.1038/35016072. 55

Munawar Hayat, Salman H. Khan, Mohammed Bennamoun, and Senjian An. A spatial layout and scale invariant feature representation for indoor scene classification. *IEEE Transactions on Image Processing*, 25(10):4829–4841, 2016. DOI: 10.1109/tip.2016.2599292. 96

Kaiming He, Xiangyu Zhang, Shaoqing Ren, and Jian Sun. Spatial pyramid pooling in deep convolutional networks for visual recognition. In *European Conference on Computer Vision*, pages 346–361. Springer, 2014. DOI: 10.1007/978-3-319-10578-9_23. 62

Kaiming He, Xiangyu Zhang, Shaoqing Ren, and Jian Sun. Delving deep into rectifiers: Surpassing human-level performance on imagenet classification. In *Proc. of the IEEE International Conference on Computer Vision*, pages 1026–1034, 2015a. DOI: 10.1109/iccv.2015.123. 71

Kaiming He, Xiangyu Zhang, Shaoqing Ren, and Jian Sun. Spatial pyramid pooling in deep convolutional networks for visual recognition. *IEEE Transactions on Pattern Analysis and Machine Intelligence*, 37(9):1904–1916, 2015b. DOI: 10.1109/tpami.2015.2389824. 61, 125

Kaiming He, Xiangyu Zhang, Shaoqing Ren, and Jian Sun. Deep residual learning for image recognition. In *Proc. of the IEEE Conference on Computer Vision and Pattern Recognition*, pages 770–778, 2016a. DOI: 10.1109/cvpr.2016.90. 77, 106, 170

Kaiming He, Xiangyu Zhang, Shaoqing Ren, and Jian Sun. Identity mappings in deep residual networks. In *European Conference on Computer Vision*, pages 630–645. Springer, 2016b. DOI: 10.1007/978-3-319-46493-0_38. 108, 111

Kaiming He, Georgia Gkioxari, Piotr Dollár, and Ross Girshick. Mask R-CNN. *arXiv preprint arXiv:1703.06870*, 2017. DOI: 10.1109/iccv.2017.322. 60, 140, 141

Geoffrey E. Hinton, Simon Osindero, and Yee-Whye Teh. A fast learning algorithm for deep belief nets. *Neural Computation*, 18(7):1527–1554, 2006. DOI: 10.1162/neco.2006.18.7.1527. 70

Sepp Hochreiter and Jürgen Schmidhuber. Long short-term memory. *Neural Computation*, 9(8):1735–1780, 1997. DOI: 10.1162/neco.1997.9.8.1735. 38

Gao Huang, Zhuang Liu, Kilian Q. Weinberger, and Laurens van der Maaten. Densely connected convolutional networks. *arXiv preprint arXiv:1608.06993*, 2016a. DOI: 10.1109/cvpr.2017.243. 114, 115

Gao Huang, Yu Sun, Zhuang Liu, Daniel Sedra, and Kilian Q. Weinberger. Deep networks with stochastic depth. In *European Conference on Computer Vision*, pages 646–661, 2016b. DOI: 10.1007/978-3-319-46493-0_39. 170

David H. Hubel and Torsten N. Wiesel. Receptive fields of single neurones in the cat's striate cortex. *The Journal of Physiology*, 148(3):574–591, 1959. DOI: 10.1113/jphysiol.1959.sp006308. 43

Sergey Ioffe and Christian Szegedy. Batch normalization: Accelerating deep network training by reducing internal covariate shift. *arXiv preprint arXiv:1502.03167*, 2015. 76, 77

Max Jaderberg, Karen Simonyan, Andrew Zisserman, et al. Spatial transformer networks. In *Advances in Neural Information Processing Systems*, pages 2017–2025, 2015. 63

Anil K. Jain, Jianchang Mao, and K. Moidin Mohiuddin. Artificial neural networks: A tutorial. *Computer*, 29(3):31–44, 1996. DOI: 10.1109/2.485891. 39

Katarzyna Janocha and Wojciech Marian Czarnecki. On loss functions for deep neural networks in classification. *arXiv preprint arXiv:1702.05659*, 2017. DOI: 10.4467/20838476si.16.004.6185. 68

Hervé Jégou, Matthijs Douze, Cordelia Schmid, and Patrick Pérez. Aggregating local descriptors into a compact image representation. In *Computer Vision and Pattern Recognition (CVPR), IEEE Conference on*, pages 3304–3311, 2010. DOI: 10.1109/cvpr.2010.5540039. 63

Andrej Karpathy, George Toderici, Sanketh Shetty, Thomas Leung, Rahul Sukthankar, and Li Fei-Fei. Large-scale video classification with convolutional neural networks. In *Proc. of the IEEE Conference on Computer Vision and Pattern Recognition*, pages 1725–1732, 2014. DOI: 10.1109/cvpr.2014.223. 150, 152

Salman H. Khan. Feature learning and structured prediction for scene understanding. Ph.D. Thesis, University of Western Australia, 2016. 135

Salman H. Khan, Mohammed Bennamoun, Ferdous Sohel, and Roberto Togneri. Automatic shadow detection and removal from a single image. *IEEE Transactions on Pattern Analysis and Machine Intelligence*, 38(3):431–446, 2016a. DOI: 10.1109/tpami.2015.2462355. 141

Salman H. Khan, Munawar Hayat, Mohammed Bennamoun, Roberto Togneri, and Ferdous A. Sohel. A discriminative representation of convolutional features for indoor scene recognition. *IEEE Transactions on Image Processing*, 25(7):3372–3383, 2016b. DOI: 10.1109/tip.2016.2567076. 72, 95

Salman H. Khan, Munawar Hayat, Mohammed Bennamoun, Ferdous A. Sohel, and Roberto Togneri. Cost-sensitive learning of deep feature representations from imbalanced data. *IEEE Transactions on Neural Networks and Learning Systems*, 2017a. DOI: 10.1109/tnnls.2017.2732482. 169

Salman H. Khan, Munawar Hayat, and Fatih Porikli. Scene categorization with spectral features. In *Proc. of the IEEE Conference on Computer Vision and Pattern Recognition*, pages 5638–5648, 2017b. DOI: 10.1109/iccv.2017.601. 94

Salman H. Khan, Xuming He, Fatih Porikli, Mohammed Bennamoun, Ferdous Sohel, and Roberto Togneri. Learning deep structured network for weakly supervised change detection. In *Proc. of the International Joint Conference on Artificial Intelligence (IJCAI)*, pages 1–7, 2017c. DOI: 10.24963/ijcai.2017/279. 141

Salman Hameed Khan, Mohammed Bennamoun, Ferdous Sohel, and Roberto Togneri. Automatic feature learning for robust shadow detection. In *Computer Vision and Pattern Recognition (CVPR), IEEE Conference on*, pages 1939–1946, 2014. DOI: 10.1109/cvpr.2014.249. 93

Diederik Kingma and Jimmy Ba. Adam: A method for stochastic optimization. *arXiv preprint arXiv:1412.6980*, 2014. 85, 86

Thomas N. Kipf and Max Welling. Semi-supervised classification with graph convolutional networks. *arXiv preprint arXiv:1609.02907*, 2016. 170

Philipp Krähenbühl and Vladlen Koltun. Efficient inference in fully connected CRFS with Gaussian edge potentials. In *Advances in Neural Information Processing Systems 24*, pages 109–117, 2011. 132, 135

Alex Krizhevsky, Ilya Sutskever, and Geoffrey E. Hinton. Imagenet classification with deep convolutional neural networks. In *Advances in Neural Information Processing Systems*, pages 1097–1105, 2012. DOI: 10.1145/3065386. 45, 74, 102, 117, 123, 140, 150, 162

Gustav Larsson, Michael Maire, and Gregory Shakhnarovich. Fractalnet: Ultra-deep neural networks without residuals. *arXiv preprint arXiv:1605.07648*, 2016. 112, 113

Svetlana Lazebnik, Cordelia Schmid, and Jean Ponce. Beyond bags of features: Spatial pyramid matching for recognizing natural scene categories. In *Computer Vision and Pattern Recognition, IEEE Computer Society Conference on*, 2:2169–2178, 2006. DOI: 10.1109/cvpr.2006.68. 61

Yann LeCun, Bernhard Boser, John S. Denker, Donnie Henderson, Richard E. Howard, Wayne Hubbard, and Lawrence D. Jackel. Backpropagation applied to handwritten zip code recognition. *Neural Computation*, 1(4):541–551, 1989. DOI: 10.1162/neco.1989.1.4.541. 43

Yann LeCun, Léon Bottou, Yoshua Bengio, and Patrick Haffner. Gradient-based learning applied to document recognition. *Proc. of the IEEE*, 86(11):2278–2324, 1998. DOI: 10.1109/5.726791. 101, 102

Christian Ledig, Lucas Theis, Ferenc Huszár, Jose Caballero, Andrew Cunningham, Alejandro Acosta, Andrew Aitken, Alykhan Tejani, Johannes Totz, Zehan Wang, et al. Photo-realistic single image super-resolution using a generative adversarial network. *arXiv preprint arXiv:1609.04802*, 2016. DOI: 10.1109/cvpr.2017.19. 141, 145, 147, 148

Stefan Leutenegger, Margarita Chli, and Roland Y. Siegwart. BRISK: Binary robust invariant scalable keypoints. In *Proc. of the International Conference on Computer Vision*, pages 2548–2555, 2011. DOI: 10.1109/iccv.2011.6126542. 14

Li-Jia Li, Richard Socher, and Li Fei-Fei. Towards total scene understanding: Classification, annotation and segmentation in an automatic framework. In *Computer Vision and Pattern Recognition, (CVPR). IEEE Conference on*, pages 2036–2043, 2009. DOI: 10.1109/cvpr.2009.5206718. 135

Min Lin, Qiang Chen, and Shuicheng Yan. Network in network. *arXiv preprint arXiv:1312.4400*, 2013. 56, 103

Jonathan Long, Evan Shelhamer, and Trevor Darrell. Fully convolutional networks for semantic segmentation. In *Proc. of the IEEE Conference on Computer Vision and Pattern Recognition*, pages 3431–3440, 2015. DOI: 10.1109/cvpr.2015.7298965. 127, 128, 130

David G. Lowe. Distinctive image features from scale-invariant keypoints. *International Journal on Computer Vision*, 60(2):91–110, 2004. DOI: 10.1023/b:visi.0000029664.99615.94. 7, 11, 14, 16, 17, 19, 29

A. Mahendran and A. Vedaldi. Understanding deep image representations by inverting them. In *Computer Vision and Pattern Recognition, (CVPR). IEEE Computer Society Conference on*, pages 5188–5196, 2015. DOI: 10.1109/cvpr.2015.7299155. 97, 99, 170

A. Mahendran and A. Vedaldi. Visualizing deep convolutional neural networks using natural pre-images. *International Journal on Computer Vision*, 120(3):233–255, 2016. DOI: 10.1007/s11263-016-0911-8. 170

Michael Mathieu, Mikael Henaff, and Yann LeCun. Fast training of convolutional networks through FFTs. In *International Conference on Learning Representations (ICLR2014)*, 2014. 162

Warren S. McCulloch and Walter Pitts. A logical calculus of the ideas immanent in nervous activity. *The Bulletin of Mathematical Biophysics*, 5(4):115–133, 1943. DOI: 10.1007/bf02478259. 40

Dmytro Mishkin and Jiri Matas. All you need is a good INIT. *arXiv preprint arXiv:1511.06422*, 2015. 71

B. Triggs and N. Dalal. Histograms of oriented gradients for human detection. In *IEEE Computer Society Conference on Computer Vision and Pattern Recognition*, pages 1063–6919, 2005. DOI: 10.1109/CVPR.2005.177. 7, 11, 14, 15, 29

Yurii Nesterov. A method for unconstrained convex minimization problem with the rate of convergence o (1/k2). In *Doklady an SSSR*, 269:543–547, 1983. 82

Hyeonwoo Noh, Seunghoon Hong, and Bohyung Han. Learning deconvolution network for semantic segmentation. In *Proc. of the IEEE International Conference on Computer Vision*, pages 1520–1528, 2015. DOI: 10.1109/iccv.2015.178. 130

Nicolas Papernot, Patrick McDaniel, Ian Goodfellow, Somesh Jha, Z. Berkay Celik, and Ananthram Swami. Practical black-box attacks against machine learning. In *Proc. of the ACM on Asia Conference on Computer and Communications Security, (ASIA CCS'17)*, pages 506–519, 2017. DOI: 10.1145/3052973.3053009. 170

Razvan Pascanu, Yann N. Dauphin, Surya Ganguli, and Yoshua Bengio. On the saddle point problem for non-convex optimization. *arXiv preprint arXiv:1405.4604*, 2014. 81

Charles R. Qi, Hao Su, Kaichun Mo, and Leonidas J. Guibas. Pointnet: Deep learning on point sets for 3D classification and segmentation. *arXiv preprint arXiv:1612.00593*, 2016. DOI: 10.1109/cvpr.2017.16. 117, 118, 119

J. R. Quinlan. Induction of decision trees. *Machine Learning*, pages 81–106, 1986. DOI: 10.1007/bf00116251. 7, 11, 22, 26, 29

Alec Radford, Luke Metz, and Soumith Chintala. Unsupervised representation learning with deep convolutional generative adversarial networks. *arXiv preprint arXiv:1511.06434*, 2015. 141, 145, 149

H. Rahmani, A. Mahmood, D. Q. Huynh, and A. Mian. HOPC: Histogram of oriented principal components of 3D pointclouds for action recognition. In *13th European Conference on Computer Vision*, pages 742–757, 2014. DOI: 10.1007/978-3-319-10605-2_48. 13

Hossein Rahmani and Mohammed Bennamoun. Learning action recognition model from depth and skeleton videos. In *The IEEE International Conference on Computer Vision (ICCV)*, 2017. DOI: 10.1109/iccv.2017.621. 150

Hossein Rahmani and Ajmal Mian. 3D action recognition from novel viewpoints. In *Computer Vision and Pattern Recognition, (CVPR). IEEE Computer Society Conference on*, pages 1506–1515, 2016. DOI: 10.1109/cvpr.2016.167. 74, 150

Hossein Rahmani, Ajmal Mian, and Mubarak Shah. Learning a deep model for human action recognition from novel viewpoints. *IEEE Transactions on Pattern Analysis and Machine Intelligence*, 2017. DOI: 10.1109/tpami.2017.2691768. 74, 150

Shaoqing Ren, Kaiming He, Ross Girshick, and Jian Sun. Faster R-CNN: Towards real-time object detection with region proposal networks. In *Advances in Neural Information Processing Systems*, pages 91–99, 2015. DOI: 10.1109/tpami.2016.2577031. 61, 123

Ethan Rublee, Vincent Rabaud, Kurt Konolige, and Gary Bradski. ORB: An efficient alternative to SIFT or SURF. In *Proc. of the International Conference on Computer Vision*, pages 2564–2571, 2011. DOI: 10.1109/iccv.2011.6126544. 14

Sebastian Ruder. An overview of gradient descent optimization algorithms. *arXiv preprint arXiv:1609.04747*, 2016. 81

David E. Rumelhart, Geoffrey E. Hinton, and Ronald J. Williams. Learning internal representations by error propagation. *Technical report*, DTIC Document, 1985. DOI: 10.1016/b978-1-4832-1446-7.50035-2. 34

Andrew M. Saxe, James L. McClelland, and Surya Ganguli. Exact solutions to the nonlinear dynamics of learning in deep linear neural networks. *arXiv preprint arXiv:1312.6120*, 2013. 70

Florian Schroff, Dmitry Kalenichenko, and James Philbin. Facenet: A unified embedding for face recognition and clustering. In *Proc. of the IEEE Conference on Computer Vision and Pattern Recognition*, pages 815–823, 2015. DOI: 10.1109/cvpr.2015.7298682. 68

Ali Sharif Razavian, Hossein Azizpour, Josephine Sullivan, and Stefan Carlsson. CNN features off-the-shelf: An astounding baseline for recognition. In *Proc. of the IEEE Conference on Computer Vision and Pattern Recognition Workshops*, pages 806–813, 2014. DOI: 10.1109/cvprw.2014.131. 72

J. Shotton, A. Fitzgibbon, M. Cook, T. Sharp, M. Finocchio, R. Moore, A. Kipman, and A. Blake. Real-time human pose recognition in parts from single depth images. In *Computer Vision and Pattern Recognition, (CVPR). IEEE Computer Society Conference on*, pages 1297–1304, 2011. DOI: 10.1145/2398356.2398381. 26

Ashish Shrivastava, Tomas Pfister, Oncel Tuzel, Josh Susskind, Wenda Wang, and Russ Webb. Learning from simulated and unsupervised images through adversarial training. *arXiv preprint arXiv:1612.07828*, 2016. DOI: 10.1109/cvpr.2017.241. 74

Karen Simonyan and Andrew Zisserman. Two-stream convolutional networks for action recognition in videos. In *Proc. of the 27th International Conference on Neural Information Processing Systems—Volume 1, (NIPS'14)*, pages 568–576, 2014a. 150, 152, 153

Karen Simonyan and Andrew Zisserman. Very deep convolutional networks for large-scale image recognition. *arXiv preprint arXiv:1409.1556*, 2014b. 50, 70, 104, 123

Fisher Yu, Yinda Zhang, Shuran Song, Ari Seff, and Jianxiong Xiao. Construction of a large-scale image dataset using deep learning with humans in the loop. *arXiv preprint arXiv:1506.03365*, 2015. 146, 147

Shuran Song and Jianxiong Xiao. Deep sliding shapes for a modal 3D object detection in RGB-D images. In *Proc. of the IEEE Conference on Computer Vision and Pattern Recognition*, pages 808–816, 2016. DOI: 10.1109/cvpr.2016.94. 136

Shuran Song, Samuel P. Lichtenberg, and Jianxiong Xiao. Sun RGB-D: A RGB-D scene understanding benchmark suite. In *Proc. of the IEEE Conference on Computer Vision and Pattern Recognition*, pages 567–576, 2015. DOI: 10.1109/cvpr.2015.7298655. 136

Jost Tobias Springenberg. Unsupervised and semi-supervised learning with categorical generative adversarial networks. *arXiv preprint arXiv:1511.06390*, 2015. 146

Nitish Srivastava, Geoffrey E. Hinton, Alex Krizhevsky, Ilya Sutskever, and Ruslan Salakhutdinov. Dropout: A simple way to prevent neural networks from overfitting. *Journal of Machine Learning Research*, 15(1):1929–1958, 2014. 75, 79, 102

Rupesh Kumar Srivastava, Klaus Greff, and Jürgen Schmidhuber. Highway networks. *arXiv preprint arXiv:1505.00387*, 2015. 108

Christian Szegedy, Wei Liu, Yangqing Jia, Pierre Sermanet, Scott Reed, Dragomir Anguelov, Dumitru Erhan, Vincent Vanhoucke, and Andrew Rabinovich. Going deeper with convolutions. In *Proc. of the IEEE Conference on Computer Vision and Pattern Recognition*, pages 1–9, 2015. DOI: 10.1109/cvpr.2015.7298594. 105, 106, 107

Yichuan Tang. Deep learning using linear support vector machines. *arXiv preprint arXiv:1306.0239*, 2013. 67

Tijmen Tieleman and Geoffrey Hinton. Lecture 6.5-rmsprop: Divide the gradient by a running average of its recent magnitude. *COURSERA: Neural Networks for Machine Learning*, 4(2), 2012. 85

Jasper R. R. Uijlings, Koen E. A. Van De Sande, Theo Gevers, and Arnold W. M. Smeulders. Selective search for object recognition. *International Journal of Computer Vision*, 104(2):154–171, 2013. DOI: 10.1007/s11263-013-0620-5. 61, 120, 122

Aaron van den Oord, Nal Kalchbrenner, Lasse Espeholt, Oriol Vinyals, Alex Graves, et al. Conditional image generation with pixel CNN decoders. In *Advances in Neural Information Processing Systems*, pages 4790–4798, 2016. 141

Li Wan, Matthew Zeiler, Sixin Zhang, Yann L. Cun, and Rob Fergus. Regularization of neural networks using dropconnect. In *Proc. of the 30th International Conference on Machine Learning (ICML'13)*, pages 1058–1066, 2013. 75

Heng Wang, A. Klaser, C. Schmid, and Cheng-Lin Liu. Action recognition by dense trajectories. In *Proc. of the IEEE Conference on Computer Vision and Pattern Recognition, (CVPR'11)*, pages 3169–3176, 2011a. DOI: 10.1109/cvpr.2011.5995407. 154

Zhenhua Wang, Bin Fan, and Fuchao Wu. Local intensity order pattern for feature description. In *Proc. of the International Conference on Computer Vision*, pages 1550–5499, 2011b. DOI: 10.1109/iccv.2011.6126294. 14

Jason Weston, Chris Watkins, et al. Support vector machines for multi-class pattern recognition. In *ESANN*, 99:219–224, 1999. 67

Bernard Widrow, Marcian E. Hoff, et al. Adaptive switching circuits. In *IRE WESCON Convention Record*, 4:96–104, New York, 1960. DOI: 10.21236/ad0241531. 33

Jason Yosinski, Jeff Clune, Thomas Fuchs, and Hod Lipson. Understanding neural networks through deep visualization. In *In ICML Workshop on Deep Learning*, Citeseer, 2015. 95, 98

Fisher Yu and Vladlen Koltun. Multi-scale context aggregation by dilated convolutions. *arXiv preprint arXiv:1511.07122*, 2015. 50, 141

Sergey Zagoruyko and Nikos Komodakis. Learning to compare image patches via convolutional neural networks. In *Proc. of the IEEE Conference on Computer Vision and Pattern Recognition*, pages 4353–4361, 2015. DOI: 10.1109/cvpr.2015.7299064. 141

Matthew D. Zeiler.   Adadelta: An adaptive learning rate method.   *arXiv preprint arXiv:1212.5701*, 2012. 84

Matthew D. Zeiler and Rob Fergus. Visualizing and understanding convolutional networks. In *European Conference on Computer Vision*, pages 818–833, Springer, 2014. DOI: 10.1007/978-3-319-10590-1_53. 44, 94, 95, 97, 170

Yinda Zhang, Mingru Bai, Pushmeet Kohli, Shahram Izadi, and Jianxiong Xiao. Deepcontext: Context-encoding neural pathways for 3D holistic scene understanding. *arXiv preprint arXiv:1603.04922*, 2016. DOI: 10.1109/iccv.2017.135. 135, 139

Hang Zhao, Orazio Gallo, Iuri Frosio, and Jan Kautz. Loss functions for neural networks for image processing. *arXiv preprint arXiv:1511.08861*, 2015. 67, 68

Hengshuang Zhao, Jianping Shi, Xiaojuan Qi, Xiaogang Wang, and Jiaya Jia. Pyramid scene parsing network. In *Proc. of the IEEE Conference on Computer Vision and Pattern Recognition*, pages 1–7, 2017. DOI: 10.1109/cvpr.2017.660. 141

Shuai Zheng, Sadeep Jayasumana, Bernardino Romera-Paredes, Vibhav Vineet, Zhizhong Su, Dalong Du, Chang Huang, and Philip H. S. Torr. Conditional random fields as recurrent neural networks. In *Proc. of the IEEE International Conference on Computer Vision*, pages 1529–1537, 2015. DOI: 10.1109/iccv.2015.179. 141

C. Lawrence Zitnick and Piotr Dollár. Edge boxes: Locating object proposals from edges. In *European Conference on Computer Vision*, pages 391–405, Springer, 2014. DOI: 10.1007/978-3-319-10602-1_26. 61, 132

Authors' Biographies

SALMAN KHAN

Salman Khan received a B.E. in Electrical Engineering from the National University of Sciences and Technology (NUST) in 2012 with high distinction, and a Ph.D. from The University of Western Australia (UWA) in 2016. His Ph.D. thesis received an Honorable Mention on the Dean's list Award. In 2015, he was a visiting researcher with National ICT Australia, Canberra Research Laboratories. He is currently a Research Scientist with Data61, Commonwealth Scientific and Industrial Research Organization (CSIRO), and has been an Adjunct Lecturer with Australian National University (ANU) since 2016. He was awarded several prestigious scholarships such as the International Postgraduate Research Scholarship (IPRS) for Ph.D. and the Fulbright Scholarship for MS. He has served as a program committee member for several leading computer vision and robotics conferences such as IEEE CVPR, ICCV, ICRA, WACV, and ACCV. His research interests include computer vision, pattern recognition, and machine learning.

HOSSEIN RAHMANI

Hossein Rahmani received his BSc. in Computer Software Engineering in 2004 from Isfahan University of Technology, Isfahan, Iran and his MSc. degree in Software Engineering in 2010 from Shahid Beheshti University, Tehran, Iran. He completed his Ph.D. from The University of Western Australia in 2016. He has published several papers in top conferences and journals such as CVPR, ICCV, ECCV, and TPAMI. He is currently a Research Fellow in the School of Computer Science and Software Engineering at The University of Western Australia. He has served as a reviewer for several leading computer vision conferences and journals such as IEEE TPAMI, and CVPR. His research interests include computer vision, action recognition, 3D shape analysis, and machine learning.

SYED AFAQ ALI SHAH

Syed Afaq Ali Shah received his B.Sc. and M.Sc. degrees in Electrical Engineering from the University of Engineering and Technology (UET) Peshawar, in 2003 and 2010, respectively. He obtained his Ph.D. from the University of Western Australia in the area of computer vision and machine learning in 2016. He is currently working as a research associate in the school of computer science and software engineering at the University of Western Australia, Crawley, Australia. He has been awarded the "Start Something Prize for Research Impact through Enterprise" for 3D facial analysis project funded by the Australian Research Council. He has served as a program committee member for ACIVS 2017. His research interests include deep learning, computer vision, and pattern recognition.

MOHAMMED BENNAMOUN

Mohammed Bennamoun received his M.Sc. from Queen's University, Kingston, Canada in the area of Control Theory, and his Ph.D. from Queen's QUT in Brisbane, Australia, in the area of Computer Vision. He lectured Robotics at Queen's, and then joined QUT in 1993 as an associate lecturer. He is currently a Winthrop Professor. He served as the Head of the School of Computer Science and Software Engineering at The University of Western Australia (UWA) for five years (February 2007–March 2012). He served as the Director of a University Centre at QUT: The Space Centre for Satellite Navigation from 1998–2002.

He served as a member of the Australian Research Council (ARC) College of Experts from 2013–2015. He was an Erasmus Mundus Scholar and Visiting Professor in 2006 at the University of Edinburgh. He was also a visiting professor at CNRS (Centre National de la Recherche Scientifique) and Telecom Lille1, France in 2009, The Helsinki University of Technology in 2006, and The University of Bourgogne and Paris 13 in France in 2002–2003. He is the co-author of the book *Object Recognition: Fundamentals and Case Studies* (Springer-Verlag, 2001), and the co-author of an edited book *Ontology Learning and Knowledge Discovery Using the Web*, published in 2011.

Mohammed has published over 100 journal papers and over 250 conference papers, and secured highly competitive national grants from the ARC, government, and other funding bodies. Some of these grants were in collaboration with industry partners (through the ARC Linkage Project scheme) to solve real research problems for industry, including Swimming Australia, the West Australian Institute of Sport, a textile company (Beaulieu Pacific), and AAM-GeoScan. He worked on research problems and collaborated (through joint publications, grants, and supervision of Ph.D. students) with researchers from different disciplines including animal biology, speech processing, biomechanics, ophthalmology, dentistry, linguistics, robotics, photogrammetry, and radiology. He has collaborated with researchers from within Australia (e.g., CSIRO), as well as internationally (e.g. Germany, France, Finland, U.S.). He won several awards, including the Best Supervisor of the Year Award at QUT in 1998, an award for teaching excellence (research supervision), and the Vice-Chancellor's Award for Research Mentorship in 2016. He also received an award for research supervision at UWA in 2008.

He has served as a guest editor for a couple of special issues in international journals, such as the *International Journal of Pattern Recognition and Artificial Intelligence* (IJPRAI). He was selected to give conference tutorials at the European Conference on Computer Vision (ECCV), the International Conference on Acoustics Speech and Signal Processing (IEEE ICASSP), the IEEE International Conference on Computer Vision (CVPR 2016), Interspeech (2014), and a course at the International Summer School on Deep Learning (DeepLearn2017). He has organized several special sessions for conferences, including a special session for the IEEE International Conference in Image Processing (IEEE ICIP). He was on the program committee of many conferences, e.g., 3D Digital Imaging and Modeling (3DIM) and the International Conference on Computer Vision. He also contributed in the organization of many local and international conferences. His areas of interest include control theory, robotics, obstacle avoidance, object recognition, machine/deep learning, signal/image processing, and computer vision (particularly 3D).

Printed in the United States
by Baker & Taylor Publisher Services